Praise

"Peter Bissonnette was the Yoda behind the Shaw Cable empire: wise, humble, and quietly powerful. His story is a testament to leading with insight over ego. This autobiography is a rare glimpse into the mind of a true corporate Jedi."
KIRSTIE MCLELLAN DAY, *ABOVE AND BEYOND: THE JR SHAW FAMILY HISTORY IN LIFE AND BUSINESS*

"With equal measures of business insights, motivational advice, and derring-do adventure, Peter Bissonnette keeps the pages turning in an autobiography steeped in humour and humility. *Count on Me* is packed full of the kinds of characters and stories that could only come from getting on a Greyhound bus with a guitar and camera and stepping off into one of Canada's most legendary business careers. Peter Bissonnette shows how to lead with heart and how setbacks and even tragedies can be turned into an opportunity for learning and growth."
TROY REEB, CO-CEO, CORUS ENTERTAINMENT

"An extraordinary life from an extraordinary man; a wonderful read!"
BRAD SHAW, FORMER CEO AND EXECUTIVE CHAIR, SHAW COMMUNICATIONS

"Peter Bissonnette's journey to becoming a key figure in shaping the Canadian telecommunications industry is an inspiration. His story shows that with hard work and determination, it's possible to overcome the obstacles in our way, prove the naysayers wrong, and go on to do great things. *Count on Me* is a gripping must-read."
MICHELE ROMANOW, CO-FOUNDER, CLEARCO, AND DRAGON, CBC's *DRAGONS' DEN*

"Using feelings of abandonment to climb the highest peaks of success while discovering the meaning of love and loyalty through chosen family (or fictive kin). This is a great read for those who want to peel back the curtain of the Shaw dynasty and gain motivation from Peter Bissonette's story of turning tough circumstances into a happy life fuelled by unwavering confidence, taking risks, and a side of musical inspiration."
DALLAS FLEXHAUG, ANCHOR, GLOBAL NEWS CALGARY

"Immediately after reading Peter's book, I went to the gym. The attendant, a premed student with brilliant marks working a summer job, had googled me and noticed my association with Jordan Peterson, Ted Rogers, Jim Shaw, Peter Bissonnette, and others, so asked me what it would take for him to achieve greatness. I told him to read *Count on Me* and integrate the lessons of Peter Bissonnette. Peter achieved his accomplishments unconventionally, but with an intense focus on what he wanted, and developed techniques to turn his visualizations into actualization. It is a beyond fascinating read by a great raconteur, an essential tool to achieve leadership and greatness."
HOWARD LEVITT, *THE LAW OF DISMISSAL IN CANADA*, AND COLUMNIST, *THE FINANCIAL POST*

"This candid memoir shows how perseverance can transform adversity into achievement across both our personal and professional lives."
KEN CARPENTER, CHIEF TECHNOLOGY OFFICER, FOUNDATION DEVICES

"*Count on Me* is a truly compelling biography of a proven leader who seizes life! Peter openly shares his life pursuits, experiences, innermost thoughts, and inspirational wisdom presented in a style that is uniquely Peter. Readers can expect to be encouraged and provoked by Peter's passion for people, purpose, and personal best."
SHANNON DONNICI, PRINCIPAL, DONNICI SOLUTIONS INC.

"I originally met Peter Bissonnette in the early '70s when he signed up for guitar lessons with me. I never would have guessed that we would collaborate on many news themes for Global together, and that was when I really got a glimpse of what a smart, fun, caring person he is. Brilliant."
JAMIE BOWERS, COMPOSER AND PRODUCER

Peter J. Bissonnette

with Lucy Lynskey

Count
on Me

MY LIFE, LESSONS, AND LEGACY
AS FORMER PRESIDENT
OF SHAW COMMUNICATIONS

INGENIUM BOOKS

Cover Photograph by Patrick McAneeley
Cover Design by Jessica Bell Design via Ingenium Books

Contents

"He's compassionate; he cares. He's wise. He was born to lead. He's someone you want to follow. He brings out the best in people, and he's not afraid to turn around and help you if you fall. He doesn't just turn away. He'll be there to support you. He'll shine the spotlight on you—he does that.

"He is always so happy to see other people being successful in whatever it is they're doing, too. He never begrudges anyone. He always wants to lift people up. Yet he has his own light that you're really drawn to.

"At big events, with lots of people, it would be overwhelming at times to see just how much everybody respected him. I want to say they love him; that might be too much of a strong word. But, you know, the hugs—they were all genuine.

"He always works hard. He's pushed through roadblocks and is proud of himself for achieving things that people thought weren't possible. He's a great example of a person who's come through challenges and a lot of hurt. He's proof that you can come ahead from that. It's remarkable."

Tracy Bissonnette

Introduction

In 1953, I was a lively six-year-old who couldn't understand what I had done to deserve being confined in a closet by my mother for hours at a time. Her disappointment in me was devastating. I have worked my whole life to prove her wrong. Her expectations were astronomically high. And I did everything I could to surpass them.

Somehow, instead of berating myself or regretting the actions that led to my closet confinement, I talked to myself the way I so desperately wished she would. Hugging my knees in the dark, isolated, and constrained quarters, I'd silently repeat, *I believe in myself.*

My father was physically present throughout my childhood, but distant. I felt detached from—and later, dismayed by—him. In the absence of a father I admired, I sought alternative father figures who inspired me. When I found them, and when they trusted me, I never let them down.

Somewhere during the early days of my education, I learned about the Parable of the Talents—and my interpretation of that passage has resonated with me ever after. It's a story about a master who entrusts his three servants with money before going on a journey. Upon his return, he finds that one servant buried his money, while the other two had made wise choices that doubled their investments. The servants who had been bold enough to take what they were given and turn it into more were praised. The servant who did nothing was punished.

I always think of this parable as being about more than just making wise decisions with money. It's about utilizing your given gifts to grow, progress, and flourish. I believe it means you will be rewarded for having the courage to work with what you have and chase your goals. I've often thought this is what life is about: harnessing your unique talents to manifest good fortune.

Time may be an illusion, but we are all caught in its mirage. As we move eternally forward in this magnetic linear fashion, we can reflect and identify the true recipe for happiness. Hindsight is an opportunity to share which ingredients have proved to work—those that added flavour to life.

Over the years, many have said to me, "You ought to write a book. You have done so much and have so much to share with the world."

I am now retired from Shaw after a fabulously rewarding career that included the RCAF, RCN Naval Reserve, Northern Radio, BC Tel, Rogers Cable, Western Cablevision, Shaw Communications, the board of Gravity Renewables, the Shaw Family Trust board, and the Shaw Communications board. I'm an honorary captain in the RCN. There are also the monastic years from my youth, and my passion for photography and music.

I feel that I have a responsibility to share this as a part of my legacy and a lesson for those who can learn from the against-all-odds story that my life reflects.

While all the events described in this book are true, some names have been changed to protect the innocent.

One — The Formative Years, 1681–1958

Conspiracies always end in tears. Or, in the case of Blessed Oliver Plunkett, who lived in the middle of the seventeenth century, in being hung, drawn, and quartered. An Irish martyr, a saint, a sober clergyman—a rarity in those days—an archbishop, and, according to King Charles II, a very naughty boy, Oliver Plunkett is perhaps the most notable of my ancestors.

Like many people who go against the grain, Oliver Plunkett wasn't, in fact, so much naughty as he was misunderstood. His grand vision of betterment and the changes necessary to enable unanimity and prosperity were deemed a dangerous threat to authority.

Today, in St. Peter's Church in the bustling town of Drogheda, Ireland, Oliver Plunkett's head—*his actual head*—is displayed in a glass case, forming part of an elaborate shrine greeting all those who come to venerate him with Plunkett's immortal toothy grimace.

Oliver Plunkett is seen by some as a patron of peace and reconciliation. After becoming ordained in Rome, Oliver formed the first integrated Catholic and Protestant boys' school in Ireland. As the only bishop in the northern province at that time, he travelled extensively to help others. At a time when religious division was rife, particularly in the highly political aftermath of the English Civil War, such prominent figures as Plunkett were feared for their uniting influence. Ultimately, Plunkett was wrongly accused of plotting to bring an army into Ireland, and was executed. To this day, Plunkett remains a positive symbol to

Catholics across the world, representing unity and harmony—ironically, the very thing for which he was sentenced to death.

While we don't know for sure what Oliver would have to say today, I suspect he would express his anguish at the horrors that have occurred throughout history in the name of religion. This thought is in line with the modern-day beliefs of many among the older generations, me included, who experienced a stricter, less-accommodating Catholic upbringing at a time when the world was different. We have come a long way since then. Perspectives shift over time, and things improve. At least, they should.

Catholicism had a significant impact on my upbringing. This was typical of the time in which I was raised. It has shaped my values, which have been integral to my success and happiness. My faith that there is a God who always has my back has oftentimes been what gives me the courage to keep going.

Family Introductions

My mother, Joan, was born in Dublin. She was the eldest of eleven siblings. Her parents were Norrises, and her grandparents were Plunketts. As a nurse in the navy, she devoted that portion of her life to caring for her patients.

My father, Edmund, was also one of eleven siblings. He was Canadian, but born in Lynn, Massachusetts. He was in the Canadian army, and his work was always his priority.

My parents met in England, somewhere close to Farnborough, where neither of them was from. Joan moved to England from Ireland when she was a teenager. She moved with my grandparents and her younger siblings. Edmund was a member of the Canadian Grenadier Guards. As he was gradually promoted through the ranks, he was relocated to posts across Canada, one of which was in Ottawa.

On December 18, 1946, I was born at Grace Hospital on Wellington Street in Canada's capital city. The temperature was minus six degrees

Celsius, and there were a few clouds and some gentle flurries. At that time, the population did not exceed 200,000. The Gréber Plan—to improve urbanization for the increasing number of civilians in the area, with an emphasis on nature preservation—was underway. Growth was expected and being prepared for. William Lyon Mackenzie King was prime minister.

I was born during an eventful year. There was Canada's largest onshore earthquake, with a magnitude estimated at 7.5, on Vancouver Island. The Canadian Citizenship Act was passed, separating Canadian citizenship from British citizenship for the first time. Canada Savings Bonds were introduced to replicate the success of the wartime Victory Bonds. Viola Desmond refused to give up her seat in a cinema, launching Canada's civil rights movement. Frank Sinatra, Perry Como, and Eddy Howard and His Orchestra provided the musical ambience. And it was the first year of the baby boomer generation.

I had six siblings: Elizabeth, Cecilia, Paul, Suzanne, Christine, and Angela.

As young siblings of the earliest cohort of the boomer generation, making our way in a world healing from WWII, our connection to one another was important. We experienced rivalry, of course, but simultaneously developed a deep loyalty and strong protective instincts. We made the best of our chaotic and nomadic early years; we had no choice but to learn about life and independence very quickly. While tough, it was an early childhood that would foster extremely useful traits and abilities for me to then call upon throughout my future career.

I've only ever met a few of my more than sixty cousins spread out across the globe. One of them, Martin Freeman, became an award-winning actor. Other cousins I admired on my mother's side included the comedian Ben Norris and the late Jamie Freeman, who was a talented musician and producer.

I was named after my mother's brother, Peter Plunkett-Norris. He was an eccentric but renowned fashion designer.

My favourite aunt—my mother's sister, Rosemary—married a neurosurgeon named Case, and the time I spent with them growing up was never dull. Uncle Case once invited me to share a cigarette with him as we looked at a fresh cadaver brain together! Because of the memories and frequent communication, I have always felt closer to my aunt Rosemary than to my own mother. At the time of writing, Aunt Rosemary was ninety-five years old and suffering from dementia, but as feisty and funny as ever.

My grandmother Agnes was a woman of great warmth and generosity, with enough love for her multitude of grandchildren. Her front door was always open. She had a big heart, a kind smile, and comforting hugs. She loved to spoil us with treats and her undivided attention.

My great-grandmother Rose had travelled extensively in the late 1800s. Her husband, Paddy, was in the military. Rose owned a quirky little sweet shop in Aldershot. I would eagerly visit it with tuppence from Granny Agnes, walking to it past bus stops at which kind little old ladies would slowly but cheerfully disembark, giving the driver a wave of thanks.

These people were finding their feet in peacetime, having survived the heartache of war. Their renewed lust for life concealed how terribly they'd suffered. They appeared to have emerged stronger for their struggles. They seemed more resilient after their pain. And they focused on their future with optimism.

Army Brats

My father didn't have much time for parenting. He was a commissioned officer and had previously served as a regimental sergeant major. He was required to relocate often for his role, and he'd always take us along. This lifestyle took me from Ottawa to Calgary, Montreal, and then England—all before I was eight years old. Though we were always following him, my father's priority was his work, and my siblings and I felt the absence of an involved and loving father.

I first went to school when we lived in the Calgary army base of Currie Barracks. I attended preschool and kindergarten at St. Monica

School. During this time, my sisters Christine and Angela—the last of the seven Bissonnette brats—were born.

While most understand the word *brat* to mean badly behaved child, the term *army brat* comes from the acronym *British Regiment Attached Traveller*, which over the years has been abbreviated and extended to all those who accompany their service-officer parents on deployment—many of whom are stereotypically unruly children. Perhaps it's due to the absenteeism of their fathers or mothers, or maybe a result of frequent moves and changes that force resilience and independence upon them from a young age.

In 1952, my mother sent my sisters Christine and Suzanne to England. They were to live with Granny Agnes in Farnborough. My little sisters, aged just three and four, respectively, travelled unaccompanied on a flight to London. A kind flight attendant took them under her wing and saw they disembarked safely into the arms of Granny Agnes at Heathrow.

For Christine and Suzanne, this was a traumatic experience. They felt scared and abandoned.

My mother must have been overwhelmed and struggling. Raising seven children while my father was occupied with work couldn't have been easy.

In 1953, we moved from Calgary to Montreal. Montreal was a busy city where most people spoke French. It felt different to Calgary. It was more diverse, with an evident arts scene. I was six years old but would often explore the streets around my new home, sometimes with my siblings, and sometimes alone.

One afternoon, when I was out by myself, I encountered a local gang of older children that I tried to befriend. I was always eager to talk to people, to play, to be silly. I followed them for a while and tried to join in their conversations. Instead of talking to me, one of the boys picked me up and began running with me. At first, I thought it was fun, and I couldn't help but laugh as I bounced around in his arms. He ran to a wooden crate directly behind a store and dropped me into it. Before I knew what was happening, he shut the lid and closed the latch, locking me inside. I thought it must be a joke, and they'd let me out soon. My laughter turned into short, sharp bursts as I choked out giggles. My muscles tightened as I heard them walk away, their voices becoming increasingly distant.

Nobody heard my determined cries for help, so after a few hours, I gave up and quietly hugged my knees. I was cold, thirsty, and uncomfortable. My only sense of time passing came from the gradually disappearing sunlight that crept in through the cracks. Eventually, I was found and released by a grocery store worker later that evening.

I don't know if my parents had searched for me. My memory of the event is a little foggy. But I was confined there alone for far longer than my mother would ever leave me in the closet. Upon my return home, my mother gave me food and water and put me in the bath, all the while giving me a stern telling off, as if becoming shut in the crate had somehow been my fault.

A Voyage

In late 1953, my father got word that he would soon be stationed to England again. Shortly thereafter, in September 1954, my parents, my siblings—except Christine and Suzanne, who were there already—and I travelled to England by luxury liner. We boarded the RMS *Saxonia* shortly after she had made her maiden voyage in the opposite direction. The *Saxonia* was a Cunard liner built for the increasingly popular Montreal-to-Liverpool service. It carried 954 passengers, of which I was one of the smallest, at just seven years old.

Though it was the first time I had been on a ship, something about it felt familiar. I was excited. The first night aboard, I should have been sleeping in the bunk with my brother, Paul, but I snuck out of my room to explore. My senses felt heightened as I took in the crisp and salty night air, listening to the waves crashing against the hull. I was awestruck by the immensity of the vast ocean mirrored by the seemingly endless sky. The rhythmic rumble of the engine and the Union Jack flag waving vigorously in the wind at the front of the bow were sounds that seemed to ripple right through me. Though the vessel was solid and mighty, its constant swaying motion was a reminder of its vulnerability. My stomach turned cartwheels, but I believed in providence and knew I would be okay.

Feeling chilled and windswept, I returned to the ship's cozy interior. I wandered the corridors, peeking through doorways. Live jazz gradually blended with the increasing volume of chatter and cheers from social gamblers eagerly betting on simulated wooden horse races, as clouds of cigarette smoke swirled around them. In another room, well-dressed people were dancing to "Rock Around the Clock" and laughing as they sipped martinis and gulped beer. Energy was high. Everyone looked happy. And there was glamour and luxury like I had never seen. It was all far too stimulating for a fascinated boy to simply sleep soundly through.

I wanted to be sure I wasn't missing anything, so my exploration continued. I opened doors, peered through windows, and ventured down hallways in every direction. Turning corners, taking stairs, wandering farther and farther. Inevitably, the sheer size of the ship engulfed me, and I became quite lost.

Meanwhile, my mother had gone to check on Paul and me, only to discover my bunk was empty. Commotion rapidly ensued as she and other mildly inebriated passengers hunted through the ship to locate me. Voices of urgency echoed through the corridors. I was relieved help was on the way.

I stood listening to the sounds of hurried footsteps getting closer, until a door at the end of the corridor burst open. A young man in a brown suit was the first to spot me, and he called loudly to those following that he'd found me. He ran to me with a wide smile, then crouched before me and put his hand on my arm. I instantly felt safe.

My mother wasn't far behind. Her steps quickened as she locked eyes with me. I knew I was in trouble, but I couldn't regret my little escapade, because opportunities for adventures aboard ships didn't happen every day. I had found the temptation too irresistible, and I wished my mother could understand that. She gripped my hand tightly as she thanked the man who found me. I could feel her shaking with what I thought was anger.

Without saying a word, my mother led me back through the corridors to my bunk, where Paul remained in a deep sleep. I felt nauseous as I waited for my mother to scold me. As she put me on the bed and began impatiently tugging my shoes off, she spoke in a loud, angry whisper. "Peter! We are on a ship in the ocean! You are seven years old! You cannot just wander off in the middle of the night! What the bloody hell were you thinking? What's wrong with you?"

When she glanced up at my face to see my response, I threw up quite violently.

My mother's sparkly dress that she had worn for her much-needed, rare, and fancy grown-ups' night was now soiled with vomit. A very foul stench had been put on her evening. Teary-eyed and no longer caring if she woke up Paul, she wailed, "Oh, for God's sake!"

I stayed in my bed for the remaining nights of the voyage.

England

My siblings and I did not spend much time at Eldon Lodge, our childhood home. The large red-brick house was on Carbery Lane in Ascot, Berkshire. Though we children spent most of the year at boarding schools, my parents lived at Eldon Lodge, and it was the setting of family gatherings over the holidays.

England was quite different from the hardy, outdoorsy Western vibe in Calgary. It was also different from the vibrant, increasingly cosmopolitan city of Montreal. To a curious, observant, and eager seven-year-old boy, there was a lot to take in.

People's accents were diverse, and dialects seemed to vary vastly from one town to the next, each with its own slang and terminology. The overall mood was different somehow—more formal, structured, and proper. Strangers weren't quite so warm and casual as comparatively laid-back Canadians.

British fashion reflected an attitude of perfection. Amid their postwar recovery, people were eager to showcase prosperity and progress. Social etiquette and class were important, and the way people dressed was considered the greatest indicator of their position in society.

We lived close to Windsor Castle, the oldest and largest inhabited castle in the world, that has served as a residence for royals for over nine hundred years. I could see the castle from the back of our home. There was so much rich history, culture, and architecture right on my doorstep that it was impossible not to be impressed by it.

I stood out as being different at school. England seemed to place more importance on collectivism, valuing community and social responsibility. This may have fuelled a greater expectation to conform to societal norms. I, however, had a Canadian accent and a bolder attitude, and I didn't readily conform and comply. I strove to be independent.

Being forced to adapt quickly to a way of life I didn't understand or agree with fostered my resilience. I learned through comparison, and grew from the experience.

My greatest growth in childhood occurred during the time spent away from my family. My mother always seemed angry and on edge, snapping at me for being loud or getting under her feet. My youngest sister, Angela, would cry a lot, and she got most of my mother's attention. My father was often either out or quietly working in his office, where the door was always closed. He never offered to go outside and play. He never sparked a conversation. He didn't seem interested in his children. Home was not a nurturing, happy place.

My time attending boarding school was a gift. Going to St. Michael's College in Hitchin allowed me to find myself and be myself. Flung into an even playing field with dozens of other boys my age, I could put to the test the adaptability and independence fostered by our multiple moves. I found great joy in playing soccer, riding bikes, roller skating, and playing hockey on metal-wheeled roller skates. I felt I had a slight advantage in the latter, being a Canadian in Britain. It was all much more fun than being at home with my parents.

Schoolyard fights were commonplace, and the hierarchy was evident. The so-called day dogs tended to be prim and proper, returning home each night to their parents. We boarders were rougher. We were the discarded, abandoned wildlings of the crowd—the ones who couldn't go home or weren't wanted there. We were the tough kids looking out for ourselves. Though I was never one to instigate a fight, I'd be the first to punch back once fists were thrown, especially if anyone called me a Yankee!

St. Michael's was run by Augustinian monks. They wore long, brown, belted robes with large, draping hoods. Oftentimes they'd pull these hoods over their heads so we could barely see their eyes. Only the small white cloth, called a scapular, that hung from their shoulders distinguished them from the darkness when they walked at night. The monks were strict, regimented, and intolerant. And they did not frown on corporal punishment.

One afternoon, right after lunch, my best friend Michael Tear and I were a few minutes early for class. The first to arrive, we were greeted by silence and rows of empty wooden desks. The largest desk, rustic and sturdy, was positioned in front of the blackboard. I opened the desk drawer to reveal a lot of white chalk. Michael grabbed a piece and dared me to write *Class is cancelled* on the board. I laughed so hard at this brilliant, mischievous idea. But I preferred to rummage further through the desk drawer, to see what else we could come up with. We found darts.

Michael and I began throwing the darts, first at desks to see if they'd stick into the wood. As our childish, excitable energy surged, we got more playful and began to throw the darts at each other. We laughed as we dodged them. Just as I released a dart aimed at Michael's leg, a monk entered the classroom. The dart had pierced the skin on Michael's knee, causing him to cry out in pain and bleed a little. My stomach lurched, and my heart pounded inside my chest as the monk grabbed me aggressively.

I was pulled by my ear straight to the headmaster's office. The monk's grip was so firm I could feel the blood rushing to the top of my ear as it became red-hot from his unrelenting pinch. The headmaster's office had a faint musty smell. There was a window on the left as we entered, through which subdued sunlight shone down, illuminating fragments of dust in the air. Beyond this one strobe of light, the room was dark, and the headmaster sat at his desk in shadow.

The monk said I had wounded Michael Tear, who was now being seen by the school nurse. I was asked to confirm this, so I nodded nervously. The headmaster rose from his seat as he thanked the monk, who then left and closed the door. Wide-eyed, I awaited my punishment.

It happened so fast. The headmaster lunged at me and grabbed me tightly by the neck. He held me there for a moment. Face-to-face, he gave me a blank stare with eyes like empty sockets. Just as I began struggling to breathe, he let go and twisted me around. He pushed me down to my knees and repeatedly kicked me in the back and ribs with his brown leather sandals. He kicked too many times to count, then left me to muffle my whimpers against the floor. After a few minutes, he told me to get up and leave.

I was bruised, aching, and quiet for the rest of the day. Nobody asked questions when I arrived late to class. Michael was there, and we exchanged a glance. I forced a smile to let him know I was okay.

That evening, I was still feeling sore. I struggled to pull off my school uniform and put on my pyjamas. Just as I was about to get into bed, the same monk who took me to the headmaster's office called me into the hall.

"Come with me," the monk said.

His face was sweaty, and he smelled like onions. We walked slowly and in silence as he directed me outside, into the cold and dark. Positioning me outside a window that allowed a view into his sleeping quarters, the monk picked up a two-by-four that happened to be right there on the ground. He struck me with it across the stomach, then again across my legs, and once across my backside. I felt like I could throw up, but adrenaline kicked in, and I didn't cry.

"Kneel down," he ordered. I knelt on the concrete, facing the window.

"You can stay here all night, just like that," he said. "You can get up in the morning when I come and say so."

At eight years old, I spent ten hours overnight kneeling outside on my own. But I did not drown in misery or feel hatred toward the monk for his actions. I thought of it as tough love and would thereafter wear a metaphorical badge of honour for having survived what seemed to be a level of initiation for any kid who dared to test a boundary. Rather than something to hold resentment about, I saw it as a success. It made me feel like I was capable of handling anything.

I did not for one moment consider these things abuse and worthy of a future lawsuit because, at that time in history, such acts were more widely accepted. Many believed that such punishments were perfectly appropriate and highly necessary. And it worked: I never threw a dart at Michael again.

When we weren't lobbing makeshift weapons at one another, Michael and I were inseparable. We loved to kick a soccer ball around, sliding in the wet mud on rainy days and taking turns in goal. Michael was a fast and agile runner and a natural with the ball at his feet. I'd ask him to show me tricks to maintain better control of the ball. He inspired me to be a better athlete, not just in soccer but in all the many sports played at St. Michael's. Off the sports field, we'd distract each other by pulling silly faces in class and leap around and lunge at each other during dramatic make-believe sword fights at recess. And on Guy Fawkes Night, we spun our sparklers side by side as the bonfire roared. The smoky scent of embers lingered on our clothing. Michael and I looked out for each other. And in a setting like St. Michael's, that's just what we needed.

Contrary to the monks' high standards, the conditions provided were rudimentary. I was among a hundred or more boys sleeping in a single dormitory. Once a week the old live-in nurse would give us a bath, the water of which would be shared among numerous dirty boys. Boils and all.

Sundays were family visiting days. We waited eagerly, excitedly, and happily as, one by one, mothers and fathers arrived, delivering hugs and kisses. They brought treats, shared news, asked questions, showed interest, and spoke with emotion and pride about how much they missed their dear children, glad they were doing well and learning a lot.

I would always be there, every Sunday, waiting hopefully with my brother, Paul. But our mother and father never showed up. Sunday after Sunday went by, and their absence grew and grew, until I learned how to conceal my sadness, hide my disappointment, bottle up my feelings, and push them way down. Instead, I'd focus on perfecting a skill, learning something new, or making others laugh until I forgot how much I was hurting.

In the painful absence of physical visits, Paul and I would receive tuck parcels containing Wagon Wheels—my favourite snacks—and brief letters that Paul would read out. On one occasion, a parcel arrived addressed to me. It was a pair of brand-new soccer boots. And for a fleeting moment I felt as though perhaps my mother thought I was good at something, that I was deserving of this expense. Excitedly, I tried on the boots, only to incur great discomfort as my toes crumpled at the ends and my heels just scraped inside. They didn't fit. Disappointment was a feeling I had become all too familiar with—one that I knew how to suppress, ignore, and accept. I couldn't dwell or get hung up on it.

One Sunday, as the Christmas holidays approached, I felt certain our parents would show up because we had handmade gifts for them—woodwork crafts I had spent hours perfecting, carving delicately with love. I was proud of my creations and so excited to share them, convinced our parents would be impressed. But they didn't come.

Paul and I were placed in the same class, due to being so close in age, with him being only a year older than me. Whereas Paul excelled in academics and his report cards repeatedly showed as much, I felt my parents' indifference toward me was in response to my below-average grades and commentary from the school regarding my apparently troublesome audacity. They didn't take our age gap into consideration when making comparisons. I wanted so desperately to prove my mother wrong, to show her that I, too, could be brilliant like Paul, if not more so.

In those days, confession was not deemed inappropriate for eight-year-olds, and I often found myself seated in the confessional box, psyching myself up to give penitence and saying, "Forgive me, Father, for I have sinned; I have been cheeky." But it was that very cheeky nature, perhaps better described as a confident attitude indicative of leadership skills, that would take me farther in my career and life than any of my more studious siblings.

The signs were already there. I loved being chosen to deliver the milk to all the boys at the boarding school every morning. It meant I got to see and talk to everyone. I was also the designated bell ringer, a privilege that suited a child who enjoyed making noise. Being helpful, being in control, and providing a needed service brought me great joy. Throughout my early education, it was clear: I thrived when given responsibility. I never let down those who trusted me, and I wasn't afraid to try anything new.

Visiting sick kids in the infirmary was another example of my desire to make a difference, to be caring and uplifting. Over time, I identified my existing traits in the Bible stories I'd study, and so began a cycle of aspiration where I would do as I was taught, while believing it was the right thing, and that God would be proud.

St. Michael's College had some of the best exam results in the country, and this, in part, was due to the firm discipline we received and the hardworking routine that, over time, became comfortably typical to us students. Whether asked to wash up four hundred dishes after breakfast while trying not to retch at the pungent aroma of leftover kippers, to clean floors until they shone or windows until they sparkled, or to march a kilometre-and-a-half and back down the road, always keeping eyes forward—they were all tasks that inspired my lifelong work ethic. The latter on the list was perhaps the hardest to do, as the girls from Sacred Heart Convent would march on the adjacent pavement. I knew my sisters were there, and I so badly wanted to run up to them. Sometimes, we'd disobediently catch one another's eye, holler, and wave, and the very sight of one another would fill us with warmth for the remainder of the day.

During Christmas and summer, Paul and I would be reunited with our parents and siblings, and our grandparents, uncles, aunts, and cousins. It took a bus rental to transport us all to Bognor Regis for the holidays. Though these trips ought to have felt relaxed and easy, automatic, and comfortable, they were chaotic and unnatural. So much time apart made our reunions feel somehow awkward. My family didn't feel as familiar as they should have, and none more significantly so than my parents. I felt painfully and confusingly distant from them, even when we were riding in the same vehicle. It was an irony I struggled to understand at that age: While I missed my family during term time at St. Michael's and longed for their closeness, when we were finally together, I couldn't wait to be back at school. At school, I could forge my own path, demonstrate my abilities, and enjoy the genuine friend-ships I'd built—without needing my parents' acceptance.

Over the few years I attended St. Michael's, those vacations would serve as reminders of the lack of faith my family had in me. The people who were supposed to support me, encourage me, appreciate me, love me, and believe in me were the very ones who doubted me the most. And while this could be a depressing realization, it only served to strengthen my motivation.

Claustrophobia

What began as a dare from a small crowd of mischievous eight-year-old boys became a traumatic addition to my claustrophobic experiences. A slightly older, slightly bigger boy along with Michael Tear giggled as we squeezed, headfirst, one by one, through the heat register in the floor and into the duct, where we slithered slowly like snakes, one behind the other. It began as an exciting adventure—one in which we imagined we'd emerge through another hole in a different part of the building, where we'd celebrate being the first to find and venture this new secret route. We were excited to think it would be something the boys would whisper to one another about in awe, for months or years to come.

But after a few metres of crawling on my elbows, the boy ahead of me had become firmly wedged, as I discovered when my head hit his feet. Seconds later, Michael's head hit my feet, and he was unable to reverse. Time seemed to slow down as the realization sank in that the three of us were trapped in a tight tunnel, where it was too dark to see, and the air felt increasingly dense and suffocating. My heart raced, my chest tightened, heat rose up my chest and neck to my forehead, and my body trembled.

Once I was aware that I was absolutely sandwiched, immense adrenaline kicked in, as I knew I could not remain in that situation for a single second longer. I frantically shuffled myself around, so I was facing upwards. I screamed, I roared, and I used all my strength and energy to push and punch and kick on the 2.5mm-thick oak floorboards above.

I could hear the boys' footsteps and urgent chatter. They were gathering, eager to help. As I punched up, they all worked together to lift the boards. The boy wedged in front of me had begun to cry in panic, which further fuelled my angst. I could feel my heart pounding in my chest as I channelled my pure terror into superhuman strength. It took almost thirty minutes of collective efforts for the boards to become damaged and loose enough to move, and hands reached out to pull us up, one by one.

My knuckles were raw and bloody, and sweat from my brow was stinging my eyes, as space finally opened for us to escape. I've never felt a rush of oxygen quite like it since. After the euphoria of freedom came deep regret, as I admitted to myself that my actions had been foolish and dangerous.

Return to Canada

In 1958, we returned to Canada on the *Empress of England*, sailing from Liverpool to Montreal. Soon after, we crossed Canada on CP Rail, going to Vancouver, where we settled for a while in Burnaby. My father had retired from the army and was appointed to the position of director of the British Columbia Centennial Council. I remember him driving his pink 1958 Ford, coloured in that way to pay homage to the BC salmon that swam up the many rivers in British Columbia. It was there that I completed grades five and six, at Suncrest Elementary School, followed by grade seven at Holy Trinity Catholic School in North Vancouver.

In 1961, I attended the Seminary of Christ the King in Mission, British Columbia, for grades nine and ten, before returning to my birthplace, Ottawa, in 1963, to join St. Pius X Seminary as a boarding student. I would ultimately graduate from Bell High School in 1965.

Two — Seminary Military, 1958–1968

I got my first proper job, a paper route, in Vancouver. I was twelve years old and excited to be given this responsibility, and to make my own money. I would enthusiastically head out before dawn, even on the coldest of winter mornings when snow was falling and icy winds blew. On these rare occasions, one of my siblings would usually join me for fun—as opportunity to slide down the hill in the snow was just too irresistible! There was one road in particular that was ideal for sliding, as it had a wider, wood-covered gutter alongside the sidewalk, designed to direct heavy rainfall flows. The angle was consistent but not too horrifyingly steep. When the weather was especially cold, it would turn into ice—a perfect slide and an invigorating start to the day!

I was surprised when my mother insisted on joining me one such snowy morning. She was normally unimpressed by the antics of her lively children. But at half past four in the morning, she was eager to go.

I gathered the rolled-up newspapers and squeezed them into my canvas *The Province* bag, telling my mother, "This is what we'll sit on to slide." With a nod, she opened the front door, and off we went. I couldn't quite believe what was happening. Just my mother and me, out in the cold and dark and silence, in what felt like it could have been the middle of the night.

It was only a couple of blocks until we reached the sliding hill. Laying the bag down, I sat on it, and she got on behind me without any coaxing.

I told my mother to keep her feet up. I pushed us off, and away we went. The fresh, cold air blew against our cheeks. Her squeals of delight likely woke the neighbours we whizzed by. She held on to me the whole way, her arms around my waist, gripping so very tight it felt as though she'd never let go. It was the longest she'd held me since I was an infant. My body filled with light and warmth; I felt as if I began to glow. A strange wave of a new kind of happiness washed over me.

Rosemary and Case

Aunt Rosemary and Uncle Case never had children of their own. They ran a medical business together south across the United States border in Yakima, Washington, where Case practised as a neurosurgeon. Rosemary managed finances, staffing, and patient scheduling.

When I was fourteen, my brother, Paul, and I spent the summer with Rosemary and Case. When we were both there, they made a point of sharing their love equally. Unlike my parents, they never showed favouritism or treated one of us unfairly.

Rosemary taught me to drive, while Case taught Paul. Rosemary would let me drive around Yakima in her 1956 Chevy. I loved the liberating feeling this gave me and the confidence and trust that Aunt Rosemary placed in me.

I felt loved and respected, and so, in turn, I worked hard for my aunt and uncle. I'd help them to plant big trees, pull weeds, and mow their lawn. In the evenings, we'd laugh together watching *The Jack Paar Tonight Show*. We were all at ease in one another's company.

When I was in the seminary in Mission, Rosemary would write to me every day. She was overly generous and recognized that a gift of five dollars in my commissary account would be greatly appreciated. So, along with words of encouragement, she would include five dollars in each letter she sent.

Case would also contribute. Always positive and upbeat, he would tell me I was brilliant at technical things, reminding me of the times I had figured out how to repair broken radios. "You know, I'm a brain surgeon, and I couldn't fix it!" he once said when I repaired his office telephone system. He recognized unique traits in me, and would tell me I ought to be proud of those attributes.

This reinforcement and acknowledgement of my strengths from a couple I saw as wonderful role models was a hugely important factor in my path to success. I would often visualize Rosemary and Case when I was unsure of how I ought to conduct myself in a given situation. I wanted to be like them.

Seminary Fathers

When I was sixteen, I thought I wanted to be a priest. It was a vocation my parents often encouraged, so I was certain it would receive their approval. My childhood education had been building toward the priesthood, and I knew it was a role in which I could help others. I felt a calling for it.

I first attended the Seminary of Christ the King, situated on Mount Mary Ann above Mission, British Columbia. It was picturesque, with its bell towers overlooking the valley. I spent two and a half years at this Benedictine seminary with ninety-eight other aspirants to the priesthood.

During my first days in attendance, I was struck by how much time we spent in prayer. From first light at 5:30 a.m., we gathered in the chapel, singing the Gregorian chants for Matins, the first chant of the day. At 6:30 a.m., when the monks arrived from their first masses, their chanting echoed through the marble-floored cloister walk and vestibule. They walked single file, heads bowed, wearing black habits with hoods covering their heads. It was an austere and somewhat intimidating moment for a young seminarian.

Prior to my entry into the seminary, we were measured for our own black robes or cassocks and were now wearing them for the first time.

Then there was silent prayer and breakfast. The first time we could speak to one another was after breakfast, going into classes. Once the long day of classes was completed, we entered a period of silence as we gathered in the chapel for Vespers. Vespers were the evening prayers, and, like Matins, chanted in Latin. From Vespers, we went into the refectory for dinner. Dinners were held in silence, except for one of the monks reading prayers aloud from his missal.

After dinner, we had a period of recreation, and then silent studies before bedtime. This routine became embedded in our very being. Was this what it was going to be like for the next years of my life? Fun seemed to have been forgotten. I couldn't wait for the weekend, during which time we could play sports, go on walks, and speak to one another.

Sundays were visiting days when our parents could come out to Mission and visit with us for several hours. During the two and a half years I spent at the seminary, this only happened once. Sundays for me were days of disillusion and emptiness. I learned from boarding school not to expect visitors because it was too painful to be disappointed each week. Instead, I would play football or lacrosse on the fields below our dormitories with the other boys whose parents hadn't visited that day, most of them because they lived too far away—in other countries, even.

When I entered the seminary, I had no desire to be a Benedictine monk. Rather, I wanted to be a parish priest like Father Kilty. Father Kilty was a priest I respected. He had convinced me that I had a vocation for the priesthood, and that I should attend the seminary. In addition to his duties as the parish priest, Father Kilty was also our basketball coach—and a very good one. Under his coaching, our team won a junior basketball tournament held on Vancouver Island. He seemed to have the best of both worlds. On one hand he had the parish to support and on the other, coaching basketball and playing golf with his brother, who was also a parish priest, in Richmond, British Columbia.

In preparation for my entry into the seminary, Uncle Case told me that if any of the priests ever said or did something that made me feel uncomfortable, to tell them that they could call him. That advice came to help me one day. Toward the end of my time at the seminary in

Mission, I was playing soccer on the main football field on the property. One of my teammates passed me the soccer ball, but it hit me in the groin. I dropped to the ground and shouted, "Shit, that hurt!" I looked up the hill and noticed that Father Placidus, our seminary headmaster, was watching the action taking place on the field below.

Later that evening, after our study period was over and we were getting ready for bed, Father Placidus asked me to come to his office. I had had a very good relationship with Father Placidus during my time at the seminary and didn't feel that this was unusual. When I entered his office, he said that he had heard me cry out when struck with the soccer ball. He then asked me, "Do you know why men get erections?" I was taken by surprise with this question, but immediately thought about the advice Uncle Case had given me. I responded to Father Placidus: "My uncle, who is a doctor, told me that if a priest ever asks me that kind of question, to have them call him directly and he will answer them." Father Placidus was stopped in his tracks and told me that I could leave for the dormitory. Though I had never directly had any problems with Father Placidus, I wasn't naive, and knew his intents were not harmless.

Enter Music

On Christmas Day of 1963, my parents gave me my first acoustic guitar. I had just turned seventeen, and for all the challenges I faced in my relationship with my mother and father, it was a slightly confusing, albeit much-appreciated gift.

Music had a profound impact on me from a young age. As a teenager, from 1961 to 1963, I attended a weekly opera club meeting held in the minor seminary's recreation area. It was run by an Italian deacon called Father Rossi. Though I wasn't especially into opera, I had an appreciation for the immensity and intensity of it. Aunt Rosemary would send me records of contemporary opera—modern renditions of old operas. The passion, powerful melodies, and expressive performances resonated with me. I didn't recognize it until later, but my love of rock music is for much the same reasons.

Expelled

In 1964, I moved to Ottawa. Here I attended St. Pius X High School, then a preparatory seminary, as a boarding seminarian.

I played basketball for the St. Pius X team, along with football. St. Pius had a reputation for excellence in the Ottawa school system and competed with secular schools in these sports. On weekends, I loved playing hockey at the school rink. Each evening, I was part of the team that flooded the rink for the next day's hockey games. When I wasn't playing hockey, I had to attend a study period for the boarders before bed—a time to revise and read up on the subjects discussed during the day's classes. Or, in my case at the time, to gaze longingly out of the window at the sports field.

On one occasion, during springtime—after the snow had all melted and the nights were staying lighter, the green grass was flourishing, and the birds sang into dusk—a pretty young woman ambled casually across the football field. I abandoned my homework, rushed out to the field, and followed her until she stopped and turned. As soon as I saw her face, I blushed.

"I don't know what I'm doing right now," I said, "but I just felt the need to come and say hello."

Being drawn so impulsively to a pretty girl was not conducive to a successful vocation in the priesthood. The girl, perhaps two years older than me, was surprisingly receptive to this spontaneous introduction and invited me to meet with her at the football field the next day to chat. And so began an unlikely but short-lived friendship between an impressionable seminarian and a young adult woman. Her father was an RCMP officer and she, her parents, and her newborn baby were living in a house adjacent to the school's football field. She must have noted the shock on my face when she revealed she was already a mother, because she rushed through an explanation about her evening strolls being a brief escape from her overwhelming home, just a short distance away. I would run on the track, sometimes three kilometres or so, and she'd arrive. I often imagined kissing her—but imagination was as far as that went. I could barely handle the adrenaline as it was.

It was a puzzling period in my life. I aspired to be a priest, yet I also had feelings for girls, which created a conflict for me. It was a dilemma I'd talk about with my friend and fellow student, Michael—another Michael from my childhood. Between classes, we'd sneak off to the bathroom and light up a couple of Rothmans cigarettes. We'd lean against the shower stall, puffing away our problems. One evening, while we were exhaling nonchalantly in that poorly ventilated space, the door flung open with a bang. In an instant, an agitated Father Redmond snatched the cigarettes from our mouths, threw them to the floor, and put them out with his foot.

"Go to your room, Michael!" he snapped. "And Bissonnette, you're coming with me."

Father Redmond led me quickly by the elbow, down the hall to his office. A large wooden crucifix hung prominently on the wall above his leather chair, between bookshelves of aging religious texts. On his desk were framed photos of other clergymen, alongside a typewriter and a large notepad upon which ink had leaked from his pen. Pungent wafts of incense circled around the room, originating from a small altar in the corner where candles dropped wax dangerously close to an open Bible.

"You're being expelled from boarding," said Father Redmond, matter-of-factly, his words landing like a punch to the gut. "From now on, you'll only be able to attend here during the day. And I plan to meet with your parents as soon as possible."

"Why?" It was the only word I could squeak out.

Father Redmond sat behind his desk and fidgeted with his hands for a moment as he stared up at me, unblinking. Eventually, he asked, "What is your relationship with the young lady who lives by our sports field?"

Realizing what this was all about had me more confused.

"We're friends. We talk about things," I said.

"Have you touched her? Have you kissed her? What have you done with her?" he demanded, his face flushing increasingly red as he shifted in his chair. "Have you had sexual relations?"

"What? No! Of course not! I've never done that!"

"Do you know she has a baby?" Father Redmond stood up hastily, his fists tightly clenched. "Do you know who the father is?"

"Yes, she told me she has a baby, but—"

"Is it yours?" The ultimate question came in an abrupt interruption as Father Redmond stepped so close to my face that our noses almost touched, and I could smell his sour breath from his visibly salivating mouth.

Taking a step backward, I insisted, "No! I only met her a few weeks ago! We've never done that! Only talked!"

"Done what, Bissonnette? Sex?" Father Redmond pulled at the front of his robe and turned away. There was silence as I stood in disbelief at this accusation. Facing away from me, he concluded, "I'll call your parents. Go and pack your things."

"But—"

"Get out now!" he yelled, still facing away from me. I left without even closing the door. My mind was preoccupied. How was I going to tell my parents?

Two days later, my parents came to get me. They had been in Toronto visiting my sister Elizabeth, otherwise they would have come sooner. As I was going to pick up my things, I could hear my friends offering to help me carry my suitcase. I heard my father yelling across the parking lot, "He can carry his own bags!"

After a car ride of silence, we arrived at our family home. My mother began busying herself in the kitchen, ignoring my father as he aggressively dragged me up the stairs. He shoved me into his office and shut the door. Before I could say anything, he kneed me hard in the testicles. Intense pain shot up through my groin and into my abdomen. I doubled over in agony. I felt instantly sick; the throbbing was debilitating, and I couldn't stand it. In my peripheral vision, I could see that my father was getting his leather military belt from a drawer. While I was still hunched over, he began whipping me with it across my back. I was too dizzy to resist, and too shocked to cry.

"Stand up like a man!" my father shouted as he pulled me up by my shoulders and then hurled me into his tall metal cabinet, making it shake. I was angry, but wouldn't strike back. There was silence for a moment. The room's only window was covered with long, heavy drapes, and a single brass desk lamp was all that lit the space. My father didn't say anything as he stood before me, casting his shadow over me. Behind him, his military medals hung on display.

"Are you done now?" I managed to ask.

"Yes, that will do for now," my father said.

Through watery eyes, I spoke to his departing feet. "I didn't do anything wrong."

He shut the door behind him.

My sisters Christine and Suzanne later told me they had heard everything from their bedroom down the hall—the thumps, shouts, clangs, and bangs—but they'd been too afraid to do anything.

In the subsequent days, weeks, and months, home life was unbearable. My mother and father didn't talk to me. She referred to me as Tom Jones. "Tell Tom Jones it's dinner time," she told my sisters. She never spoke directly to me at the dinner table, and they were instructed not to either. Now that I was a day student, I would hitchhike to and from the seminary every day, which meant a very early start each morning to ensure I'd find a ride on time.

Life wasn't fun.

At the dinner table, where I was not supposed to speak, my sister Christine was talking about her friend, who wanted to sell her a piece of his car—specifically, a tailpiece—which we all laughed about.

Eavesdropping and unimpressed, my mother snapped, "A piece of what?"

Nobody responded as our bowed heads and side glances tried to stifle chuckles.

"Come on, a piece of what? *A piece of what?*" she demanded angrily.

"Oh, Mother, a piece of tail," I said.

My mother erupted in anger. Picking up the giant wooden salad bowl from the centre of the table, she threw it over my head in a fit of rage.

In that instant, I made a spontaneous but very definite decision to leave home. I ripped my salad-covered shirt off and went upstairs to pack a bag of clothes. I had had enough! My cheeky nature, which I had sincerely apologized for many times during confession as a child, could not be suppressed, for it was who I was and who I am to this day. I couldn't be myself around my parents.

For three days and nights, I stayed in a laundromat not too far from St. Pius X. It was cozier than the cold basement to which I had been banished at home. It was clean and warm, with a pleasant smell of dry sheets, and the rhythmic whirr of the washing machines was somehow comforting. There were plush benches where I could lie down at night.

People would come and go, and many of them stopped to make small talk, so I rarely felt lonely. And before I'd left home, I had told my sisters that's where I'd be, so they would visit. It was a place we could finally talk as much as we wanted, about whatever we wanted. It was liberating.

One evening, about supper time, I made a point of visiting my spiritual director, Father Bill MacDonald, who was also a teacher at St. Pius X. He was still very angry at Father Redmond, whom he referred to as an asshole. From Antigonish, Nova Scotia, Father MacDonald was forthright and a very likeable and honourable person. Each seminarian was assigned to a spiritual director, and I was fortunate to have been assigned to him. He recommended that I find a way to go back home, as no good was coming from my running away.

Eventually, my father discovered my whereabouts and came to the laundromat. With less compassion than authority, he unapologetically talked me into returning home. I knew I couldn't live at the laundromat forever, so home I went.

Ultimately, I learned that the seminary was not for me. Maybe it was the realization that a life of priesthood, devoted so intensely to the Church, would not enable the vibrant life of variety and experience that I craved. Maybe it was the desire for change, built into me by my upbringing, where new places and new people had been an ongoing theme. Or maybe it was, ironically, divine intervention. A guidance from God not to put too much weight in God.

Expectations

That same year, I worked at an ice cream stand along Highway 7 outside of Crystal Beach in the suburbs along the Ottawa River.

At the King Cone, where I worked alongside my brother, Paul, and sister Suzanne, it was easy money: scooping ice cream into cones and then secretly licking off the leftovers. We would work on Sundays too, when there was more traffic on the highway.

Reminiscent of my days delivering milk at St. Michael's, I loved seeing grateful, smiley faces. I'd save every cent and count my earnings at the end of each week. I couldn't wait to spend it!

There was a record store near home that always had elaborate window displays of the latest LP releases stood up between second-hand guitars and amps. I'd often gaze longingly, hoping one day I could have them all.

Finally, I had my own money, and I could spend it as I chose. I went straight to that store after my last shift of the week, cash in hand. Eagerly, I flicked through the endless rows of smooth record-album sleeves depicting colourful artwork or moody photographs of the artists, admiring them all. I chatted with the long-haired, knowledge-able salesclerk, who shared my admiration for rock music. His left arm was covered in tattoos, which was not a common sight those days, but I thought they looked cool. Eventually, I decided to buy a Conway Twitty album that cost me four dollars. I ran all the way home, excited to show my sisters and listen to it together.

At home, Christine and Suzanne squealed with delight as I proudly presented my purchase. Keen to know what we were all so excited about, my mother peered over our shoulders. Seeing the record, she snatched it, pulled the record from its case, snapped it in two, and threw it in the garbage. It happened in a flash, and I was completely devastated. Suzanne and Christine watched sympathetically as I stormed off. Retracing my footsteps in the direction of the store, but without any cash this time, I tried to make sense of what had just happened, and why my mother had broken the first record I had ever owned.

It was only a year after that incident that she moved out of the family home for several months, leaving us and my father to stay with her brother, Peter, in Vancouver. Clearly, they had been experiencing a rocky patch in their relationship that was casting a constant dark cloud over her. Conway Twitty was known for his emotional country ballads. Perhaps this was too much for my mother amid the peak of her own melancholic love story.

When my mother left, my father had to manage his now nearly adult kids on his own at our home in Ottawa. Though I didn't miss my mother, her absence amplified my father's expectations. I suddenly felt as though pleasing my father was more important than ever.

Shortly thereafter, I went down to the recruiting office in Ottawa to sign up for service with the Royal Canadian Air Force. It was a direction I didn't mind being swayed into by my father. Much about the lifestyle appealed to me, as a viable alternative to the church. It sounded like it could be an honourable career with meaning and opportunity. My father told me it would be well-paid, and well-perceived. I was already a member of the Navy Reserves, having joined at HMCS *Carleton* immediately upon my departure from the seminary. So, I had already had a glimpse of what life in the military might be like.

On one occasion while in the Navy Reserves, I was serving aboard an older ship called the HMCS *Porte St. Louis*, which was moored in Hamilton Harbour. This ship had been a minesweeper that served the Royal Canadian Navy during the Cold War period. Its main task was to clear mines from harbours, coastal waters, and other strategic areas. When I was aboard, it was being used as a training vessel for the Reserves. Hamilton was a heavily industrialized area, and a hub for steel production. The grey and gritty landscape was dominated by factories, mills, and shipping infrastructure. The ocean breeze mixed with the odours of metallic fumes and burning coal. Docks were prominent along the shoreline, where chemicals were killing the fish in the sea, so hungry seagulls had grown all the bolder, often swooping low overhead those who dared to picnic here. The uninviting scenery gave me little distraction from my work.

It was there that I had my first alcoholic drink. It was a bottle of Labatt 50 Canadian ale. I drank this simply to fit in with the crowd and to be initiated into navy life, where I soon learned that beer in large quantities was a daily staple. Thereafter, I chose to remain on watch, as I preferred to do my job on the ship rather than spending nights ashore in other pursuits.

My apprentice role at that time meant I worked a great deal in the engine room, which was a locked-off, dark, windowless space. Constant rumbling mechanical sounds made it impossible to hear other workers, as the escaping steam from boilers periodically hissed, pumps clanked, and engines whirred. It was a tight squeeze through narrow spaces to access the specific parts requiring maintenance or repair. I would sweat profusely in the heat, and the lack of air made my heart pound.

As a young ordinary seaman, I enjoyed learning about the navy tradition. I loved the discipline. I spent many hours on the parade square at HMCS *Carleton*, and the opportunity to play basketball, a sport I loved, on the navy's team fulfilled me.

I soon learned, on my first voyage, that the navy was rife with intemperance. During downtime hours, women would come from the dock area to the harbour. Some would even come aboard our ship. Even the married men would take them out on the town and late at night sneak them onto the ship.

Incorporating multiple expletives into every sentence was the language of naval personnel at the time. Sexually transmitted disease was rampant, alongside the prevalent attitudes of aggression, exhibitionism, risk-taking, entitlement, and superiority. I had sought change and adventure, but the sex, the booze, and the constant swearing were all too conflicting with the life I had known before signing up.

As I thought about where my life might go if I stuck with a career in the navy, I decided it was better to move on, sooner rather than later. I knew it wasn't for me, and staying would have been a waste of my time. I began researching alternatives.

During the 1960s, the Royal Canadian Air Force—the RCAF—played a crucial role in Canada's military forces. The Cold War was ongoing, and tensions between superpowers were high. Equipped with some of the most advanced aircraft of the era, the RCAF played a key role in NATO's air defence system, with Canadair CF-104 Starfighter aircraft stationed in Europe and the Arctic to provide surveillance and deterrence against potential Soviet aggression. It was a time in which they were involved in several peacekeeping operations, including a deployment in Cyprus in 1964 as part of a UN mission to help restore order after a coup. These successes, along with seeing the Golden Hawks perform thrilling aerial displays across Canada and the United States, were among the motivations of young men to join—to make a positive difference, to help others, to protect and defend their beloved country, and to contribute their strength, skills, and courage for a broader purpose and a greater good.

For me, too, joining the RCAF in 1965 was a proud moment in my young life. It was an achievement that felt like a calling in my life's journey. Two weeks after I signed up, I was sent to Saint-Jean, Quebec, for basic training. My father drove me to the bus station, handed me a carton of cigarettes, and shook my hand goodbye.

I undertook ten weeks of basic training in Saint-Jean. If I proved myself during that time, if I performed well, I would then be invited to choose a trade in which to specialize. There was everything from cooking to policing, but I wasn't interested in most of the options. The one that really interested me was electronics.

I was an eager learner, and because I found it all so interesting, I absorbed new information like a sponge. It was a time in my life when I progressed quickly, feeling very much like I was on the right path, doing something I excelled at and enjoyed.

After a year of electronics training at CFB Clinton, I was assigned to the advanced radar training facility in Camp Borden, Ontario. There, specialized training specific to ground and airborne radar systems was taught by air force instructors who had served on bases across the country. I loved being stationed in Borden and focused on learning as much as possible, knowing it would have a bearing on my next posting. I wanted to be assigned to an active air force base where I could work on jet-propelled or large transport aircraft. Their radar systems were diverse and complex. I did not want to work on remote, ground-based radar systems in northern Canada. I was ill-suited to isolation.

I was driven to succeed because the fifty airmen in my class would have the opportunity to choose their next posting based on their performance. I was delighted to learn that my top-two rating allowed me to select the air force base in Trenton as my next assignment. Trenton is the Canadian Forces Air Transport Command's headquarters. In stark contrast to my struggles with learning during my time at boarding school in England, I discovered that having a clear goal motivated me to elevate my performance. Daily, I reflected on what success could look like for me. Life on the base, however, wasn't all roses.

One evening, as my roommates and I prepared for bed, a primal roar suddenly resonated from the far end of the barracks, interrupting our lighthearted banter. Approaching rapidly through the rows of cots, stomping like an angry giant, was a uniformed airman whose furrowed face I barely recognized. He was a man I had seen but never spoken to. He had one arm raised high above his head, brandishing something shiny, sharp, and large. The moment I realized it was a combat knife with a 15 cm blade, I saw the man's unblinking eyes were angrily fixed on mine as he continued his almighty, unbreaking scream.

Fortunately, my reaction was instantaneous as he lunged toward me. My heart was pounding in my chest. With the full force of my weight, I pushed the man two metres backward, keeping my hand gripped tightly on his weapon-wielding arm. As I held him against the wall, he struggled, trying to twist his hand free, pushing against me while maintaining his firm hold of the knife. It was all happening so fast, and

I had to make quick decisions while others were still frozen in disbelief. With my free hand, my body still pressed up against his, I slammed his head as hard as I could into the wall. His head broke through the plasterboard. He slumped to the floor, unconscious.

Breathless and shaking, I took a step back, worried for a moment that I might have killed him. My squadron mates gathered around the man, whose raspy breathing cut through the otherwise silent room, reassuring us he was alive. The military police were called as I sat on the nearest bunk, processing what had just happened. I was in shock, but relieved.

With multiple witnesses to the event and the attacker already known to authorities for aggressive behaviour, he was put behind bars. I was commended for my quick response, and did not receive any disciplinary action for the head injury I caused the man. We were military men who were not at war, and such things should never happen in the safety of a training base.

The next day, I saw the attacker shuffling in his orange overalls, escorted by the military police with the big *D* for *detention* on his back.

The incident made me realize that, despite unwavering faith in humanity as a whole, I should be aware that there might be someone seeking to harm me or others without reason, when I least expect it.

Hercules Crash

It was a routine night training flight in Trenton for six Royal Canadian Air Force crew members aboard the Lockheed C-130E Hercules, a relatively new four-engine transport plane built just two years earlier, in 1965. The evening was brisk for mid-spring, with temperatures at just six degrees Celsius and a strong, constant breeze, as is common with the change of season across much of Canada, when evening temperatures dip. Wind gusts reached thirty kilometres per hour. Touch-and-go landings were routine manoeuvres that occurred most evenings at Trenton. We didn't pay them much heed.

Two weeks earlier, two other airmen and I decided to leave the crowded barracks and rent a unit in a small community trailer park called Bayside, situated close to the end of Trenton's runway. We made the move to gain more independence and approach our roles in the air force more like a job. In our tired-looking, ten-by-nineteen-foot trailer, which offered less space per person than the barracks, a small propane furnace kept us warm. It wasn't luxurious, but we valued the privacy.

On the evening of April 27, 1967, my roommates and I were enjoying a typical post-supper card game of three-handed euchre. I was feeling confident, about to play my highest trump card for my fifth winning trick, when we were interrupted by an increasingly loud and resonant low-frequency hum that began to shake the small table we sat at and make the dishes in the sink lightly clatter. The growing deep rumble overhead was the unmistakable sound of an extremely low-flying Hercules. A sudden and powerful whoosh of air rattled the thin, single-pane glass of the small trailer windows. The rumble became deafening. Then, a heart-stopping, thunderous boom accompanied a tremendous explosion that lifted our trailer a few centimetres off its wooden moorings, slamming back down as a blinding flash of bright orange light filled the room.

Without a second thought, I leaped into action. I pushed open the trailer door. The air felt instantly thick and warm. I sprinted faster than I ever had in my life, directly toward the blast, which had occurred just 800 metres away. An intensely bright fuel fire was now raging where the force of impact had generated a monumental fireball, leaving much of the plane's undercarriage and engines buried in the soft mud of farmland just a short distance from the runway.

As I got closer, panting and full of adrenaline, I scanned the wreckage for any signs of life. Flames roared upward, and I felt the burning heat turn my face red. It had been mere minutes since the explosion, but already military police officers were hurriedly arriving to the hectic scene. I approached them, presenting my military ID card and identifying myself as a member of the RCAF. Grateful for the assistance, the military police officer quickly placed a security identifier on my arm and led me to an area several metres beyond the remnants of the plane.

There was little time to process the horror I saw, the tragedy that was evident, and the scale of destruction, before the mounting chaos around me propelled me into action. I assisted with securing the area and preventing civilians from getting too close.

There was a pungent odour intensifying and swirling around on the night breeze. It was metallic and coppery, with strong wafts of ammonia mixed with kerosene and smoke. Though the smell was unbearable and overpowering, I couldn't help but inhale deeply as we approached a deceased aircrew member. It was one of the first times I had seen a dead person. He was still strapped into his seat. Though his face was covered in heavy clumps of dark red blood, his eyes and mouth appeared gently closed, and he looked almost peaceful, as if in a deep sleep. His skin was smooth and clear. His features were symmetrical. He had a defined jawline and full cheeks. His hair was thick with a healthy shine. My eyes glazed over as I kept them fixed on his once perfect face. I needed a moment before I could take in everything that was in my peripheral vision.

It was a miracle the man's face had stayed intact. I later learned that was not the case for the other victims. The seatbelts had somehow kept his head and torso together. But one shredded leg barely hung on at the waist. The rest of his limbs were scattered. Surveying the scene to locate them, I could see the remains of the other airmen strewn across the field. Unintentionally, I absorbed every detail in slow motion.

I was relieved to be distracted by shining car headlights. Half a kilometre away, along a country lane separated from the field by a small wooden fence, vehicles began lining up. People were gathering at the fence, being held back by officials. Word of the incident was circulating already in nearby Belleville, and residents were flocking to view the morbid scene.

I never saw active service during my years in the military and would never have anticipated experiencing such a heartbreaking catastrophe in my home country, in the relative safety of a training base. All six crew members aboard had perished. They were all young, they were all ambitious, and they all had families and histories and lives before them. And in an instant, they were gone.

I couldn't dwell on my feelings or let my mind overthink. I tried to physically shake off the immense shock by moving my body. I paced a little to distract myself from the urge to vomit. I pushed the intense sadness way down, so I could focus on my responsibility.

As hours went by, in contrast to the ghostly silence of the wreckage, air force personnel were steadily gathering. Investigators were tasked with retrieving significant parts of the Hercules so they could reconstruct the event and examine thoroughly whatever had gone so horribly wrong. Large tents were erected. Herman Nelson heaters attached to generators ran to keep the tents warm.

At sunrise, a stray dog wandered across the field.

As witnesses shared information, a clearer picture began to emerge of the sequence of events. The farmers spoke of how the plane had flown mere metres above the roof of their barn before crashing, and described how the ground trembled like an earthquake. Many of the avionics radar systems were embedded deep in the soft mud. As the day warmed, the gut-wrenching, inescapable smell became one of carrion and decomposing flesh.

Along with many others from Trenton air base, I spent a week at that site. At nighttime, we'd try to keep warm, standing by large firepits fuelled by the wooden fence we had repurposed from the farmer's land. We had an important job to do. I understood this to be a reality you signed up for when deciding to join the military, and despite how traumatic it was, never for a moment did I regret my choice to be there.

It was concluded that an elevator trim failure upon takeoff had caused the crew to lose control completely. There was nothing they could do. It was a catastrophic malfunction that was out of their hands and ultimately deemed the fault of nobody.

The six lives lost that day would ever after remind me of the fragility of life, of how fortunate I am, and that those who are living and capable owe it to the departed and helpless to have sincere and eternal gratitude. To appreciate every day. To work hard, do one's best, and never take a single moment for granted.

Rivers

At age nineteen or twenty, the responsibility of repairing and maintaining radar systems instilled in me a profound sense of pride and inspired me to strive for reliability and accuracy. The lives of the aircrew depended on the systems I worked on.

During my time at Trenton, it seemed like nothing could distract me from my role and career goals. That was until I met Peggy Hill. Peggy was attending a party in Belleville with her dad, an airframe technician about to be transferred to Rivers, Manitoba.

I had never heard of Rivers, but was told it was only thirty minutes northwest of Manitoba's second-largest city. That made it sound big and exciting. Knowing that this very pretty girl would be there only added to that excitement! But I soon learned that the city was Brandon, with a population of just 29,000 at the time. It was a place where the climate was harsh, poverty was evident, and crime rates were high. Several months later, having volunteered to accept a posting to Rivers, my excitement evaporated rapidly upon arrival.

Nevertheless, it was only a short time later that I left Trenton and drove with Peggy and her parents, Irvine and Laura, for a brief getaway in Shediac, New Brunswick, to celebrate Canada's one hundredth birthday on July 1, 1967, before I made my journey to Rivers.

Only a Canadian—or maybe only I—would add twenty-six hours of driving over 2,700 kilometres to a road trip to attend a party in the East before heading back west. Given it was quite a way, I did spend several days in Shediac, watching the tidal bore and digging up clams. I drove alone to Manitoba, on a journey that took me thirty-six continuous hours along the Trans-Canada Highway in my 1964 Chevy II. Adrenaline powered me through, but this is not a route and schedule I recommend! On arriving just short of Brandon, exhausted, I pulled over to the side of the road and fell asleep before I could so much as turn off the engine. I slept deeply for a solid eight hours in the driver's seat.

The next morning, I arrived at Rivers—a very large army base where army paratroopers were trained. On arriving at the gate, an older, stern-looking army sergeant major appeared unimpressed by my dishevelled look, pointing at my tousled hair and asking, "What is that?"

"Hair," I responded.

Unsatisfied with my response, the sergeant major questioned me twice more before screaming, "It's hair, *Sir!*"

It was not the warmest welcome I had ever received.

I was oriented into my new job in the air force hangar, where I worked on TACAN—tactical air navigation system—radar beacons and other radar technology that was used on the T-33 Silver Star training jets. I was disappointed that there were no Hercules or other large transport planes like the ones I had worked on in Trenton, and was quickly regretting having made the move, telling myself not long after arrival that I would not stay there long. And though Peggy and I had never developed a serious relationship, when I saw her kissing a man one night at a party, I made the decision to move on as soon as my one-year commitment to Rivers was completed.

In late 1968, the integration and rightsizing of the armed forces led to the shutdown of the base in Rivers. Air force personnel were offered transfers to Cold Lake, Alberta, while the government sought volunteers for discharge due to military downsizing.

I felt my time in the military had become stagnant, leading me to voluntarily apply for and receive an honourable discharge from the RCAF. This decision marked a pivotal moment in my life, as I sought to redefine my future outside of military service. On July 28, 1968, I embarked on a lengthy drive from Rivers to Ottawa. This journey stirred feelings of emptiness and vulnerability. A sense of uncertainty came over me as I faced the future without a job, income, or guaranteed security.

My relationship with Peggy had evolved into a platonic friendship. We both recognized the need for change. We agreed that when we reached Ottawa, Peggy would travel with her parents to Irvine's next posting, in

Greenwood, Nova Scotia. Despite the challenges, I felt a sense of hope in returning to Ottawa, a city with which I was familiar. I understood the importance of moving forward, and was determined to take steps toward building a new chapter in my life.

After two hours of driving, we arrived in Winnipeg, following Peggy's parents in their station wagon, which was filled to the brim with their belongings. While driving though an intersection at a traffic light, a motorcycle with both a rider and a passenger unexpectedly veered in front of the car in front of me. There was a collision with the rear of the motorcycle, resulting in both the rider and passenger being violently thrown through the intersection. Irvine's car came to an abrupt halt, and his driver's door flew open. He jumped out of his vehicle and rushed across the intersection to assist the passenger who had been thrown off the motorcycle. His gaze was fixed on her as he rushed to help; I could see the anguish in his eyes as he realized what had happened. Laura remained sitting in the Renault, her hands covering her eyes, sobbing.

Reacting quickly, I slammed on my brakes and pulled over to the side of the road. I could see the passenger of the motorcycle lying on her back. She was screaming, her left leg contorted and hanging by the fabric of her pants, which were quickly saturating with blood.

A woman from the sidewalk rushed to assist, providing comfort and applying a makeshift tourniquet to the injured woman. Across the street, I saw someone attending to the driver, who, though appearing uninjured, was in a state of shock from the incident. It happened so fast that I struggled to grasp what had occurred. A sense of helplessness overwhelmed me as I wanted to reach out and extend my support, but I was uncertain to whom I should reach out—her parents, the injured victims, or Peggy. I crossed the intersection and put my arms around Irvine while he was on his knees trying to console the young woman, who had reached up for help. Soon after, several ambulances and a police car arrived at the scene. Officers began interviewing Irvine and Laura, as well as Peggy and me, given that we were witness to the accident.

The events of that day dramatically altered the course of our journey. Due to the injuries sustained and the uncertainty surrounding insurance liability, we found ourselves needing to find a motel in Winnipeg for the night. Irvine, not wanting to inconvenience me, had suggested that I carry on without them, but I told them that I would never leave them in the lurch.

The following day, after being cleared by the police to continue our journey, we learned the heartbreaking details about those involved in the accident. The motorcycle driver and passenger were identified as an Indigenous couple. Tragically, the young woman had to undergo an amputation of her leg, while the driver remained hospitalized, nursing multiple abrasions and bruises. This entire incident, like others I had witnessed, brought to light the impact of unforeseen events and the emotional weight they carry.

Three — One Small Step West, 1969

Upon my arrival in Ottawa, my priority was to find a job that would allow me to leverage my air force experience and training, and begin a new chapter. Before diving into my job search, I felt compelled to visit my parents, whom I hadn't seen in several years. The longing to reconnect was strong, as I hoped to bridge the distance that had grown between us. Arriving at their apartment, I was met with silence. Despite the ringing of their doorbell, they refused to let me in. Their rejection felt painful, perhaps stemming from their inability to reconcile their expectations with my life choices—first, leaving the seminary, and then resigning from the air force. Despite my best efforts to maintain communication, my attempts to visit were met with silence. Each time I buzzed their high-rise entry phone, I faced the same disheartening response—silence.

On one occasion, I rang the buzzer for over an hour, holding on to hope that they might let me in. Eventually my mother responded over the intercom.

"Go away!" she snapped. "You're not welcome here."

Before I could ask why, she accused me of stealing her jewellery, claiming my sister Suzanne had told her that I had taken her most treasured rings years before. I insisted that I had never taken anything and would never dream of doing such a thing. I asked how that would even be possible, as I hadn't seen them in several years.

It was an accusation that hurt me deeply, reflecting the rifts that had developed in our relationship over the years. Ultimately, I felt defeated by their continued rejection and chose to walk away, recognizing that my efforts to see them and mend our relationship were met with barriers I could no longer scale.

After I had left the air force, and was settling into an apartment in Ottawa, I received a pension cheque of approximately six hundred dollars from the government. For me, that was a lot of money. At that time, my sister Suzanne and her husband, Steve, who had been married for less than a year, were struggling financially. One night while playing euchre with them in their apartment, Steve asked me if I would give them a loan. Despite my own limited resources, I agreed to lend them the full amount from my pension, emphasizing that I needed it to be paid back due to my own financial situation.

When the first month came for repayment, I was taken aback when Steve nonchalantly claimed he owed me nothing. His apathetic response shocked me, especially considering the help I had extended to them. My sister's support of him was equally as shocking. More than hurt, I felt betrayed. I confronted them about their obligation, expressing the seriousness of my need for the money and urging them to honour their commitment. Not getting anywhere, I turned to the law.

Several months later, when the situation had escalated to the small claims court, I reflected on my initial desperation for the funds. However, by that time I had a job, albeit low paying, and had reached greater financial stability.

After the judge read their letters to me acknowledging the loan, she ruled in my favour. I informed the judge that I no longer needed the money and did not want to pursue the case any longer. In response, she suggested that Suzanne give me a big hug after the proceedings.

However, post-court interactions created further tension within my family. Suzanne inaccurately informed our mother that they had won the court case, painting me in a negative light. This reinforced the misunderstandings and conflict between my mother and me, as she believed I was in the wrong for taking my sister and her husband to court.

I asked myself why Suzanne would act the way she did—to lie without reason. It occurred to me that throughout her life, she had done whatever she could to ingratiate herself with our parents. Our parents rejected Suzanne when they sent her to England at the age of four. I felt she would do anything to avoid experiencing that rejection again. This realization helped me make a difficult decision: I was going to break the cycle with my parents. I was no longer going to expend my energy trying to convince them that I was deserving of their love. I chose to move on without them in my life. What a liberating experience that was: I could move forward and make decisions without needing their approval. I realized that I thrived living my life on my own terms, away from my family, away from drama and accusations.

The Town That Fun Forgot

Shortly after arriving in Ottawa, I was called by Phil White, the manufacturing manager of Northern Radio, who informed me that I was the successful applicant for the quality control technician job. What a weight that took off my shoulders. Northern Radio was an electronics manufacturing company that designed communications devices for CN/CP used on their transcontinental rail systems. The interview conducted by Phil was quite detailed. It included testing my knowledge of analog and integrated electronics systems. Fortunately, I had been exposed to these technologies while working on the C-130 Hercules and Buffalo aircraft. As a quality control technician, I oversaw the final testing of the telecommunications equipment they had built in their factory in Ottawa. Several switching systems I designed and built to test their communications equipment were integrated to great success. This test setup saved countless hours of testing for each rack of equipment that they shipped to their customers. Phil confided to me that these devices affirmed his decision to hire me, and that I would have many opportunities going forward. While I felt proud of my achievements at Northern Radio, I was in a low-wage position that did not reflect my level of responsibility, and that did not motivate me to excel.

Despite my low income and need to budget, the nine-to-five schedule gave me time to embrace my early twenties. I shared an apartment with friends, socialized in local bars in the evening, took on creative projects, and got into minor mischief during the day. I could cope with being poor, as long as I kept busy. Poverty was a challenge, but boredom was painful.

The Rideau Canal stretches 202 kilometres through the heart of Ottawa, all the way to Kingston, connecting various lakes and the Rideau River en route. Constructed in the nineteenth century, it was originally intended as a military supply route in the event of war with neighbouring Americans. Fortunately, it has never been needed for that purpose and has instead played a crucial role in the region's economic development. This historic waterway provides a touristic backdrop to Parliament Hill, creating a picturesque scene that enhances the charm of an otherwise dull and grey downtown. I found something oddly alluring about it that I couldn't resist.

The Rideau Canal draws people year-round. During colder months, the canal is transformed into the world's largest naturally frozen skating rink as it becomes the Rideau Canal Skateway. Offering almost eight kilometres of icy pathway, it attracts skaters of all skill levels from around the world. During the summer months, it is not a place for recreational swimming. Aside from the dangers presented by underwater structures and fluctuating water levels, the inevitable pollution produced by nonstop boat traffic within this busy city-centre waterway makes it utterly filthy and far from desirable for those seeking a refreshing summer dip. But it's tempting, nonetheless.

On a sunny summer day in 1969, I put on my cut-off blue jeans and entered the canal. It was warmer than I thought it would be, so I comfortably swam back and forth across the canal. Aware that people were watching me, I maintained a confident rhythm, keeping my strokes strong and controlled to showcase my speed and athleticism to onlookers.

My little escapade in the Rideau Canal was part of an impromptu black-and-white photo shoot with a budding photographer who knew my good friend Rick Begin. He requested Rick and I pose at some iconic Ottawa settings. Other shots would include the two of us, post-swim and still dripping, each hanging by one arm twelve metres high from the cement wall of the National Arts Centre. Adrenaline and excitement around getting a fabulous photo drowned out both our fear and common sense. We were models.

Rick and I chased accomplishment and exhilaration, pushing ourselves out of our comfort zones, testing our personal limits, and conquering challenges. In hindsight, all of this pointed to restlessness elsewhere in my life. My career didn't excite me. I wasn't progressing as I had hoped. My intellect wasn't stimulated, and I felt disengaged.

Rick and I had met during basic training in the air force. He talked about wanting to be a lawyer, and I admired his ambition and his follow-through. In Ottawa, he and I attended night school. I was taking a math course to gain a deeper understanding of the numbers side of technology, which I found so interesting, and Rick studied law. We kept our heads down and worked hard during classes, but out of hours, when our brains were disengaged, we had adventure on our minds.

As the saying goes, "The devil makes work for idle hands." Without meaningful productivity, a person is more likely to turn to mischief, fall into temptation, and land themselves in hot—or, in my case, just reasonably warm—water. Rick and I proved this further with other shenanigans we got into at the time.

The Chaudiere, a bar across the bridge from Ottawa, in Hull, Quebec, was known for being a bit of a wild place. It was affectionally known as The Chaud. Rick and I would go there for a few hours on a Friday after work. We'd drink several beers and narrowly avoid getting involuntarily pulled into fights with the array of characterful and rowdy patrons. Many workers were riled up at the end of a busy week and needed to let loose.

On one occasion, I suggested we depart for a quieter, more elegant location to enjoy a nightcap in a more peaceful setting. I needed a change of scenery. Novelty was always appealing to me, and there was one bar in the city we had not yet been to.

The Fairmont Château Laurier hotel is one of Canada's most iconic landmarks. Open since 1912, it sits in a prime location adjacent to Parliament Hill and can be seen from afar with its impressive French Gothic-style turrets, copper roofs, and intricate stonework. High-profile guests appreciated Château Laurier's luxury and charm; it was a place frequented by politicians, celebrities, and royalty. I wanted to enjoy it, too.

On arriving in the glamorous lobby, I noticed two busmen. Dressed in their regal attire, standing duty, they were stationary and serious. My eye had also been caught by a large, ornate, beautiful royal-looking chair that shone like a beacon. Reminiscent of the furniture seen in Windsor Castle, it triggered memories of my childhood in England and seemed to call out irresistibly.

Under my breath, I suggested to Rick that we liberate that chair from its position in the lobby to the great outdoors. I knew the challenge would give us a great adrenaline rush. Rick knew this, too. He accepted the mission with a nervous but determined grin.

Rick and I waited for the guards' backs to be momentarily turned, then with haste, we stealthily hoisted the enormous chair and moved swiftly toward the main entrance. But it quickly became apparent we had underestimated the suitability of this elaborate throne to be carried through the revolving doors. As we attempted to navigate the situation, performing difficult pivots of the heavy chair—wiggling and squeezing as quickly as we could to get it unstuck—the duet of pompadours had noticed the commotion and rushed toward the scene.

Fuelled by dopamine, I gave a mighty push, which flung the chair onto the stone entranceway. Rick and I stumbled behind before sprinting away as fast as we could. Glancing back over our shoulders, we could see the busmen picking up the chair and struggling comically to get it back through the doors. That's how we had fun in Ottawa.

One Small Step

I was beginning to see indications that I ought to strive for better. On July 20, 1969, my two boozy and rambunctious roommates and I sat together on a tired, secondhand couch to watch history in the making. Around the world, eyes were glued to TV sets and ears were open to the radio. Then, Neil Armstrong hopped out of Apollo 11's lunar module onto the surface of the moon.

"I can't fucking believe this," said Rick, beer in one hand, cigarette in the other, his mullet dishevelled, as he stared in open-mouthed awe. "This TV actually fucking works!"

And that was admittedly impressive. Two days earlier, I had salvaged that television from a pawn shop for five dollars. It wouldn't turn on. Its days were numbered. It had ceased to be. It was an ex-TV. But I troubleshot that dead appliance for two days, dismantling and reassembling, rewiring, and testing. I was patient and meticulous. Determined and persistent. I believed I could bring it back to life. And I did.

The TV finally turned on mere moments before Neil Armstrong took one small step. It lit up with glorious black-and-white images and complementing audio that was only as distorted and crackly as the moon landing footage itself.

Watching men set foot on the moon made my job at Northern Radio feel even more insignificant. I wanted to be significant. I had to shoot for the stars. 1969 is the year I consider my life to have truly begun.

Psycho-Cybernetics

In the summer of 1969, I took a Greyhound bus from Ottawa to Vancouver. I had with me just a single suitcase of clothes, my Super 8 motion picture camera, fifty dollars in my wallet, and a book called *Psycho-Cybernetics* by Maxwell Maltz.

During the multiday, cross-continent journey, I had plenty of time to read and reread the words of Maltz. *Psycho-Cybernetics* taught me how to achieve success and happiness by harnessing the power of my own mind and have greater appreciation for, and belief in, myself. Maltz theorized that the way people think about themselves has a profound effect on their ability to pursue the life they truly want. He explained that our self-image is the cornerstone of our personality. The way we see ourselves greatly influences our thoughts, actions, and accomplishments. I learned that the brain operates like a guided missile system with a target in mind. By setting clear goals and using feedback, it's possible to train the brain to strive for what we want. I knew I wanted to be successful. I had to believe it. I had to visualize my success. It was an inspiring book to read on such a significant trip.

It was a long time to be on a bus. It would have taken around forty-eight hours if there were no stops for gas or to let passengers on and off along the way. I don't enjoy sitting still and quietly for long periods of time. So, over the course of those three days, I befriended a girl around my age. Having been reluctant to talk to me initially and attempting to ignore me for the first several hours, she eventually decided I was the least threatening-looking person on board, and took me up on my offer of a game of cards. This made my confinement to the bus more bearable.

By the second night, the girl was comfortable enough to fall asleep on my shoulder. Something felt quite special about two strangers journeying this great distance together at full speed toward our next, unknown chapters. We had different circumstances, backgrounds, and motivations, but we were travelling side by side.

When we finally arrived in Vancouver, we decided to grab a late-evening coffee at the White Lunch restaurant on Hastings Street. Our intention was to go back to the bus station, where we had left our suitcases, and head our separate ways after having a coffee. Unfortunately, when we went back to the bus depot, it was closed. We couldn't get our luggage until it opened the next day. Neither of us knew where we planned to stay that night or the next, so after walking about a kilometre from Hastings Street to Robson, I found the Ambassador Hotel on Seymour Street. We took separate rooms.

About fifteen minutes after getting settled in my room, I heard a tap on my hotel door. My friend said that she was afraid as she went to the shared bathroom on her floor, and felt uneasy. I invited her to come into my room. Even though I had spent the last few nights sitting upright on a Greyhound bus, I remained a gentleman and slept on the floor beside the bed.

Upon awakening in the morning, I heard chimes and bells. I later came to learn that it was the signal of the time coming from the BC Hydro building some blocks away. It was noon and I had slept for ten hours. I looked out the hotel window overlooking Seymour. The BC Tel logo caught my eye, but I was drawn to the activity in front of that building. Striking picketers with placards were marching up and down, shouting at the passing cars and their passengers.

My friend and I parted ways that day. As I watched her cross the street, I accepted that I'd probably never see her again.

I needed to go to the bus station to get my luggage and then call Uncle Peter.

Uncle Peter

My uncle, Peter Plunkett-Norris, was a warm and wise character who had always praised and encouraged me. Knowing I could not afford to stay in hotels, I called him. Though we had not seen each other for years, his tone indicated instant delight when I told him I was in Vancouver and ready to start a new life.

Uncle Peter directed me to take the bus through downtown and across the Lions Gate Bridge to North Vancouver. The sights along the way triggered memories of the years I had lived in Vancouver as a kid. I noted how rapidly the skyline was growing. The city was clearly thriving. I felt I had entered a great land of opportunity.

Uncle Peter had a wonderful house. It was large and full of character and charm, with ornate details and an interior that reflected his highly creative, artistic eye. He lived with his partner, Douglas. The two of them spoke proudly of their home as they showed me around.

Uncle Peter and Douglas gave me a grand tour of Vancouver, driving me in their yellow Chevrolet convertible to all the tourist hot spots I had not been to as a child. They helped me as I researched employment possibilities, contributing ideas with enthusiasm. I took the bus to job interviews, which Uncle Peter and Douglas would chat with me about beforehand and debrief afterward. When I received a rejection from Lenkurt Electric, it didn't slow my momentum or dampen my spirit. I was excited about this journey in a place that fit me far better than Ottawa ever did, and I knew I'd made the right choice.

During my time staying at Uncle Peter's home, I paid my way by doing work around the house. I built a large sundeck, installed a new roof, and assembled furniture. I enjoyed keeping busy and was so grateful to be in the company of family who loved and supported me.

Uncle Peter was the designer of Margaret Sinclair's trousseau wardrobe ahead of her marriage in 1971 to Prime Minister Pierre Trudeau. The collection of clothing he created for Margaret would be photographed and seen around the world. Margaret had specified that some of the garments incorporate Russian-inspired design, as she would be touring Russia shortly after the wedding. It was a project that Uncle Peter began working on not long after my arrival in Vancouver, and though he kept very quiet on the details and didn't broadcast his involvement ahead of the big day, I and other family members were so very excited and proud.

Babe I'm Gonna Leave You

I began dating a beautiful girl named Barbara McMichael. I was excited to bring her home to introduce her to Uncle Peter and Douglas. Together, we'd hang out on the sundeck I built. My sister Suzanne would often join us for musical jams on the porch, singing as I played guitar. Suzanne had divorced Steve about a year after our court case, remarried about a year later, and moved to Vancouver with her second husband, Gerry, about a year after that. We had reconciled soon after they had arrived in Vancouver.

Barbara was the perfect person to spend time with as I got to know the city and settled into my new chapter.

For Christmas that year, I bought Barbara a wonderful stereo system consisting of a turntable, speakers, and an amplifier. To test it out, I played Led Zeppelin's first album. As the song "Babe I'm Gonna Leave You" played so hauntingly through the stereo speakers, I had no idea that Barbara was about to break up with me the very next day—on Boxing Day.

I didn't have a lot of money, so I felt upset that I had just spent a significant amount on Barbara only one day before she ended our relationship. Barbara's father, a prominent businessman, convinced her she should return the gift to me, which she did. I then took the stereo to a pawn shop on Seymour to recoup my money.

After that, every payday, I returned to that same pawn shop to buy back the stereo, only to pawn it again midmonth when I was low on funds. I became such a regular there, repeatedly selling and buying the same item, that a year after I'd first bought it, the manager invited me to their Christmas party!

I learned three things about myself from this: to be more cautious about whom I give gifts, that I needed to make more money to afford the things I wanted, and that invitations can come from the most unexpected places!

Four — Who Am I? 1970–1976

When I applied to work at BC Tel in 1969, I had no idea that thirty years later, that company would merge with Telus, the greatest rival of the company where I would eventually become president: Shaw.

BC Tel was established in 1904 to provide telephone services in Western Canada. As a longstanding company, it had a reputation for reliability.

I saw exciting potential in the telephone industry. There were familiar elements—the same technology, the same transmission properties— that I had worked on as a radar technician in the air force. All the things that made radar work were what made transmission over coaxial cable work.

Recognizing this connection and that my skills would transfer well to this industry that temptingly offered immense opportunity, as it was clear to me that the demand for those offerings would only increase considerably, I proactively studied for and took the National Cable Television Institute—or NCTI—exam to obtain my NCTI rating before I dove into this new career path. It was a big decision and probably the best one I ever made.

I was interviewed by a woman who later revealed to me that despite my less-than-exemplary reference from Northern Radio, who were disgruntled that an employee dared quit over inadequate pay, she very much appreciated my sharp and stylish, impeccably tailored brown suit and cool Beatles-like vibe—an outfit recommended by my highly fashionable Uncle Peter.

My aesthetic, not my resume, had got me that job.

Early Communications Career

When I started at BC Tel, I knew I had more to prove than just being good at my job. Determined to show my commitment, I went above and beyond my regular duties, working hard to earn the respect of my supervisors. Before long, I was chosen as one of only three technicians for an intensive forty-eight-week training course on the new Traffic Service Position System—or TSPS—which was Canada's first digital toll-switching system. It was a massive project, involving complex technology and a lot of long hours. But I threw myself into it, even taking night classes to keep building my skills.

Binary code is the foundational language of computer systems and is at the core of modern technology. Binary code forms the basis for all our communications and digital displays, and it was essential to understand to succeed in electronics. First attributed to the mathematician Gottfried Wilhelm Leibniz in the seventeenth century, binary code is a way to represent information using only two options, typically represented as zero and one. Upon being introduced to binary code, I found I had a natural aptitude for following the step-by-step approach and evaluating a process from start to finish. It was an approach reminiscent of how I had fixed radios and telephones in my younger years.

Perhaps it's what Pythagoras was talking about when he said, "All is number," bringing all that is seemingly complex down to the simplest of principles. We are surrounded by numbers all day, every day, in everything we do: from dates in the calendar to hours of the day, balancing income and expenses, clocking up more kilometres on the car. Everything is measured, everything is formed—and at the root of it all is numbers.

This deeper understanding of numbers, coupled with a desire to learn more and specialize, led me to pursue further training. From signal processing to data analysis and system calibration, my comprehension of binary code and its use in electronics offered a solid foundation for this progression. And like with electronics, it's all about translating numerical data into actionable information.

Working under my supervisor, Tom Porteous, pushed me to take on extra shifts, solve every service ticket on my watch, and tackle complex problems head-on. I was proud to be on the TSPS team, especially working alongside the experts from GTE—General Telephone & Electronics—who'd flown in to help us. Tom counted on me, and I wanted to make sure I earned the trust he'd put in me. When the project launched successfully, I felt like all the hard work had been worth it, and Tom let me know how proud he was of my dedication.

A few years later, I was promoted to TSPS supervisor after scoring the highest on a management test designed to gauge leadership skills. Tom had been an incredible mentor, showing me by example the importance of fairness, reliability, and respect. It was a huge step forward, and I felt honoured to follow in his footsteps. Even after I left BC Tel for new challenges, Tom stayed a trusted friend and mentor. Later, he would even join me at Shaw's golf tournaments.

Independent efforts are obviously necessary to move forward in your career, but having supportive co-workers and effective mentors is a significant help. I was fortunate enough to be surrounded by highly experienced leaders who valued my ambitions and work ethic.

A Life Saved

In 1974, I would often work the night shift, from midnight to half past seven in the morning, in the SATT—Strowger Automatic Toll Ticketing—office located on the sixth floor of 768 Seymour, under the supervision of Tom Porteous. It was a complicated switch of step-by-step analog relays, but it was configured like a common control switch, similar to how early computers shared resources like memory and core switching. In its day, it handled all calls coming in from Vancouver without operator intervention.

One evening, I was working on trouble tickets that had accumulated during the day shifts. At around three in the morning, I noticed that one trunk light on the main console was still lit up, indicating that a call was still in progress. I went to the monitoring console and listened to ensure the trunk was in use rather than hanging up with a fault.

I heard a very deep voice speaking harshly. The voice was distinctive and ominous, making very disparaging remarks about someone. As I listened further, I heard the deep voice instruct the person on the line to *take out* or *ice him*, referring to whomever they were talking about. My heart raced as I realized that I had clearly intercepted a call that was going to result in someone being harmed. I needed to help.

I went over several aisles from the main console to the trunk ticketer that the call was using and took the cover off the unit so I could access the many relays that were used to store the telephone number the call was going to. Eleven relays were engaged, and I could decipher these to acquire the telephone number.

It was a number from the Pacific Telephone and Telegraph Company in Oakland. I contacted the Oakland Police Department and told them what I'd learned. I got the number of a Pacific Tel technician on duty in Oakland. I told them that I was calling from Canada and that I had overheard a call in which a person, whose name they referred to as Whitey, or something similar, was going to be killed. I asked to ensure that he was protected. I took the officer's name, and he thanked me.

A few days later, with this incident still on my mind, I contacted the Oakland Police, and they assured me that they had been able to locate the person and that I had indeed saved him from a potentially life-threatening incident.

The Apology

That wasn't the only interesting phone call to occur in my earlier days at BC Tel.

Shortly after arriving to work one afternoon in 1974 and making a start on the twenty-five tickets I needed to resolve on that busy shift, amid the buzz and noise of the telephone switch and my nine co-workers, I picked up the phone to a familiar voice. Though it was shaky and emotional, the words came slowly between breath-catching and sniffs.

"Peter. I want to apologize for just how horrible I was to you when you were growing up."

The pause might have been as long as thirty seconds before I responded, as I processed what was happening with disbelief. My mother was calling me. We hadn't spoken at all in at least four years. She always ignored me. She was always cold toward me, disappointed in me, even enraged by me.

Yet, presumably, having got it from Uncle Peter or Aunt Rosemary, she dialled my number and was on the line. In that moment, she sounded remorseful and genuine as she tearfully told me she was horrible.

I took a deep breath.

Oh my God, I said in my mind, before telling her out loud, "It's okay, Mom, you don't need to apologize. That's over with. I'm making my way in life now, and I'm doing okay. And so, actually, I have to thank you."

I could tell from her breathing patterns that she was only crying harder as she insisted, "No, Peter. No, I was an awful mother. I'm so sorry."

Her emotional distress was evident as she sobbed loudly.

"Can you ever forgive me?" she asked.

I wanted to calm her down. I didn't like hearing her so distressed. I reassured her: "It's okay, Mom, there's nothing to forgive. I don't feel that way. It's okay."

It was an out-of-the-blue call that caught me off guard, but as her words sunk in, I realized that maybe this was a significant turning point. Perhaps we were making some progress in our relationship.

"I was so unfair to you," she said.

I knew it must have taken my mother immense gumption to make this phone call. I admired that. I was so grateful for that. And I knew I needed to tell her I understood a little. I had to share my perspective on it so she could see I truly forgave her.

"Mom, I knew you weren't happy," I said. "You were so young when you married. You had seven kids. One after the other. Bang, bang,

bang, bang. You'd been taken away from your home country, away from your own parents and siblings and friends. And Dad was never very animated, expressive, or affectionate. You know, he was a military man. A businessman. You're different. You've always been more gregarious.

"You probably felt trapped, and you needed so much more. So, I attribute the way you treated me and the things you said to your unhappiness. In fact, I even wondered if being sent to boarding school was because you couldn't handle us all. I always thought it was probably just too much for you."

The call lasted more than ten minutes, and my mother cried the entire time. But it felt liberating to acknowledge our reality, to share our feelings.

It was the most important conversation we ever had. And though we weren't suddenly and miraculously the best of friends thereafter, the door had been opened. We could communicate again. And we could be mother and son again.

It was probably the most distracted I'd ever been at work. Still, after a few minutes of contemplation, allowing what had just happened to sink in, I snapped myself back into the present moment at BC Tel, returned to my customer-centric focus, and completed all twenty-five tickets by the end of my shift.

Salt Spring Island

By this time, I was living with my wife Amy, in a studio apartment just off Broadway, right behind the Denny's restaurant. Numerous flags adorned the few walls we had, including a Canadian flag that I had removed after shinnying up a pole in front of City Hall on 12th and Cambie. We'd listen to Gordon Lightfoot and Kris Kristofferson records and marvel at the genius of Pink Floyd.

Amy was an orthopaedic nurse. We had met in 1970, when she and several other young ladies were washing cars in downtown Vancouver to raise money for healthcare facilities. I paid her to wash my car, and she was undeterred by my long hair and beard. We flirted and exchanged numbers. One thing led to another, and before I knew it, I was going over to her house in a very swanky neighbourhood and being introduced to her parents, who were visibly aghast when they saw what a hippie she'd brought home.

Despite her parents' initial reservations, they grew fond of me, which was fortunate because Amy and I got engaged just two months later—before I was even twenty-four years old. During this period, we had spent most of our free time getting to know each other, and although it happened fast, I felt absolutely certain she was the one and that marriage was the right thing to do. I knew I would feel proud to call Amy my wife.

At the time, I was often juggling night shifts at BC Tel with classes in music, photography, and technical courses to build my skills. Amy, a year younger, came from a very different background. She was the daughter of Joe Green, the founder of one of British Columbia's largest Ford dealerships. Despite our different upbringings, Amy was unpretentious, well-educated, and had an outgoing personality.

Amy and I had a lot in common, especially a shared passion for music and photography. While I was more of a rocker with my long hair and beard, she was a classically trained pianist with a love for folk music, and we took guitar lessons together at Bill Lewis Music—I from the rock instructor and she from the folk teacher. We also enjoyed sports, from hockey and karate to skiing trips up to Grouse Mountain and Whistler. Despite our differences, these shared interests and experiences brought us closer and made us feel at home with each other. The connection we had—exploring each other's worlds and pushing ourselves to new experiences—gave me the confidence to propose just a few months after we met.

Shortly after, we moved into a modest basement studio on 10th Avenue, pooling our resources to make it work. Our space was small and simple, decorated with guitars on the walls and shelves of quirky collectibles, but we found it cozy and filled it with things that made us happy. Amy's parents were a bit shocked by our engagement at first, but we didn't let that deter us.

In the early years of our marriage, Amy and I would spend our weekends on Salt Spring Island, where her family owned seventy-eight acres of oceanfront land. We would take the ferry on a Friday after work and spend time with her parents on their incredible property. It was so wild and beautiful, tranquil, and serene—a vast contrast to the nonstop hectic lives we led in the big city, and something I'd look forward to all week.

Joe was building a house, and I was keen to help. I liked being the hammer-and-nail guy. He had big machinery and tractors that I just loved to drive around.

With the electrical knowledge I had, I was able to help with the house wiring. But I also learned carpentry and how to frame and drywall a home. I thoroughly enjoyed the construction process from start to finish. It was educational and rewarding. There's something quite special about building a house.

It was a period in my life when I became very tempted to take a significantly different path—a path of simplicity and calm. I began to consider becoming a telephone technician on Salt Spring Island.

It would be a low-stress, easy life where I'd still provide a service, but to a much smaller community—a community in which I'd get to know every single person in no time.

I imagined playing my acoustic guitar barefoot in the forest and writing NDP-inspired songs about shovels and spades and the importance of making your way by working with your hands.

I pictured growing my own vegetables, swimming in the sea every morning, taking artistic photos of wildflowers on the mountainside, shearing sheep, and selling my own brand of neon-dyed wool sweaters at the local market in Ganges every Saturday. I imagined my neighbours would buy them and say, "Peter, since you've moved here, I've had absolutely no trouble at all with my telephone."

What a wonderful, worry-free life it would be. I could stay there forever. Retire there.

And that would be it.

Luckily, it was only a momentary aspiration. A lifestyle like that would never have sustained me. I would have become restless, climbing the walls and seeking something big and exciting to do, something monumental to accomplish. Without escape, I would most certainly have died of boredom. Atrophy would have eventually killed me. I'd have fallen into a passive state of laziness, and my energy would have simply dissipated. I'd be gone.

This became even more evident as, back in Vancouver, I strove to fill every hour outside of my full-time job with learning, sports, and creativity. I sought greater challenges as I pursued my career, and took on courses to gain further qualifications. Everything I engaged in was for my own personal growth and future job prospects—I wanted leadership roles.

Amy was equally busy. She was brilliant at her vocation and, in addition to being the lead nurse in the orthopaedic operating room, was working toward her master's degree and teaching nursing at the University of British Columbia.

We had ambition and a strong work ethic in common. We wanted to be challenged and successful. To be the best in our respective fields. To make a difference to others and have an impact. And as such, we didn't spend all that much time together.

The Queen's Sword

I have always been very protective of my sister Suzanne. Though we had our ups and downs in our young sibling relationship, she was always one of my very best friends. We would spend a lot of time together. Sometimes on double dates. Sometimes with my sister Christine or my brother, Paul.

Like me, Suzanne has claustrophobia. In fact, most of my siblings do. I've often wondered why, as I was the only one ever to be shut in a closet. Despite this, Suzanne and I went no fewer than five times to see *Premature Burial* at the movie theatre. It was a horror film based on the short story by Edgar Allan Poe wherein the main character becomes obsessed with a fear of being buried alive. Every time we watched it, we were as captivated as we were terrified. There was something tempting, almost alluring, about staring fear in the face.

It's a funny juxtaposition, taking pleasure in one's worst nightmare. But we did. Maybe enjoying *Premature Burial* was indicative of our own burial of psychological trauma. Mine from being confined in the closet, and Suzanne's from being sent away from her parents and all but one sibling to England on a plane when she was just four years old. As we'd become adults, I'd begun to realize just how scared and sad she must have been. Having recognized that absence of protective parents, I felt a greater need to protect her myself.

One night, at eleven o'clock, I had already gone to bed in our home in Tsawwassen when the ringing phone woke me up.

I picked it up to hear Suzanne sounding worried.

"Peter, you need to come quickly," she said. "The people we had to evict have broken into the neighbouring apartment and threatened us. They said they're going to come back. We're scared."

Suzanne was an apartment manager in the West End of Vancouver, and some tenants could be difficult. But her husband, Gerry, was a black belt in jiu-jitsu, so I thought she should be safe. On this occasion, they felt they couldn't handle the potential violence coming their way, stressing this was serious and backup was necessary.

It was a forty-five-minute drive from my place to their apartment building. I felt I ought to take something to protect myself with, or to at least make me feel safer—something for show.

In my sleepy state, trying to think quickly, I grabbed an enormous Queen Victoria officer's sword that I had bought at Windsor Castle when visiting with Amy just a few months prior.

I drove to Suzanne's quickly, where I sat with Gerry and her for just an anxious few minutes before there was a buzz from the front entrance. I answered it and went downstairs to the entryway. I opened the front door and told them loudly and firmly to get their shit and get out, or else I'd deal with them. My surging adrenaline served me well as they flinched at the intensity, grabbed their stuff, and left, much to the relief of everyone. No weapons were necessary.

Deciding the threat was over, Suzanne and Gerry were grateful as I took my sword and left—concealing it down my pant leg for the short walk back to my vehicle.

On approaching my car, through the darkness of the night sky, I saw three menacing-looking guys sitting on the hood.

"What the fuck are you guys doing? Get off my car!" I yelled from around four metres away.

One of them rose up and responded, "Fuck you, make us."

My heart pounded and my hands trembled as I pulled that huge, elaborately decorated sword from my pants and brandished it toward them. Truthfully, I wasn't sure how much damage a hundred-year-old officer's sword could have done—or if I'd have even known how to wield it—but the audacity of it seemed enough. Maybe it wasn't the sword itself but the sight of a crazy-looking guy in the middle of the night, waving around an over-the-top blade, that sent them fleeing. Like frightened rabbits, they took off as I climbed into my car, my pulse still racing, and drove home.

Tom Porteous

We all need protectors. And we all need mentors.

Protect and mentor has become one of my mantras throughout life. I hold such high regard for the people in my life who mentored and motivated me, recognizing how powerful their encouragement was, that I, in turn, strive to do the same. Teaching, guiding, supporting, and uplifting wherever I can—wherever I see potential—I do my best to help people flourish.

I became a good mentor because I had good mentors. It was a domino effect of positivity.

Tom Porteous was instrumental in my early career as someone who recognized my strengths and encouraged me to pursue my life goals.

During my early years at BC Tel, Tom saw potential in me and selected me as one of just three people to complete an intensive forty-eight-week computer and hardware course to prepare us for the more-than-a-year installation and acceptance testing of the TSPS system.

Tom and the three of us worked hand in hand with the computer specialists from the telephone equipment manufacturing company, GTE, for over a year. When completed, we were proud to take control of the systems as the GTE representatives returned to their home base in Chicago. We were flying on our own. What an exhilarating but daunting feeling.

Tom told us how proud he was of our accomplishment as we took control of the daily operations of the system and all that entailed. As he was my supervisor and someone who had trusted me, I wanted Tom Porteous to know that he could count on me no matter what the circumstances.

I registered for various courses to enhance my understanding of computer languages and systems. I completed a course in the programming language Fortran at the British Columbia Institute of Technology, as well as a course in digital transmission, both of which I found straightforward due to my previous training as a radar technician and my previous technical position at Northern Radio.

There's a creative aspect to technology. You need to visualize how systems can function, how you want them to work, before testing the science. I enjoyed the complexity of it all and sought greater challenges. Tom recognized this about me and supported me as I worked my way into leadership roles at BC Tel and progressed both technically and administratively during my twelve years at the company.

Sadly, Tom would die all too young of prostate cancer. He was a wonderful man, and I am forever grateful that he was a part of my life.

Building My Soundtrack

During my years at BC Tel, I led an extremely busy life with very few hours of sleep. Outside of work, I played on numerous sports teams, signed up for various courses to enhance my resume, took photography classes, and immersed myself in my love of music.

I sometimes wonder how many times I've listened to my favourite songs and try to remember where I was, what I was doing, and who I was with the very first time I heard them. It's not an easy task—even for those with the best memories.

Though we might be unaware of it in the moment, each of our lives builds its own soundtrack—a playlist that reflects our journey, our challenges and triumphs, our romances and our heartache, our willpower and our rebellion, our joy, and our sorrow.

There are tracks that will trigger memories, nostalgia, emotions. They'll remind us of certain people, certain places, certain events. There are songs we'll sing many times in the car or in the shower, songs we'll dance to at weddings, at milestone celebrations, at Christmas parties. There are songs that will carry us through hard times, offer messages of hope, or serendipitously play on the radio at the very moment we need to hear them the most.

I consider music to be the communication of the soul. It's a window to something beyond the three-dimensional world we inhabit. It can spark an idea, aid the process of grieving, offer a means to express euphoria or melancholy or determination—even inspire a revolution.

Music can make me feel challenged, contemplative, utterly fabulous, or at absolute peace. I have always believed music played a hugely important role in my own development and growth. It was my passion, my escape, a gift I honed for myself and would always offer up for others.

Music is an international language that transcends status or circumstance. Those who attend the same concert or festival are united in an endorphin-filled aura created by the merging array of feelings experienced by a crowd listening to the same powerful melodies.

If you can play an instrument, you can access the world of creating and re-creating music, getting lost in the endless possibilities—the limitless array of infinite tunes, each unique to the performer's style.

In 1971, I decided to take my interest in guitar-playing more seriously, and began lessons with Craig McCaw of the Poppy Family. The Poppy Family was a Canadian psychedelic pop group that had several international hit records in the late 1960s. Their most well-known and successful song, "Which Way You Goin' Billy?" featured introspective lyrics that resonated strongly with audiences. The track reached number one on the Canadian charts and peaked at number two on the U.S. *Billboard* Hot 100.

During one of my first lessons, Craig taught me Jimi Hendrix's "Little Wing," which became one of my all-time favourite songs.

Craig knew every Mountain song note for note, and I was particularly moved by "Mississippi Queen," which still today evokes feelings of nostalgia for the 1970s Vancouver as I recall my days of after-work music lessons. I developed a huge respect for Craig, whom I recognized to be a superbly talented musician during a very interesting time for the progression of the genres he played.

At the same location I had taken lessons with Craig, I was also taught by Jamie Bowers, who became another significant influence in my life. Inspiring and creative, he encouraged me to pursue my artistic side. I considered Jamie to be a savant. I had never been in the presence of someone so talented and rooted in music or its theory. I took lessons twice per week for eleven years.

As was my nature, I needed to understand more about music and how it was made. How it was literally made. I needed it to make sense in my mind how every component of every sound was produced. So, I took a guitar-building course from Jack Lewis—Bill Lewis's brother—in 1973 to learn how to build acoustic guitars. Jack had formerly been in the logging business and had begun harvesting and resawing western red cedar, which, in the brothers' opinion, was the optimal material for guitar-building.

I was learning from the absolute best in the business. From the late 1960s to the early 1980s, Bill Lewis Guitars on Broadway and Dunbar in downtown Vancouver was *the* guitar store to visit. His guitars were works of art appreciated by some of the finest musicians of the era.

They were owned by the likes of Led Zeppelin guitarist Jimmy Page and Pink Floyd's David Gilmour—one was used in the recording of *The Dark Side of The Moon*. Eric Clapton played a Bill Lewis guitar when performing in Vancouver in 1969. There aren't many of them out there in the world, and they're worth a lot of money!

Photography

I'm drawn to preserve memories, to tell stories, to reflect emotions, and am perhaps motivated by a heightened awareness of mortality, of the speed at which time passes by, of the need to document it all— never wanting to lose a single bit of life. Capturing moments through photography felt like a way to preserve tiny pieces of life and forever keep a memory fresh.

I had the technical skills necessary to quickly learn about cameras and lenses, and to understand lighting and composition, and I had the patience and perseverance to get the best shots, knowing the wait would always be worth it.

I would find beauty in everything, transforming my vision into hopefully captivating images that would effectively illustrate my perspective.

Photographs are a window through which to view history and culture, and showcase the vast array of brilliant, intriguing, and awe-inspiring differences in people and places.

I have great respect for the power of photographs, knowing they can stir emotions and even ignite social change: They can drive people's decisions, affect their viewpoints, and offer greater explanations in the absence of words worthy of the scene.

Analog cameras offer a unique look and feel that exudes authenticity through their slower, more intentional processing—not just in the darkroom but also in taking a picture more purposefully. The absence of instant on-screen previews and limited film rolls forced me to be more deliberate with my framing, timing, and lighting.

Though photos are seen as a tangible record of past experiences that can connect people across time and distance, we now live in a digital age that has made it possible—easy, even—to manipulate and edit photos. The rapid evolution of artificial intelligence threatens the value of photography as we know it. While I encourage and applaud technological progress, I fear the loss of authenticity that such advancements will spur.

I was aware from quite early on in life, when I found great enjoyment in history and learning about the past through documentation, that I was, in fact—as is everyone—a part of history in the making. And I felt a strong desire to record the present day so that I and others could look back on it in the future—to document my own history and everything that was going on around me. I felt others didn't take that idea as seriously as I did. They didn't see the importance or significance of photographs or film.

It was something I desired to do long before it became a trend. I wanted to be able to share with others my reality—whether it was what it's like in an aircraft hangar, working in avionics and seeing impressive jets taking off, or how my friends and I lived and what our lives were like in a specific era, at a specific time. I wanted to remember all I was experiencing, because I knew it would be over tomorrow.

When I arrived in Vancouver in 1969, with my Bell & Howell Super 8 mm movie camera, I decided to pursue my passion for photography and learn how to do it better. I subscribed to photo magazines and enrolled in many specialized photography courses.

In 1973, Focal Point: The Visual Arts Learning Centre opened at 4474 West 10th Avenue, offering diplomas and part-time programs. At Focal Point, I befriended other aspiring photographers, developed my camera and film-processing skills, learned about composition, techniques, colour, light, and angles, and honed my creative eye.

I tried to cram in as much learning as possible during that time: guitar lessons, a photography course, hockey once a week, karate three times per week, and school at night. I fit it all in by averaging four hours of sleep, and somehow, I sustained that for a few years.

In 1976, I graduated from Langara College with a major in photography.

While working with Walter Evans at Focal Point, I had access to a large studio and a well-equipped darkroom that I set up in my home. The darkroom allowed me to develop and print photos quickly, often showing clients the results on the same day. My process included working in black-and-white, C4 colour, and Cibachrome, which produced vivid, high-quality prints with excellent colour saturation and archival properties. This efficiency and range of options appealed to local modelling agencies, and set me apart as a photographer who could deliver both quality and speed.

The agencies valued my approachable style and unique approach to lighting. I preferred fixed lights over flash photography, as they allowed me to see and control shadows, creating a softer focus that gave my portraits a natural look. This approach made clients feel comfortable and confident in front of the camera, and they appreciated the artistic softness and immediacy I brought to their photos. My reputation grew quickly, and I became known as a dependable photographer with a style that models and agency managers valued or sought after.

In 1974, I photographed the Mr. North America contest for *Looking Good* magazine, which aspired to be the equal to the very popular *Muscle Builder*—later renamed *Muscle & Fitness*. Italian bodybuilder, power-lifter, and actor Franco Columbu, who was Mr. Olympia at the time, was there. The Mentzer Brothers, Robbie Robinson, and the up-and-coming Arnold Schwarzenegger were all showing off their strength and toned physiques.

The Weider Brothers, who owned *Muscle Builder* magazine and whose names were inscribed on most barbell and weightlifting equipment, were there. In fact, my role as photo editor for *Looking Good* magazine was to show them around Vancouver. Both brothers were wonderful ambassadors for the industry. We hosted them at the restaurant atop Grouse Mountain overlooking Vancouver and its harbour.

In addition, I would make money by doing wedding photography on the weekends, processing the film in my at-home darkroom. I had wonderful camera systems, including a Nikon F3 and Mamiya RB67, a large-format camera that produced very high-quality images.

These were exclusively film-based, so once the shoot was over, the work began. I always had a fear of losing the film or that the shots wouldn't come out great. A wedding wasn't an event you could re-create or do again, so I was always nervous waiting to see the results.

There were so many things that could go wrong, and I was always aware of these pitfalls, as wedding photography is so important to the couple. The pictures I would take would be the photos they'd cherish for life.

Wedding photography was my least preferred type of photography, as it demanded considerable effort for the potential risks involved, particularly since money was never my incentive. I was motivated to pursue opportunities that contributed to my portfolio of diverse shooting situations.

Most of the weddings I photographed were done as favours to friends or word-of-mouth references following those. I'd occasionally get unusual requests, such as the one from the couple who requested I take their photo as they snorted cocaine together in a vestibule off the main church hall. Both bride and groom resembled Rod Stewart.

The bride pulled a huge baggie of cocaine from her purse and invited me to join them in their post-nuptial ceremonial high, but I politely declined.

I was far too busy to delve into the world of mind-altering substances. The only occasion I ever partook was in 1969 at Silver Lake in Ontario with Rick. After about twenty beers, Rick had told me to try a little red pill he pulled from his pocket. It would be my first and last experience with LSD. As the seventeen-minute-long psychedelic rock song "In-A-Gadda-Da-Vida" by Iron Butterfly played, I lay looking up at the star-filled sky as a gargantuan owl with fire shooting from its talons swooped down on me.

After that terrifyingly real hallucination, I made the decision never to take drugs again.

Art Phillips

Art Phillips was the thirty-second mayor of Vancouver, in office from 1973 to 1977. He was considered a progressive mayor who advocated for environmental sustainability alongside heritage preservation. Most notably, he's known for creating the downtown waterfront park, today known as Jack Poole Plaza, which served as the site for the 2010 Winter Olympics' cauldron.

Driving to work one morning, I stopped to grab a newspaper and was thrilled to see my photograph of Art Phillips on the front page of *The Vancouver Province*. I had been paid fifty dollars for that photo, an action shot of Phillips at the Gastown bike rally with an ice cream cone sticking out of his mouth. Incidentally, he was married to Carole Taylor, who was on the board of Rogers at that time.

It was an image that generated a lot of humour that morning, with most of Vancouver talking about it. It stirred conversations and got people talking politics.

BC Pen Hostage-Taking

The weekend prior to a hostage-taking, I was playing baseball with our BC Tel team, against the very prisoners who instigated it.

Arriving at the jail that Saturday, we left our belongings at the holding area and were escorted by prison guards to the ballfield, where we were met with whistles from the inmates who were watching their team from the bleachers. We were the recipients of catcalls and other crude jeering by the inmates. Although it was initially unnerving, the teams transitioned to more typical rivalry banter and settled into their usual competitive mindsets. One of the more unusual sights was that of a prisoner dressed in a bikini, prancing up and down the third base line, hurling insults at us. This was received by spontaneous cheers from the stands.

And it became like any other game. It was fun, adrenaline-boosting to have such a rowdy crowd of spectators. We were evenly matched teams, which kept things interesting. The BC Pen prisoners were exceptionally talented. After all, they had nothing but time to excel. After seven innings, the game was tied. Consequently, the prisoners requested two additional innings, after which they emerged victorious, winning by one run. Not only did they exhibit excellent skills, but they played fairly.

It was difficult to imagine that so many of these young men, now confined to spend their days behind the walls of this nineteenth-century federal jail, had done such abhorrent, evil, hurtful things. They played with passion, energy, and obvious ability even as they jeered and cheered and smiled and laughed, as they dove and jumped and ran and slid.

It was evident that for this short time, none of them were thinking about the horrors they'd committed for one reason or another—because they had made horrendous decisions, been unable to control their impulses, had regrettable moments of rage or an attitude that was never reined in or disciplined throughout their troubled and love-deprived childhoods.

Was it because they were seeking vengeance or acting in self-defence? Were they jealous, addicted, threatened? Maybe they'd had a mental breakdown, a delusion, or an irrational fear. I wondered if they were remorseful now, or full of arrogance and hatred. Did they have sadness upon reflection, and empathy for others, or only contempt for authority?

Here were two teams playing a game of baseball. One side had committed crimes severe enough to put them in a high-security federal prison; the other side worked for a telecommunications company. But we were all individuals, with our own stories, our own motivations, our own failures and hopes, and inevitably, our own mental health problems—present from birth or developed due to a lifetime of unfortunate experiences, neglect, or trauma.

It was a few hours on a single sunny day, in which all those prisoners must have momentarily felt a childlike freedom that transported them back to boyhood and perhaps a longing to return to more innocent days with an opportunity to start again.

Maybe that baseball game further fuelled a desire for escape, that taste of liberty, those minutes of genuine enjoyment. I don't know.

The following Wednesday, June 11, 1975, Mary Steinhauser, a thirty-two-year-old social worker from Vancouver Island's Cowichan Valley, was unintentionally shot and killed by a police officer during a stand-off with three inmates that had lasted forty-one hours at BC Penitentiary in New Westminster.

The inmates—Andy Bruce, Dwight Lucas, and Claire Wilson—had taken fifteen people, including Steinhauser, hostage by knifepoint to escape the prison.

Steinhauser was a psychiatric nurse with a master's degree in social work. She was an advocate against solitary confinement. Arguably, her approach was progressive for the time and considerably more empathetic than was commonplace.

CKNW's most popular broadcaster, Jack Webster, was on the scene at the hostage-taking and even participated in negotiations. It was something that journalists today might not be encouraged to do, but it was at the prisoners' request that he acted as a mediator in the situation.

From the 1950s to his retirement, Jack Webster was known as King of the Vancouver Airwaves. He was an abrasive Scotsman who'd been a major in the British army, serving several years in the Middle East before emigrating to Canada. Perhaps these experiences were useful to have in a person on hand as these events unfolded at BC Penitentiary.

It was quite the dramatic juxtaposition, the energy and fun of a friendly baseball game and the ultimate killing of a young woman who'd done nothing to harm or hurt those who used her as a bargaining tool. She'd, in fact, been one to advocate for more humane conditions and greater understanding and compassion toward the inmates. How tragically unfair, how devastatingly unjustified, how heartbreakingly cruel.

And as I watched it all unfold from my office at BC Tel, in the knowledge that I had just been at that very place with those very people, it reminded me of life's unpredictability and my good fortune.

Brothers

For many of us, the first team we ever join is that of our family. We have no say in this. We are born into a group of people we may or may not like but are forced to live with for a time and, regardless of whatever future distance we might put between ourselves and them, will forever be connected to.

Families are teams that inevitably face a lot of internal competition.

I always considered my slightly older brother, Paul, to have a sense of entitlement that came from a mollycoddled childhood that contrasted starkly with my own experience of our parents.

Though Paul was older and smarter—at least on paper—I always felt the need to protect him. When I was twenty-eight and Paul was twenty-nine, the two of us joined a karate dojo in Vancouver that was run by a husband-and-wife duo who had received their black belts while training in a dojo in Japan.

During our training session, Paul was confronted by a much larger student who felt intruded upon by us newcomers and wanted it to be known that he was king of the hill.

We'd spend time learning kata. These are defined movements and techniques performed in a specific pattern that are often performed in solo training exercises. They simulate combat situations, containing combinations of kicks, blocks, stances, and strikes that must be executed in a precise, predetermined sequence. Practising kata is said to enhance balance, form, and mental focus. It's an essential part of karate training that develops muscle memory, skill, and discipline in the martial art.

After about a year of attending karate two evenings per week, Paul and I and others from the dojo were practising the noncontact kata and sparring techniques. Though it was supposed to be noncontact, it was fast and competitive, and accidents could happen, particularly to a person's solar plexus—the vulnerable area of the upper abdomen. Striking this sensitive area below the rib cage can temporarily incapacitate an opponent and is frequently taught in self-defence training. The big guy hit Paul so hard that he collapsed and couldn't breathe.

A rush of adrenaline rushed through my body, and I declared to the sensei, "I wanna fight him!" It was an overwhelming instinct to immediately avenge my winded brother.

"Are you sure?" asked the sensei.

"Yes, I want to fight him right now!" I said, full of adrenaline.

I beat the shit out of that bully, humiliating him in front of all forty members of the dojo. Though I did not consider myself to be a particularly good athlete, when the offer of competition arose, I was always enthusiastic.

During my first karate tournament fight at the Forum in downtown Vancouver, I was disqualified for punching an American's teeth out. My opponent had travelled from Oregon for the competition, and that morning, I had overheard him telling a friend he'd been set up to fight *a real mark*—an insult that echoed in my mind for the full three hours between that moment and our match. I had not intended for the guy to lose teeth; it happened in a flash, and as blood-spattered flags went up around me, I heard the word *disqualified* reverberate around the venue. My sensei was up in the stands, yelling at me to apologize. So, I did apologize before saying, "If you're not able to fight, can I take your place?"

My opponent was not very happy, shouting, "Fuck you!" through a very bloodied mouth.

Hockey

I first donned skates at age three, in Ottawa. I'd skate in locations around the city with my older siblings, on outdoor rinks and the Rideau Canal. I also skated in Calgary as a kindergartner, and in Montreal.

That first time, as I skated on a pond in the evening, I enjoyed hearing the swooshing sound of the blades on the cold, hard ice. Later, during my secondary school years, I played hockey with friends on Hatzic Lake in British Columbia's Fraser Valley, pushing the puck through lines of built-up snow atop thin, clear ice that moved in gentle waves as I skated over it. I never really feared the reality that this motion was a sign the ice could break at any moment. Fortunately, it never did.

As a teenager boarding at the seminary in Ottawa, I had the rink to myself every evening with nine other friends. We practised together, then prepared the rink for the next day, playing in all temperatures, with red noses and frozen eyelashes.

As an adult in Vancouver, I got serious about hockey. I played at the Four Rinks in Burnaby, which had both indoor and outdoor arenas. I joined BC Tel's team playing in the industrial league, and, although underdogs, we won the championship in the mid-1970s. My linemates were Ted Parker and Marv Brubacher.

BC Tel News would proudly share pictures of the team. Our line was fortunate to have scored the most goals in that tournament. One of my teammates from those days, Drew McCarthur, continues to play recreational hockey well into his seventies.

The sport caused me multiple injuries and required no fewer than six shoulder operations after I experienced complete acromioclavicular separations. Try saying that with a mouthful of donuts! Fortunately, Amy worked in the operating room in orthopaedics, so I had an expedited route to treatment—perhaps this subconsciously reduced my resistance as, time and again, I engaged in a high-speed, fiercely determined, rough-and-tumble approach to the game. It wasn't just shoulder injuries; I also broke multiple ribs, insisted on playing with broken ribs, and then broke some more and punctured my lung. It was painful, but I considered it all part of the joy of playing competitive sports.

I would frequent Vancouver General Hospital so often that I even appeared two years in a row on the exact same day with the exact same injury caused in the exact same way by the exact same player from the exact same rival team. His name was Dave Adams, and he had stuck his stick between my legs when I was on a promising breakaway with a clear path to the goal for a prime scoring opportunity, causing me to trip and slam hard headfirst into the boards—a sequence that unfolded as if in slow motion. The surgeon declared feeling a strong sense of déjà vu.

Despite the setbacks and the months I spent healing, the BC Tel team won our division championship. The victory was exhilarating and demonstrated the power of a unified team. My motivation only grew when facing bullies, obstacles, and doubt, and my desire to prove others wrong was a powerful force that drove me to persist against all odds. Each challenge I encountered fuelled my determination to succeed, and became a catalyst for my growth. Winning that championship felt like winning the Stanley Cup, and I was immensely proud.

This relentless commitment to sports tied into my deep belief in team-based values and personal accountability. Whether in hockey or baseball, I found joy not just in the game itself, but in contributing to the team's success. The bonds I created with my hockey line mates, for example, have lasted for over forty years. I always felt an obligation to give my all, even at the risk of injury. Similarly, in baseball, I thrived on being in pivotal roles, such as pitching, where strategy and execution determined the game's outcome. Before each game, I would visualize playing the perfect game, and those images propelled my performance on the field.

For me, the principles of sports carry over into business. In both, teamwork is paramount, and success hinges on positive relationships and accountability. Just as I respected my sports teammates and competitors, I applied that same respect in negotiations and business. It was never about domination—it was about creating win–win scenarios where everyone walked away feeling valued. Interestingly, a 23andMe analysis later revealed that I carry what is referred to as an elite athletic marker in my DNA. While I can't say for sure how much that contributed to my love of sports, it does align with my lifelong drive for competition and high performance.

Five — Crossroads, 1977–1983

The day Elvis died, I was stung by a jellyfish in Greece—and a scantily clad, hippie young woman kindly offered to pee on me.

Despite the agony, I respectfully declined. I was a gentleman. A married man. And not partial to being urinated on.

It was August 16, 1977, and just as I had not been able to help falling in love with Amy, I was also unable to halt the growing distance between us as I gradually fell out of love with her.

We were in Greece for five weeks, a romantic destination where we had ridden Vespas, visited islands, and explored the historic city of Athens, much of which I had artfully captured on my camera.

It was an idyllic setting for a young couple. It was time away from work, an opportunity for some well-deserved R & R; the weather was perfect, the scenery spectacular, the food delicious, and the ouzo flowing. Despite this, Amy and I seemed to be becoming more distant, unable to appreciate each other's company. And if that couldn't be done under such circumstances, then it certainly did not bode well for our future.

I felt terribly sad as I thought back on when we first met and how I once felt about her. There is something elusive about love—that it truly cannot be prevented or forced. It's a power greater than human control, as all the Elvis fans who mourned the day he died will attest.

Thomas

In 1978, I decided I needed to move on from my marriage to Amy.

Having begun our relationship so young, we were growing apart as we were growing up. While we had ambition in common, we had each become so busy with our own careers, often working conflicting hours, frequently taking night shifts—she as a nurse and I as a technician. In addition to my work, I pursued photography, karate, and hockey during my off-hours. As our paths barely crossed, our relationship became increasingly platonic—almost as if we were housemates. It was respectful but not loving. It was no longer a harmonious unity where we shared the same visions for our future. It was a quiet, disconnected, unfortunate conflict of hopes, beliefs, and ideals that was not conducive to progress or happiness.

I cared about Amy, and I felt great nostalgia for our relationship and appreciation for our memories, but I could not see making more memories with her. We could remain friends, perhaps. We could end things amicably, and it would be best for both of us. We could move on. There was more out there awaiting each of us. New chapters beckoned. It was over.

The day I planned to talk to Amy, to tell her I wanted a divorce—that word my young Catholic self never thought would apply to me—Amy had something to say, too.

"I'm pregnant."

I couldn't hide my disbelief and compulsive honesty. I could not pretend to be thrilled by this news. Suddenly, everything I'd planned out and hoped would happen was thrown into uncertainty, and I was caught between my desire to do the right thing and the need to be true to myself.

As Amy and I sat in the kitchen, I tried to form my sentences. I didn't want to hurt her, although I sensed that I would. This was a deeply emotional and pivotal moment in our lives. I found it incredibly challenging to express my feelings about love and our relationship, particularly when I knew our conversation involved ending it, and all the significant change that would mean. I was trying to balance honesty with compassion. But there was no easy way of expressing what I wanted to say other than by stating my true feelings.

"I want to move out."

Amy was silent, trying to comprehend what I had just said. "Even Margie our sister-in-law called me to congratulate us. What am I going to say to her?" she sobbed. "What am I going to tell my parents?"

She was wiping her nose as tears filled her eyes. I truly cared for her and wanted to ensure that she felt supported, especially with the impending responsibility of parenthood. I told Amy in that very moment what I knew in my heart, what I thought we both knew, in fact: that we weren't in love. I said I would be a supportive father, that I'd do all I needed to do for our baby. But I'd do it in a world where we were separated.

It was a horrible, difficult, emotional conversation. But it was a crucial acknowledgement of our situation.

That evening, feeling emotionally exhausted, we decided to consult someone who could possibly help us. But after several months of couples therapy, we parted ways.

And so—after eight years of marriage—it wasn't the joyful, exciting pregnancy that young married couples hope for. I often wondered why God had chosen to bestow a baby upon us at that time.

Speaking to my father-in-law, Joe, about the breakup, I felt sadness that we'd no longer be related. But I knew we'd keep a connection, as we'd become close. I admired everything about him. His ambition, his work ethic, and his openness. We could always say whatever was on our minds. As Joe did when I told him Amy and I were separating.

"Are you fucking stupid?" Joe said. "Do you know how much you're going to be worth?"

Joe Green was a multimillionaire. Should I have remained married to Amy, I would have eventually been joint recipient of his impressive empire.

Though I was influenced somewhat by the passionate notions of the left-wing liberal hippie movement, it was not because of that that I declined money in favour of love.

"You can have all the cash in the world, but what does that matter if you're not happy?" I told my father-in-law.

It sounded a little poetic and probably borderline nauseating to your stereotypical mogul, but Joe understood my sentiment and respected my decision—and my honesty. I told him I could never bullshit him.

Since my marriage to Amy, I had come a long way in my career. I was getting recognized for my skills and positive can-do attitude. I had been promoted. My reputation was growing. I was well-groomed. I appeared tidier. I suppose, I looked like a businessman.

A lot of that was owed to the influence of my impressive father-in-law. He was a man who knew that the only way to get what you want in life is to go and fucking get it. He was an influence so great that he had perhaps changed the trajectory of my life. His influence was evident now in my decision to reject a free ride, in my choice to move on from my unhappy marriage, and in my determination to pursue my own success and my own joy. Joe succinctly stated his amusing business advice to me about his secret to success: You slide farther on shit than rocks! I thought of that often when the urge to push back was replaced with the wise advice to practise restraint.

It was the most stressful time of my life, and I broke out in hives. My hands were covered, and it was painful. I was prescribed prednisone. It's amazing how the body physically responds in these moments of psychological distress.

But none of that took away from the love I felt for my newborn son the instant he arrived.

Thomas was the one who first made me feel like a father. He was the first child whose birth I was present for, the first whose diapers I changed. He was the first newborn I held close and carefully, experiencing that confusing mix of awe and fear—fear of the monumental, inescapable responsibility that many parents feel during those early, sleepless, life-altering days.

Baby Thomas Bissonnette had been named after my much-loved and highly respected uncle on my mother's side, who had served as a Grenadier Guard at Buckingham Palace. He was a loving man with a black belt in jiu-jitsu—sort of strong but gentle.

I continued to pay my way, contributing to the mortgage and bills that kept Amy and Thomas in their home. Irrespective of the fact that money was no object to Amy's family, I did what would be expected of any man in that situation. After all, I was the one who chose to leave and change their set of circumstances. And it was the annual increase in these payments that further motivated me to ascend my career ladder more expeditiously—to increase my salary, to ease that financial strain, and to take full responsibility for my obligations.

As a child, Thomas excelled at school. He was a natural genius, gifted, and quick to grasp even the most complex scientific concepts from a very young age. Though I also had an aptitude for the technical, I was more excited by the idea of playing sports and music with my son— which we did, but Thomas never truly enjoyed it.

As Thomas grew up, we grew farther apart until he ultimately made a choice to cut me out of his life entirely. There had been miscommunications, unspoken words, hurt, and disappointments on both sides. And we evidently share a stubborn streak in what I feel is a very sad father–son breakup.

The piercing pain of rejection I felt may subconsciously be reminiscent of the way my parents rejected me. But, despite my efforts, I too failed at fatherhood, and that failure was not easy to accept.

Over the years, I've tried to find him, tried to speak with him, attempted to reconcile. I sent him cheques for birthdays and special occasions, five or ten thousand dollars each time, that were uncashed and returned to sender. I tried going to his place of work in Vancouver—hoping I might bump into him at his downtown office in the old Sinclair building.

I found out through social media that Thomas and his wife had a baby. A grandchild I may never meet. Thomas's wife is a doctor, and on one occasion I went to the hospital where she worked to see if she would speak with me. She would not.

I would have loved to have kept a natural father–son relationship with Thomas. I think about him often and miss him greatly. I've tried to make sense of our estrangement, and though I've often wondered if it's related to money and that perhaps he thought I had more than

I did—and should have given him more than I did—he has never needed money.

Men are not born with an inherent, natural capacity to be brilliant fathers, just as women are not born with an instinctive ability to thrive in motherhood—to know what to do, how to love, how to nurture, how to guide, educate, discipline, and bond, simply because society says this is a role in which they should automatically excel.

There are guidebooks, and advice and support systems and research and information, but none of it can change the way you feel. None of that can guarantee a soul connection, unbreakable blood-ties. It cannot build and strengthen unconditional love.

I feel the absence of Thomas. I know I cannot alter the past to be a better father. It is my life's biggest regret.

St. Anthony

It was around the time Thomas was born, as I was facing the new challenges of early fatherhood, navigating a separation and heartache, managing a busy life, big changes, and the side effects of stress, that I needed reminding of my faith.

One evening, after a few drinks with friends at the Rose & Thorn—the much-loved and frequented pub of all BC Tel employees, just steps from our building on Seymour, where I was now a TSPS supervisor—I met one of my guardian angels.

It was 1:00 a.m. as I was getting into my car. As I sat down, and put on my seat belt, before I could shut the door, an arm reached in, grabbed me by the head, and proceeded to punch me repeatedly in the face. Flashes of light hit me as he pounded my face and eyes.

He was yelling, almost spitting at me, "You fucking piece of shit! Why you, and not me?"

Pushing back with an explosion of energy and strength, I forced my way out of the car and spun this mystery hooligan onto the hood.

Holding him down, I yelled, "What the fuck are you doing? Who the fuck are you?" No sooner had that come out of my mouth than I recognized my assailant. I knew the guy. It was a workmate from BC Tel named Jerry. I was shaking from the wave of adrenaline that had surged in me. It was the same feeling I had felt when I was confined in a small space and had to break free. As my mind cleared, I shouted at him, "What the fuck is going on?"

He was incoherent and just mumbled, "You got all the breaks!" as he stumbled away. I recalled that Jerry worked in the long-distance switching centre at BC Tel, but not on the same floor as I did. I would run into him occasionally in the hallway and at lunch, but he was never communicative with me; in fact, I had a feeling that he didn't like me. Now I knew that for sure!

The most upsetting thing about the incident was that in the altercation, I had my gold chain ripped from my neck—something I didn't realize until I got home.

At 7:00 a.m., I returned to the parking lot and looked around the area where my car had been parked. There was nobody around, and it was eerily quiet. But as I looked up, I saw a person who appeared to be homeless, wearing round glasses with cracked lenses and long, unkempt hair.

"What are you looking for?" he asked in a low and calm voice.

I told him that somebody had attacked me last night and I lost a gold chain.

"You will find it," said the man.

No sooner had he uttered that than he simply disappeared. Perplexed, I did a 360-degree scan, looking around for him. He was nowhere to be seen in any direction. But there, in the very spot where he had stood, on the ground was my gold chain.

I immediately thought of Saint Anthony of Padua, the patron saint of lost and stolen articles, and got goosebumps, as I knew something spiritual had just happened to me.

Upon returning to work on Monday, I told Tom Porteous of the incident. He shared with me that Jerry had some challenges with drugs and alcohol. Taking the compassionate approach, we agreed it was not an offence he should be fired for, but rather we wanted to help him. So, we arranged a period of rehab—which ultimately was the best option for everyone, as it delivered a more positive outcome all around.

The gold chain had an ankh pendant on it. It was of sentimental value. It was symbolic of my journey, my past, and my love of life. It was representative of hope. It was a reminder that the opportunity to travel far and wide is ever present and that there's always more to explore.

I wore that necklace all the time for many years, until I eventually passed it on to my youngest son, Michael.

Manifesting and Visualization

Manifesting and visualization are concepts that involve focusing on goals and dreams, and imagining them as if they have already happened. In doing so, the idea is that we attract these forces into our lives to make our desires reality.

Though it might sound too good to be true, there is considerable evidence supporting this theory, both anecdotally and through comprehensive studies. Specifically, research on athletes shows that those who visualize themselves achieving something unique or setting a personal record tend to perform significantly better than those who do not. The lack of visualization, in turn, may invite an element of self-doubt.

This is not to discount luck, which is entirely separate. It is not to say that those who exude negative energy are at fault when tragedy befalls them. That isn't how it works. Misfortune and circumstance, the actions of others, nature, and the coinciding of time and error will, of course, result in bad luck that is beyond individual control.

However, when we're actively chasing a dream, training for a marathon, prepping for a job interview, embarking on a creative project, envisioning ourselves living in a certain place, or preparing for an upcoming exam—these are the moments when we need to build up our enthusiastic spirit, upbeat attitude, and optimistic outlook. We need to gather all those good vibes and fill our aura with them. Proceed with confidence and determination!

This might seem obvious, but it's a notion that people around the world have not adopted en masse. Feelings of unworthiness, fear of rejection, imposter syndrome, and inferiority complex can take hold of far too many of us—particularly in a modern world that combines high expectations with an aversion to embracing anything too original.

Doubt can become a self-fulfilling prophecy and ultimately lead to failure.

People will tell us that daydreaming is a waste of time, that we should keep our feet on the ground and not get lost in the clouds. But it's not about floating around aimlessly; it's about aiming high. Without daring to imagine these scenarios, without picturing the life we long for, without practising our Oscars acceptance speeches, the universe will have no idea what we want.

The more detail we envision—the sensations, the emotions, the reactions—the better. Writing it down makes our goals all the clearer. By setting timelines, stepping stones, benchmarks, and waypoints, we begin to see the end goal coming ever closer as we check off these lists, reflect on achievements, and witness our own personal growth and progress.

Of course, it must be doable. People confuse the idea of manifesting with believing in the impossible, setting unrealistic expectations. But that's not how it works. It needs to be within the realm of human capability, or it will only lead to disappointment. The point is that our capability is infinitely greater than we realize, and we'll never know how great it is until we push ourselves to find out.

The vocations we're drawn to, the passions we feel, the purposeful activities we enjoy, the skills we were born with—all offer us opportunities to climb much, much higher.

Many books relate to this idea, including Maxwell Maltz's *Psycho-Cybernetics*, which I read back in 1969 on the bus to Vancouver. It was life-changing for me!

Lou Tice

I appreciate the expression "You are what you eat." In Lou Tice's perspective, "You are shaped by your own words."

The author of *Smart Talk for Achieving Your Potential: 5 Steps to Get You from Here to There*, Lou was a renowned personal development trainer and founder of The Pacific Institute, an organization that specializes in providing training programs aimed at improving personal and professional performance.

Lou Tice facilitated the weeklong session at The Pacific Institute that would remind me how impactful Maxwell Maltz's book had been, and how stimulating and encouraging his exciting and powerful ideas truly were.

Like Maltz, Tice offered inspirational teachings on the power of the mind that ultimately impacted millions across the world. Focused on helping others achieve their goals and realize their potential, he developed Smart Talk, an effective communication training program aimed at improving students' communication skills and teaching them how to interact with different types of people to build positive relationships in all walks of life.

My experience at The Pacific Institute had a significant influence on me. The time I time spent with Lou Tice was especially transformative. It reinforced the things I had read in *Psycho-Cybernetics* all those years prior. I was reminded of my own individual powers and that I had control of my destiny.

There, I could develop my natural leadership skills and make anything possible with a recipe of hard work, relationship building, constant positive energy, and self-belief. I knew I wanted to lead a company. Becoming the president of Shaw was no accident. My career progress and success were entirely intentional. I imagined it, I hoped for it, and I put in the work and the steps to make it happen.

Father Kilty

Sometimes, sadly, there are people we will look up to and admire for a time in life who might not be the people we thought they were.

Father John Kilty died in 1983. Since 2003, several people have come forward accusing him of assault and sexual abuse—including the rape of a six-year-old boy. These incidents are said to have occurred during Kilty's time as pastor of Holy Trinity Church in North Vancouver during the 1960s and 1970s.

Back in 1972, Father Kilty officiated my marriage to Amy.

From the earliest days, my life was filled with a theme of fathers—not least of all, the Father, to whom I pray, have faith in, and believe guides me.

There were good fathers, bad fathers, and my own father. I became a father biologically, and I chose not to become a Father when I left the seminary. In the absence of my own parents for much of my childhood, particularly during my time at the all-boys' boarding school of St. Michael's in England, priests were my influences, my educators, and my protectors.

I consider myself to be a good judge of character, and I had trusted Father Kilty not only as an ordained minister but as a friend, so this news was gut-wrenching. It was confusing and devastating and unignorably nauseating day after day, for a long time. Considering all I had learned through my devotion to Catholicism, it was painfully perplexing to speculate. I wondered what happens to people who do such things. Do they still go to heaven?

I found it impossible to come to terms with learning something so abhorrent about a man I thought I knew so very well and admired. I never suspected he could do anything remotely bad, let alone so horrifyingly awful.

At a time when Father Kilty and priests across the country and the world were supposed to be inspiring, mentoring, teaching, and caring for people, approximately 4 percent of them—which is a scarily large number in reality—were, in fact, traumatizing, humiliating, and hurting people.

But beyond the claims made about Father Kilty, this sickness within the clergy is undeniably deep-rooted, evident, and systemic. It's dismantling the institution, degrading the religion, and transforming the faith of the people.

The Church's diabolical treatment of children, tragically, is not limited to those 4 percent of priests. The recent discoveries of mass burial grounds at former residential school sites across Canada have triggered investigations uncovering unimaginable horrors, as the government apologizes for tearing children away from their families, stripping them of their culture and identity, and mistreating and starving them. The last of these residential schools closed as recently as the 1990s.

The Catholic reputation is in rapid decline. With debatably archaic ideas and non-diverse leadership, it's hard to imagine how the religion will survive without a sincere and comprehensive combination of apologies and reinvention.

I have faced internal struggles trying to reconcile what I naively thought I knew about people and events with what I know now.

But ultimately, my faith is not tested. I was born and raised in Catholicism. It formed the basis of my education, and the values I have embraced throughout my life were at the core of that learning.

Father Kilty had been someone I looked up to. He was a coach, a mentor, and, in my eyes, through all the time I knew him in life, he appeared to be nothing but a genuinely wonderful person.

I attribute my improvements in basketball during my younger years to the tough coaching style of Father Kilty, who took the role seriously. Inevitably, the skills and attitude honed on the basketball court would translate to other sports throughout my teens, twenties, thirties, and beyond.

During my time at Holy Trinity, I dedicated myself to serving the church. Every morning after my paper route was completed, I would walk to the church on 17th and Lonsdale to serve Mass as an altar boy. On the weekends I would cut the grass and weed the gardens at the parish grounds. On Sundays, after all the masses were completed, I would take the donations baskets and count the cash for the parish.

Through all my memories of him, Father Kilty was a significant guide. Upon hearing the news of what had been going on behind closed doors—and a side of him that I never caught a glimpse of—disappointment and horror accompanied a gut-wrenching realization of how close I might have come to that fire.

Six — Strike! 1984–1986

In September 1981, I left BC Tel and began work as the operations manager at Vancouver Cablevision, which had just been acquired by Rogers. It was there that I and others would write the contingency plan for the anticipated strike as part of the negotiating committee for ALMCO—the Association of Lower Mainland Cable Operators. The strike did indeed occur on July 14, 1986, and disruption of services was limited thanks to the effective implementation of our plan.

The Strike Contingency Plan

Perhaps nothing highlights the line at which teammates become competitors quite so profoundly as a confrontational union strike.

While I had unknowingly embraced the modern mantra of *Be less scared by being prepared* by completing a comprehensive and effective strike contingency plan just months earlier, the events that unfolded during this combative and antagonistic standoff were intimidating and unsettling to many in the industry at the time.

I engaged Scott Atkinson and Tom Hobley, operations and engineering supervisors respectively, to work with me to develop a comprehensive plan. We would meet once a week at work, and then at night I would commit the plan to writing. The contingency plan had taken me a year to write. We had taken time to focus on all potential eventualities and how to address and solve the problems that would arise from them, so business and much-needed services could go on uninterrupted. It was not only a sensible thing to do, but ultimately, it enabled the almost smooth continuation of operations amid the chaos of the riled-up masses.

It was with my direct knowledge from experiencing two strikes at BC Tel that we considered all possible scenarios and how to tackle them—that saw me lead the effort through what became a six-month-long labour dispute in Vancouver in the summer of 1986.

While managing the day-to-day challenges of the ongoing strike required unwavering strength along with calm, determined leadership, there were also technical emergencies—and fewer people available to handle them.

Going back to my experience at BC Tel, I had only recently become a manager, yet everything was happening all at once and very quickly. And amid the disorder and passionate anarchy of the strike, I was called upon to revive an integral switching system. It had been sabotaged in Kelowna. It was a brand-new system that, fortunately, I was familiar with, having supervised its operation in Vancouver.

Workers initiated the strike to demand higher wages, while unions sought greater jurisdiction to expand their roles and limit company management's powers.

Despite the contention, I maintained good relationships with those who opposed our views. Friends from the BC Tel hockey team were striking, while I worked extra hours as a manager to cover their absence. Yet, there was mutual respect—they understood my role as a manager and my responsibility to keep vital equipment running.

The strike escalated quickly, perhaps in part thanks to the comprehensive media coverage it received. All the local news stations were on the scene, talking to picketers and showing footage of the passionate crowds. It became a very public event.

It also turned scary. Strikers took over the BC Tel building, refusing to leave. They wanted to stall operations by forcing all management out and occupying the building.

I refused to leave, standing firm and arguing my case for staying and doing my job. Hours turned into days, and though I kept up my resolve, I started to feel the tension in the air. *Maybe they're bluffing,* I thought, hoping the mob would eventually tire out. But that illusion crumbled quickly. When they began damaging equipment and sabotaging the plant—actions none of us thought they'd take—I knew I might have underestimated them. I watched as they tampered with systems, feeling a sinking realization: They weren't going to stop. When I saw that they were prepared to physically throw me out, I had to accept defeat. There was nothing left but to leave. Remember the sage advice from Joe Green.

A court order eventually forced the strikers out a day or two later, but although we could reenter the building, I still had to cross a picket line to park my car every day. My arrival at work was met with insults and intimidation.

Though far from fun, this experience gave me valuable insight into handling strike situations and helped me develop an effective plan for managing future disruptions.

By the time the strike of July 14, 1986, happened—the result of a Rogers labour dispute—we were prepared with a plan.

In addition to my firsthand experiences of strikes, I had read books on contingency plans and represented Rogers in negotiations in the Lower Mainland that involved all the major players of the time—Vancouver Cablevision, Western, and Shaw.

In preparation for the strike, we trained a hundred workers on a cable system on Bowen Island. They needed to know how to troubleshoot and build cable plant.

We had a backup fleet of trucks parked in leased basements. A designated contingency crew of technicians and engineers included great leaders like Scott Atkinson and Tom Hobley. It was like preparing for a battle.

On the opposing side, Rogers' technicians had also prepared, using preset trigger points to short out coaxial cable drops situated on disparate telephone poles. With the use of a metal device such as a screwdriver, someone could walk by the telephone pole, apply the metal shorting device to the end of the drop, and cause a short circuit to occur at the amplifier downstream. By exchanging the fuses in the amplifier with metal busbars, they could blow the power supplies feeding that portion of the cable plant. With the main power supply failing, a much larger section of plant was taken out of service. Part of our job was anticipating and preventing these tactics, while also coordinating the legal efforts to deal with the consequences of these actions.

Unlike the more respectful relationships I had during the BC Tel strikes, this situation was far more hostile. There were death threats, injunctions, and plenty of contention. Still, amid the animosity, some technicians I had played baseball with knew and respected me, as I did them.

We had a supervisor named Cliff Rowe, who'd been in the union a long time prior to joining management, and who was strongly disliked because of his position. In a move spurred by my instinctively protective nature, I made Cliff my work partner.

At a not-so-secret warehouse where we were parking our trucks, the union guys had figured out the location and were picketing angrily. As Cliff and I walked toward the warehouse, the crowd began to get violent with him, pushing him and spitting at him. I grabbed hold of Cliff's arm and pulled him through the line—a moment caught by CTV cameras that were on the scene.

When I reemerged from the warehouse with a large orange Rogers truck—the kind that carried all the equipment and was fitted with lifts—I recognized an enraged face in the crowd. It was Rory Sharpe, someone I knew from working with his father years before. Rory charged at the vehicle, pounding on the window and yelling a string of insults at me, the most repeated being "You fucking scab!" He ripped off his shirt in a Hulk-like display of fury.

Never one to appreciate intimidation attempts, I opened the sliding door of the truck alongside where Rory stood, red-faced and scowling.

"You are the ugliest fucker I've ever seen!" Rory said.

I replied, "Well, you obviously haven't seen my wife!"

Rory was flummoxed as people around him began to laugh. Among them were technicians who knew me, who knew I was the VP of operations and that I had to do this. I had no choice. They weren't working, and my role was to keep things running. Nothing was going to change that, not even if every man there ripped his shirt off in a manly display of outrage.

Rory turned around and walked away. I drove on and did my job.

It was a strike that tested people's mettle. Steve McDonald approached me and said, "I have been watching you in action, and we'd like to talk to you about a role in our company."

And so, in the middle of the chaos as the strike went on, I met them for lunch, where they offered me the role of executive vice president and general manager at Western Cablevision Ltd.

Though it pissed off my boss, Frank Eberdt, at Rogers Vancouver at the time, one week after I started at Western the strike was settled and technicians returned to work. It was October 3, 1986.

I always believed the purpose of the strike contingency plan was to ensure the company could keep running, not to break the union. I made this clear to the employees, telling them that their role was to work together to make Western a better company. From day one, the tone was set: We weren't competitors; we were a team.

Further Education

In 1984, I attended executive management courses at Queen's University in Kingston and the University of British Columbia in Vancouver.

My deep passion has always been working with people. I recognized that, in addition to my leadership skills, I needed to pursue specific courses focused on business management to unlock new opportunities. Although I was primarily managing most of the operational and engineering efforts at Rogers Vancouver, I understood that greater challenges lay ahead.

I sought out people who valued the course at Queens as much as I did: those with skills and ambition who could push me further. I connected with people I believed had the qualities of strong leaders and shared my drive. Surrounding myself with them motivated me to aim higher.

At Queen's University, most of the students were determined to succeed, and many went on to achieve great things. This both humbled and inspired me. I eagerly wrote notes, absorbing everything I could from each class. At one point, I even considered pursuing a full-time course or a master's degree, but I had bills to pay, and my career was already moving forward. Over the years, I continued taking courses in various subjects. I attended public-speaking and writing courses at the University of British Columbia, including one with Keith Spicer, author of *Winging It: Everybody's Guide to Making Speeches Fly Without Notes*. That education gave me the confidence to stand in front of large audiences and speak for over an hour about culture and values in a way that was memorable and impactful. It prepared me to be the good shepherd, guiding others along their path.

My desire to learn was so strong that I attended courses during my vacation time. Education was monumentally important to me, and I took every chance to expand my knowledge and develop my leadership skills. When I wasn't in a classroom, I was reading—studying business strategy, understanding human nature, and learning how different personality types respond to stress and urgency. I took a deep interest in how to lead people effectively. Classes often included mock negotiating sessions with senior management from prominent companies, which helped me hone my skills and understand the complexities of leadership.

That period had a profound impact on me. It marked a transformation where I adopted a positive, can-do attitude, feeling that nothing was impossible. I wanted to be prepared and have the right tools to become a senior leader. I knew, despite Keith Spicer's book title, that I could never just wing it.

I met Louise at Vancouver Cablevision's Christmas party in 1984. She was a petite, assertive woman who navigated the crowded dance floor, showcasing provocative moves aimed directly at me. Dressed in a tuxedo penguin suit, she approached with confidence, closing the distance between us.

In the new year, Louise sought me out in the hallways, asking for a tour of our new facilities. I suggested having Scott Atkinson, our operations supervisor, give her the tour, but she insisted it had to be me. Louise was remarkably forward, and a year later, on Valentine's Day, we got engaged after an evening of enjoying too much sake.

By July 1986, despite her earlier claim that her doctor had said she couldn't conceive, she was four months pregnant, and we were preparing to get married.

Last Rites

In 1986, my father, Edmund, passed away. Around the time I started my new role with Western, he had a seizure and was diagnosed with a brain tumour. Living alone in Victoria after my mother left him a few years earlier, he was in his final days. My sister Suzanne and I sat by his bedside as he received the Last Rites.

Reconciliation and Anointing of the Sick are given to those of Catholic faith to forgive their sins before ascending to heaven. I didn't know the specifics of my father's sins, but something within me made it hard for me to show him affection during those final moments. Perhaps it stirred a reminder of the need for forgiveness for past mistakes.

Arranging for the Last Rites was my way of helping him to receive absolution for his failures, his absence, and the often-heartbreaking way he approached fatherhood—likely a reflection of his own harsh upbringing, having lost his mother at just eight years old.

Before receiving the sacrament, my father mumbled incoherently, as if asking me to help him. He was trying to tell me something. When the monsignor standing at the head of his bed said, "May the Lord Jesus Christ protect you and lead you to eternal life," my father visibly relaxed, becoming peaceful and calm, as though he believed finally his sins had been forgiven.

My father's dying moments, marked by the sacrament and the monsignor's affirmation that "You will never know the power of the gift you gave your father," illustrated to me the profound connection many people have with faith, especially during times of great emotional turmoil. The peace my father found in that moment provided great comfort not only to him, but also to me. He slipped into a coma shortly after and never woke up.

Three days later, on December 15, 1986, my son Michael was born. Three days after that, I turned forty.

Loss and new beginnings. While experiencing grief and loss, new life and hope arises, in unexpected ways.

A good father has faith in his children. He celebrates their successes, expresses pride, and leads by example. His presence inspires, motivates, and shows the way. He is reliable, supportive, and loyal. A good father sees the best in his children and wants the best for them. These qualities overlap with those of an exceptional teammate, a trusted advisor, a mentor, or a leader who inspires confidence. I have tried to be all of these things in both my personal and business life.

Michael

There were many influential father figures in my life, though my own dad was barely one of them. Teachers like Father Bill MacDonald of Antigonish, my uncles Peter and Case—each played a role.

From the moment my son Michael was born, it was the most conventional father–son relationship I've had—full of love. That's not to say it's been without its challenges. Parenting rarely is. But overcoming those challenges, tackling setbacks, and working through difficulties can strengthen relationships, stretching them until there's no doubting the unbreakable bond. In that love, trust, and commitment, any teen facing an uncertain world stands a better chance of growing into a secure, successful person.

I was putting out fires, keeping the business running, and tackling monumental tasks—all while Louise was pregnant. It was an exciting time, and knowing I was about to welcome another child only fuelled my motivation. Michael's early years were fortunate, filled with love and abundance.

From an early age, our similarities were clear. Michael's zest for life, his cheeky nature, and his boundless energy made it easy to bond with him. Parenting felt more natural the second time around. Michael was a happy, adventurous child who loved our time together. He was a born athlete and a fearless competitor.

Rogers

During my time at Rogers in the mid- to late 1980s, I was part of the talented team who proposed and planned for a complete rebuild of the Vancouver Cable System. Ted Rogers fully backed our bold recommendation, and signed off on the $30 million capital requisition, giving the green light for the project—a moment that brought smiles to all of us who had just presented the long-term benefits of this crucial investment. It became the largest capital project at Rogers in Vancouver at the time.

In business, rivals and teammates drive growth. Even the strongest teams need competitors to challenge and push them to be better. I've been fortunate to work with some of the most effective management teams in Western Canada's telecommunications industry. Though I'm a fierce competitor with a strong passion for winning, I've always held my competitors in high regard. I respect their dedication and skill, recognizing that they challenge us to push our limits and strive for excellence. Without their presence, the journey wouldn't have been nearly as rewarding or as enjoyable. Yes, we would get pissed at them because they mischaracterized our products or oversold their own, but they motivated us to elevate our game or die doing it!

Seven — Enter Shaw, 1989–1999

When I joined Shaw in 1989, it was with eagerness, zeal, and drive. The company was a great fit, and I was determined to excel. I wanted to make an impact, contribute, learn, grow, and make progress; I was dedicated.

And while nobody can predict how things may unfold when they start a new job among new people, in a new place, this much is certain: A person going into a new role with a keen attitude and positive thoughts has an infinitely greater chance of success than one who is unwilling, uncertain, or half-hearted.

My path to Shaw might have seemed daunting to many. But with dogged determination, eyes set upwards, and an unshakable inner belief that I had much more to learn, experience, and achieve, I moved forward with confidence.

Shaw's core values—teamwork, accountability, balance, customer focus, integrity, loyalty, and a positive, can-do attitude—weren't just defined; they were lived and celebrated. These values resonated deeply with me and aligned perfectly with my own beliefs. They were embedded in every employment contract, promotion, and transfer, ensuring that anyone joining the company agreed to uphold these principles as a foundational aspect of their role. Shaw was ahead of its time in how much it cared for its employees, and we always felt that this commitment was noticed and respected.

Hole-in-One

In an article published by *Forbes* in May 2016, the bold claim was made that "Golfers Make Better Business Executives." According to *Forbes*, 90 percent of *Fortune* 500 CEOs play golf. It's considered a valuable networking activity that enables the establishment of new business relationships. Contrary to stereotypes, it's not a gentlemen-only game, and neither are the networking and job opportunities limited to corporate ladder ascension. Katharine Hepburn, for instance, played golf in Bel-Air, California, in the 1920s while discussing and bargaining for her potential movie roles.

Clearly, it's a leisure interest beneficial to all. As you stroll around scenic courses, converse while waiting for your turn, and perhaps enjoy a refreshing cocktail, you can present yourself as both athletic and charmingly relaxed as you take your swing.

Golf was slower and less exciting than the high-energy sports I typically enjoyed, but I loved the social aspect and was a reasonably good golfer. It didn't come with the dangers of the team sports I favoured, which may have been a good thing—I have yet to break my shoulder playing golf.

Mingling with characters on the golf course served me well on many occasions. Innumerable handshakes, profitable decisions, investments, collaborations, ideas, and the jokes that linger in the minds of those I worked with—all evidence that deals do get done on the golf course.

When my journey with Shaw began on the golf course in the summer of 1989, I was working at Western Cablevision for David and Steve McDonald, who had just agreed to sell their cable systems in Surrey, Langley, and Abbotsford/Matsqui to Rogers—a merger that cemented my decision to move on.

On this occasion, I had been invited to join the Shaw corporate group for their annual golf tournament in North Vancouver. My current boss, Steve McDonald, was present, along with over a hundred attendees from the industry and friends and employees of Shaw. The event was hosted by Jim Shaw and his father JR, both of whom I knew at the time, though I couldn't have foreseen that they would one day become like family.

During that tournament, I was paired with JR Shaw—an undoubtedly intentional move to allow JR some time to get to know me better. Although any occasion mixing business with pleasure fosters relationship-building, it wasn't the first time I had interacted with the Shaws. Jim knew me from my involvement in the successful labour negotiations, and I had developed a reputation for getting things done. And Jim loved to get 'er done!

I had also met Jim in social settings, where over a few drinks we quickly realized we were alike: ambitious, unstoppable, and lively presences in any room.

After the golf tournament, JR addressed the participants, announcing that Shaw had a new opening for a vice president of operations in British Columbia, covering Vancouver, the Lower Mainland, and Vancouver Island.

This news excited me, not only because I had already decided to leave Western without knowing what opportunities lay ahead, but because the job title and location seemed tailor-made for me.

Soon after, I reached out to Richard Morris—who was vice president of operations at Shaw and whom I had worked with during labour negotiations—to inquire about applying. He enthusiastically affirmed that it was the right move.

About six months prior to this, Steve and I had met with JR and Jim Shaw to go over the financial models we had developed at Western. These models were for sensitivity testing of certain sales models for the basic and extended basic tiers that the industry was wrestling with.

Shaw was leaning toward launching the extended basic discretionary tiers based on projected penetration rates of that tier over basic carriage. We at Western were advocates of this approach, as the modelling showed it to be the most positive revenue generator of the two options.

Shaw agreed with us and proceeded to launch the extended basic discretionary tiers around the time we met at the golf tournament. This may have been the icing on the cake, given my experience, work ethic, and enthusiasm.

I got the job.

Icebreakers

The first day in a new job is always a little daunting. However prepared I was, there were inevitably unknown elements ahead. It was a new beginning, one I hoped would go well.

December 15, 1989, was my first day as vice president of operations at Shaw. I arrived at work at 5:30 a.m., where that morning's agenda was negotiating a collective agreement with the International Brotherhood of Electrical Workers—IBEW—in North Vancouver. Alongside me were Terry Medd, system manager at North Vancouver, and Richard Morris, vice president of operations for the Interior of British Columbia—both highly competent executives who welcomed me warmly.

On entering the meeting room, I gave what I supposed was my usual approachable yet professional, driven, and resolute smile. It was a look I'd naturally honed over the years—automatic and genuine, not forced or deceptive—and I always hoped it would become the face of a man who gets what he wants.

To my surprise, seated at the bargaining table was none other than Rory Sharpe, the man who, just three years prior, had attempted—and failed—to intimidate me in front of a large crowd of his riled-up employees.

Before I could say anything, in what seemed like an attempt to appear confident and unfazed by this unexpected reunion, Rory leaned casually back in his swivel chair—a move he instantly regretted as he fell over backward in noisy, dramatic fashion, ending up quite red-faced on the floor.

After a brief silence, which probably felt like an eternity for Rory, I said, "What a wonderful icebreaker, Rory! Now, why don't we get on with what we're here to do—reach a settlement between the union and management—and let's forget the accidental histrionics."

There was no further discourse between Rory and me during the meeting, but Rory had clearly mellowed. It had been a moment from which he couldn't possibly make a cocky comeback. The meeting proceeded with a reminder that behind every difficult deal are real people with real feelings, which is never a bad subtext in a negotiation where the combined best interests of everyone moving forward are the top priority.

For Shaw, it was ultimately a successful negotiation—and a memorable first day for me.

Expanding

Fuelled by a relentless pursuit of success, we refused to settle for anything less than extraordinary. Shaw constantly sought new challenges and pushed boundaries with unwavering determination to rise above mediocrity. We envisioned a future of boundless possibilities, committed to creating a lasting and influential legacy. We strove for advancement, excellence, and meaningful impact with energy and optimism.

This mindset reflected Shaw's tenacious and visionary ambition. JR and his sons, Jim and Brad, embodied this attitude so strongly that everyone who worked closely with them shared the same enthusiasm and drive. That was certainly the case with me. I was supercharged and loved everything about working at Shaw. Many families were deciding to sell their cable systems. Shaw, however, had chosen to grow rather than sell. Our growth was to be through acquisitions, new product launches, and investments in new technologies.

As the decade turned and we approached the end of the millennium, the timing was ideal for expansion, fuelled by rapid digital development that united and inspired people. Expanding our service territory in British Columbia was crucial for the scale of growth JR and Jim envisioned. However, it wasn't just about acquisitions. Shaw's long-term success relied on building relationships, trust, and loyalty. This endeavour required sustainability, continued opportunity, and a respect for reality. Everything had to be done well and executed with integrity.

Change often brings about resistance, which is a natural human reaction. The fear of the unknown means that anything new or different comes with inherent risks. My role was to facilitate this change effectively, advising Jim and JR toward their vision while minimizing disruption. This involved engaging and motivating stakeholders, ensuring they felt heard and valued throughout the process. My focus was on building support and fostering understanding to ease the transition.

Most of Shaw's technical personnel were not in the union. As we expanded our company through acquisitions, we recognized that some family-owned companies came with unions. This presented a challenge, as there was often little incentive for ongoing loyalty to the union. To address this, we needed to establish a robust foundation that fostered commitment and pride amongst our workforces.

I proposed transitioning all contracted technical installation employees into owner-operators. By doing so, we aimed to shift the perception of employment from being owned by the company to being part owners themselves. Although this approach required a significant initial investment, it would ultimately strengthen both the company and its workforce. This model not only enhances employees' sense of responsibility and pride in their work, but aligns their interests with the success of the company, creating a motivated team dedicated to achieving common goals.

In Vernon, British Columbia, a system we acquired in 1991, I met with the IBEW business agent and our employees, accompanied by Richard Morris. The atmosphere was tense as the employees were entering collective bargaining.

To ease the tension, I told their bargaining agent, "I'm putting this imaginary button on the table. If I cross a line or say something you don't agree with, just press it."

The button remained unpressed as I laid out the option to decertify and become owner-operators, with the alternative being potential layoffs. While some employees seemed open to the idea, one angry worker stormed out. Moments later, I spotted a similarly dressed man through the door, carrying what appeared to be a holster.

"Holy fuck, I think he's back—and he has a gun!" I whispered to Richard.

Fortunately, it was a Loomis armed driver, completely unrelated to our meeting. No one got shot, no one pressed the button, and Vernon's installation employees became owner-operators.

Shaw's expansion spree accelerated in 1990 and 1991. This was the role for which I had been hired. We acquired systems in Ontario, Saskatoon, and Manitoba, purchasing companies like Cablecasting and CUC—Conway Upper Canada—as well as Classicomm, Cable Net, and later, Hamilton.

B.B. King—The Thrill Is Gone

Originally written by Roy Hawkins and Rick Darnell, "The Thrill Is Gone" became most famously associated with B.B. King after he recorded it in 1969. A defining moment in his career, it tells the story of lost love and emotional detachment.

During our time working and playing music together in North Vancouver, Terry Medd and I would regularly drop into bars to see live music together. One evening, in a small hotel not far from our office, B.B. King was playing. It was typical of him to perform in small venues at that time.

Keen to meet him, I introduced myself, and we ended up chatting about music and blues for half an hour. He was such a classy guy and made us feel important. I would play with the guitar pick that B.B. King had given me until it was worn beyond recognition.

At a later occasion, at the much larger venue of Queen Elizabeth Theatre, I saw B.B. King a second time. He remembered me—or at least he said he did—and was wonderfully friendly and engaging. For me, it was a treasured opportunity to be able to speak with such a talent, whose lyrics had spoken to me so often over the years. The thrill is never gone, with B.B. King!

Margaret Parker

Canada is the second-largest country in the world, at a whopping 9.985 million square kilometres. There are almost eight thousand cities and towns across all provinces. The population today is over forty million, a number that has steadily increased since 1960, when it was just under eighteen million.

There are 1,440 minutes in a 24-hour period.

So, a chance meeting in a single place, with a single person at a particular minute in time, twenty-plus years since having last seen them with no contact in between, at a time when technology was rudimentary compared to now and keeping in touch with people from your past was not a typical or easily done thing, must be considered more than a simple coincidence.

My first love was a girl named Margaret Parker. We met as teenagers in Ottawa after I had left the seminary and returned to high school for grade twelve. As the new boy at Bell High, rumoured to have come from the seminary, I guess I was intriguing.

Margaret and I quickly formed a unique bond that, in line with my Catholic beliefs, was respectful and platonic. We were best friends.

At a time when my home life was turbulent and my future uncertain, beautiful Margaret Parker showed up like a nurturing angel—someone who made me forget the unpleasantness and pain of family strife and liked me very much simply for who I was, encouraging my true personality to bloom and believing in my abilities. She made life fun and positive and bright. There were times when I truly believed Margaret was The One.

Later, while I was assigned to electronics training in Clinton, Ontario, after my basic RCAF training, Margaret became a flight attendant in Syracuse, New York, moving across the border to live there with her father, who was a wing commander in the RCAF on special assignment with NORAD—the North American Aerospace Defense Command.

Clinton to Syracuse is more than a five-hour drive these days, with efficient roads, fast cars, and GPS replacing the need to map read while driving. Back then, it would have taken even longer. And I didn't have a vehicle.

But nothing stands in the way of young love. So, occasionally, on my days off I would hitchhike the distance to see Margaret. In all weather conditions.

Penniless, in uniform, I would stick out my thumb and walk along the highway, hoping for kindness. How fortunate I was that I'd always get picked up—and not once by an axe murderer. Although there were times when I was picked up by drivers who were clearly attracted to a young man in uniform. In those instances, I respectfully declined their advances and ordered them to stop the car and let me proceed unharmed.

I've always had trust in the human spirit, never doubting that the majority are kind. Perhaps without knowing it, it was this firm belief that manifested my safe reality.

On New Year's Eve, in 1966, I braved this journey in a snowstorm with nothing but ten cents and a meal card in my pocket.

This snowstorm is often referred to as The Blizzard of 1966. The storm dropped more than a metre of snow over several days and caused several disruptions. Once on the road, there was no turning back. I was blocked by a customs agent at the Buffalo border. She wouldn't let me through. I tried to appeal to her matronly senses, but she wouldn't change her mind. I was cold and tired. I had travelled with a cardboard sign on which I had painted in gold letters the word *Syracuse*.

I lay down in my air force greatcoat on the Canadian side of the border and waited and waited for a car to pick me up. I didn't know if I was going to make it. By this time, it was past midnight, and very little traffic was coming across the border. Almost miraculously I heard the sound of air brakes, and this large semi-trailer truck pulled to the side of the road, three metres from me, and the driver opened his door.

"Get up here!" he yelled.

The snow was blowing in and around the cab as I stepped up the slippery steps to get into the cab.

"Fuck me, man, what are you doing out here?" he cursed.

My lips were frozen as I mouthed the words, "Heading to see my girlfriend in Syracuse."

"I hope she's worth it," he said, followed by, "Better get laid. You are one lucky motherfucker. I'm going to the truck stop beside the Howard Johnson in Syracuse."

Then he opened me a beer and offered me half of his bologna sandwich, wrapped lovingly in wax paper. I was never happier to be out of the weather and safe in the warm cab of this semi. Perhaps my love of driving my own diesel pushers came from this moment.

"Who knows?" I said to myself. "Maybe I will get a midnight kiss after all."

On my return trip early the next day, after seeing Margaret for a few wonderful hours, her father drove me to the outskirts of Syracuse, where I began my hitchhiking trip home. The weather hadn't improved.

The storm of monstrous proportions continued to descend on northeastern New York, with blizzard and whiteout conditions escalating quickly. Cars were buried and power lines came down.

After fifteen hours on the treacherous roads, I became stranded in Centralia, an air force base in Ontario not far from Clinton. Fortunately, I was in my uniform and had been found by a Canadian wing commander from Centralia. With my meal card and ten cents, I was able to eat and hunker down while waiting for the monumental snow to be cleared. After a week on that base, I was transported by an air force bus to Clinton. The things we do for love.

Despite my efforts to see Margaret, my evident military aspirations at the time—which one would think might appeal to a former air force squadron leader—and my caring approach to his daughter, Margaret's dad did not like me at all. He had low estimations of me; he felt I was going nowhere and had nothing to offer. He also didn't like that I was Catholic.

It was the first time someone had expressed dislike for me because of my faith, and when I learned of it, it surprised me greatly.

As time went on, it became increasingly evident that this long-distance relationship was impossible to sustain. As we each pursued our busy and ambitious lives, hundreds of kilometres apart, I reluctantly conceded to end our courtship via heartfelt letter. And that was that.

Almost thirty years later, with no contact in between, I saw Margaret again.

It was in 1991, at Shaw's headquarters in Edmonton, more than three thousand kilometres from where we first met in Ottawa.

Margaret was paying her Shaw bill in the retail centre of the building just as I walked in with JR Shaw, who had taught me the value of MBWA—Management by Walking Around: a way of surveying the goings-on of day-to-day operations to understand the roles and thoughts of employees across the company. This was one such occasion: a brief but beneficial meeting-interlude to conduct some valuable MBWA.

As a familiar-looking woman fumbled in her purse at the counter, I did a double take. Could it be? Surely not.

"Margaret? Is that you?" I asked.

Confused, she looked up from her purse.

"Yes," she said, with a puzzled look.

"It's Peter Bissonnette," I said.

Utterly flummoxed, Margaret was speechless for what felt like a full minute as a thousand memories flooded my mind.

"What are you doing here?" she asked, as if I'd hired investigators to track her down during her mundane errands.

"Well, I'm the vice president of operations for Shaw. I'm here for meetings, but I work out of Vancouver," I explained.

She stared open-mouthed for a moment, then grinned widely.

"Wait till I tell my dad. He thought you were going to be the biggest loser."

Some might take offence at such a comment, but I was completely delighted to have proven her father wrong.

She gladly accepted my invitation to catch up over lunch, which became the most unexpected and spontaneous opportunity to reconnect with our past and revisit the people we once were.

It was cathartic to look back and see how far I'd come. It was nostalgic to recall moments, feelings, and decisions, and to gain new insight with the benefits of maturity.

Margaret told me she had to pinch herself at the idea of telling her dad all this—that his predictions of my demise had been unwarranted. I told Margaret how much her encouragement had influenced me, how her faith in me—her belief that I could and would be better—played a part in my success.

It was undoubtedly a serendipitous meeting, one that invites acknowledgment of providence.

Nashville Network

The Nashville Network was a much-loved service, particularly in Alberta. Country music was thriving in North America in the 1990s, and the channel attracted a considerable viewership.

It was an era that marked a period of success for several Canadian country music artists who achieved international recognition. Shania Twain, Terri Clark, and Paul Brandt were gaining fans by the minute. The genre's appeal was expanding beyond its traditional fan base, generating increased mainstream popularity. In short, music channels were a hit.

Jim Shaw and I flew to Atlanta, Georgia, to meet with the president of The Nashville Network to negotiate service rates. They had proposed price increases, and Shaw was not prepared to pay them.

When we arrived, we were informed the president was upstairs in another meeting, and we'd have to wait. As a typically punctual person, I was unimpressed by this disregard for timekeeping, but assumed we wouldn't be waiting long.

As time ticked by and minutes became hours, The Nashville Network's representative apologized, though not profusely, that the president was too busy to meet with us. It was both perplexing and infuriating. We had travelled more than 2,000 miles—Jim from Edmonton and I from Vancouver. That's not just a short trip!

Did the president consider Canadians insignificant? We were a country with a potential consumer base of over thirty million people and one of the most stable economies in the world. Did he think we were too polite and friendly to be upset by such blatant disregard for our time? He couldn't have been more wrong.

Upon returning to Edmonton, Jim and I attended a senior management meeting chaired by JR. After being informed of what happened in Atlanta, JR agreed with our recommendation that Shaw would no longer carry The Nashville Network.

We had already started negotiating with CMT—Country Music Television. At the time, CMT was a fledgling channel offering twenty-four-hour music videos and live performances. I believed we could secure a long-term, advantageous affiliation agreement with them.

During the meeting, the vice president of Alberta operations expressed his disagreement with our recommendation. "This is the stupidest thing I've ever heard! How could we think about taking down The Nashville Network? It's one of our most popular channels!"

What followed was an extremely rare and angry response from JR—one I had never seen before.

"Do I have to listen to your shit?" JR said, surprising everyone in the room who had never heard him swear.

He continued, "We need to be a united company. The Nashville Network didn't have the courtesy to meet with Peter or Jim, and they are arbitrarily raising their rates. I fully support this recommendation, and now we just need to do it right."

It was a moment that reaffirmed the mutual loyalty among Shaw's senior leadership. It demonstrated JR's trust in Jim and me and his intolerance for disrespect.

As it turned out, CMT, a sister channel to MTV, saw the value of being broadcast through Shaw's network. We negotiated a rate of ten cents per subscriber—an amount that Mike Ostopowich, Shaw's chief financial officer, had bet I couldn't secure.

CMT gained a growing viewership throughout the 1990s, expanding its programming to include lifestyle and entertainment shows, further cementing its prominence. Meanwhile, The Nashville Network ceased to exist by September 2000, after undergoing a series of rebrands that took it away from its country music roots entirely.

Hawley Chester, who was leading negotiations for CNN at the time, saw how Shaw handled The Nashville Network, and as a result, negotiations for CNN's rates went much more smoothly.

During my first decade at Shaw, there were many deals like this. Michael D'Avella and I, affectionately known as Jim's Henchmen, were partners in affiliation negotiations. We took a good cop, bad cop approach—with me being the former—which helped us communicate effectively with all types of personalities.

Eight — Toronto Calgary, 1995–1999

In April 1995, Jim and JR Shaw asked me if I would move with my family to Toronto, Canada's largest city and an economic powerhouse of global status.

We had acquired a significant number of cable systems in the region, namely CUC, Classicomm, and Cablecasting. I immediately agreed that I would move to Toronto, as it had become more and more challenging to fly back and forth from Vancouver to manage the integration of these systems into Shaw. Shaw needed to have a local presence, and I relished the opportunity to take on this challenge.

The companies we had acquired served more than 650,000 customers in the Toronto region. That was more subscribers than all of Shaw's Western systems combined. It was in the best interests of Shaw and its newly acquired customers to reorganize these systems to take advantage of the economies of scale and the synergies that existed between the support staff and management of these previously disparate companies.

In April 1995, Louise, Michael, and I moved to Stouffville, a small, rural community north of Toronto. Surrounded by picturesque farmland with numerous parks and trails nearby, it was a peaceful and more relaxed contrast to the hustle and bustle of a big, busy city.

Quaint but convenient, it also offered great schools and amenities for kids, making it a desirable family location and an exciting move for the three of us.

When I exited the vehicle at Shaw's offices in Toronto, JR welcomed me with tears in his eyes. He expressed that he was emotional because he understood I was taking on a significant responsibility and that the challenges ahead would be formidable.

I was aware from earlier conversations with JR that these acquisitions expanded our banking limits, and it was essential for us to improve the financial performance of these companies to adhere to the bank covenants. Both Jim and JR clearly placed their trust in me. I deeply appreciated this trust and was determined to surpass their expectations. I promised myself that I would never disappoint them.

I recognized that this would be a challenging task. We had reviewed the financial statements from these companies and compared their cost structures to those of our systems in the West. I was confident that with the right team in place, we could improve their performance.

While living and working in Toronto, I frequently put in fifteen-hour days. It was a brief but critical period in my career during which I needed to effect change and make a positive impact in key areas of the company. Our success during this time ultimately led to another opportunity: a promotion to Shaw's headquarters in Calgary.

Toronto was the setting for my introduction to the broader Shaw leadership team, to the national competitors, and to the impressive and expanding scale of the company.

It was where I first worked with Michael D'Avella, whose deep understanding of the country's regulatory and public policy environment, combined with his significant role in Shaw's business strategy and planning, proved invaluable as we collaborated on the company's growth.

As a graduate of St. Michael's College in Toronto, Michael knew the city and the industry well and was a great friend.

Collaborating on numerous projects, our role as senior leaders was to shine the light on the company, rather than to run to the light to have it shine on us. We used to jokingly refer to the bumps on the heads of managers from similar companies from running to the light and crashing heads in the process.

JR and Jim rewarded humility and encouraged that value in all their leaders. Some called it self-effacing, but we referred to it as the secret sauce of success!

Windsor

In July 1995, just a couple of months after relocating to Toronto, I had an important issue to manage in Windsor.

Shaw had recently acquired Cablenet, a company with several cable systems located throughout Canada. The system in Windsor was part of that deal. At the time of the purchase, Windsor was a nonunion system, but the technicians had grown increasingly concerned due to unverified rumours that Shaw intended to sell to Rogers, a company whose reputation regarding employee rights and benefits, although unwarranted, was less than favourable among the workers.

Unaware of these rumours, I received a call from the operations manager, Rick Therrien, who informed me that an application for certification had been submitted by the employees of Windsor; they were seeking to unionize.

When I heard this news, I was floored. Nobody had ever certified while working at Shaw.

"I'm on my way," I told Rick.

"Right now?" he asked with a surprised tone.

"Yes, I'm going to fly there right now," I confirmed.

Rick was clearly in disbelief at my immediate response and could see this was being taken very seriously.

I flew there alone—a moment filled with disappointment and adrenaline. It was a situation that should never have occurred, an unexpected problem that needed immediate resolution.

Upon arriving in Windsor, I met with the management team to ask why this was happening. I didn't get clear answers, and it quickly became evident that no one had their finger on the pulse.

"Tomorrow, I'll meet with all the employees in the lunchroom," I said.

The next day as I came into the room where our employees were gathered, I could sense a mix of anticipation and apprehension among them. We decided that Shaw's corporate lawyer, Howard Levitt, would stay in another room with a close friend, in case we needed him. I was concerned that his presence would unsettle the employees, and I was confident that I understood what I could and could not say during this delicate period. My focus was on connecting with the employee team.

I took a deep breath, scanned the faces before me, and began. "I understand there have been a lot of changes lately, and I want to ensure that everyone feels informed and supported. Many of you haven't had the chance to meet me or Shaw's corporate team, as it's been a short time since we acquired this system in Windsor. Today we want to get to know you better, as well as have you get to know me."

The employees shifted slightly, their expressions reflecting a mix of curiosity and concern.

"We respect that this decision to apply for certification wasn't taken lightly, but I am here to listen to your concerns and address these in a transparent and open manner."

I didn't want to dive right in without first allowing the team to get to know me a bit, so I began with a friendly introduction. I told them about Shaw as a company—its history, values, and goals—and expressed how happy we were to now be in Windsor.

I then invited them to share, openly and honestly, any concerns they might have. I told them that I was prepared to take whatever time it took to understand their concerns. Over the course of about four hours, those employees who were leading the group became apparent. I focused on reassuring them that Shaw had great respect for its employees and wanted them to feel fulfilled in their roles. I also emphasized that, in keeping with Shaw's compensation and benefits practices, they would receive competitive salaries and a generous benefits package.

I reassured them that a shared vision of our company's plans for success was an integral part of Shaw's culture. I emphasized that our commitment to collaboration and open communication would foster a strong sense of community among us. I articulated my belief that pursuing external union representation was not only unnecessary, but in conflict with our reputation for fairness and our commitment to share the benefits of our success. As I spoke, I noticed a change in the body language among the employees; the tension began to dissolve as they nodded in agreement. The atmosphere shifted to one of optimism and camaraderie.

The following day, as promised, I introduced Bill MacDonald and Roger Welsh, VP of sales, to the Windsor employees. They reaffirmed the cultural benefits of working at Shaw.

One week later, I received the news that the application for certification had been revoked by the Windsor employees.

It was an unprecedented move; typically, once a union application was submitted, it would proceed through the process. The decision to revoke it spoke volumes about the employees' confidence in our company's culture and their ability to be heard in matters of compensation, benefits, and working conditions.

My return flight to Toronto was much cheerier. The sun streamed through the airplane windows, and I reflected on the past week's events with a sense of gratitude. I was delighted to call Jim with the great news of this resolution.

Jim and I spoke every day during this time to ensure we were in lockstep on operating strategies for this important cluster of systems in Ontario, where Shaw had invested almost $2 billion in acquisition costs.

Within one year, the operating margins of these systems improved from 30 percent to 52 percent. This had a significant impact on Shaw's overall performance, where financial discipline was critical to meeting the more stringent bank covenants.

Shaw Launches Internet

It's difficult to remember a world before we offered our customers internet access. But there was a time—a time of phone books and library visits, of reference publications and encyclopedias. Personal and business correspondence was sent via postal mail, documents were transmitted via fax machines, printed newspapers were delivered to your door, and magazines were purchased from newsstands. You browsed shops physically, making purchases while in the store. You took cheques to your local bank branch, attended in-person meetings, and relied on personal networking.

Back then, nothing could have just been an email.

The internet has revolutionized how we live, work, and connect with the world. The immediacy of information, real-time communication, collaboration across borders and time zones, on-demand entertainment, e-learning platforms, online banking, remote work, and instant live news from around the globe are things we now take for granted. But it wasn't too long ago that companies like Shaw were betting on its success, trying to predict its future, and finding a way to provide this revolutionary, magical thing called the internet reliably and affordably to millions of customers across the country.

Canada's initial involvement with the internet came in the late 1980s, when the government funded a project called the Canadian Network for the Advancement of Research, Industry, and Education, or CANARIE. It was an ambitious project aimed at expanding the internet in Canada—primarily to provide access to universities and research institutions.

The first nonacademic internet service provider in Canada, Netcom Canada, was established in 1993, marking the beginning of a transformative era in telecommunications.

Following Netcom's lead, players like Shaw, Simpatico, Rogers, and Bell entered the market in 1995, leading to a rapid adoption of the internet among Canadians. At that time, Shaw and Rogers had a great advantage over the telephone companies, as our networks were higher capacity broadband distribution systems compared to the telephone companies' ADSL twisted pair networks. Some jokingly referred to ADSL as *Another Darn Slow Line.*

In time, the telephone companies invested billions building their own fibre-based broadband systems. This surge in demand for connectivity led Shaw to quickly become one of the fastest-growing internet providers in North America, achieving impressive profit margins of up to 53 percent.

Despite this success, the landscape of digital services had shifted dramatically. The capital investments required for infrastructure and digital networks were significantly higher than during the pre-internet days. As the number of internet customers exploded, so did the demand for increased bandwidth and capacity. Our customers clearly differentiated our service from the telephone companies based on two key factors: faster network speeds and superior service response times.

In a rapidly evolving digital landscape, it was essential for us to understand what truly mattered to our customers, and we found that our commitment to exceptional service was a significant advantage. Our strategy involved maintaining service centres in Canadian cities rather than outsourcing calls to offshore call centres. Local expertise was paramount. We ensured that our representatives had a thorough understanding of local geography; they did so because they lived locally amongst our customers. This translated into a more personalized customer experience.

The CEO of Telus was annoyed by this, and he asked us informally to stop focusing our advertising on this shortcoming. Even his own union representatives took umbrage with this outsourcing of jobs offshore. In fact, they approached me several years after their call centres were closed in Canada, to do an interview with me detailing the benefits of made-in-Canada call centres. I reluctantly agreed to do this, and during the interview, I took the high ground, sticking to the benefits rather than the adversarial aspects of competition. It would have been obvious to anyone viewing this video that that was the message.

AC/DC—"You Shook Me All Night Long"

Parties that go on all night have been far from unheard of throughout my life. Perhaps most notably, in 1996 in Stouffville, at our home in Blue Ridge, a subdivision of that community, we held a going-away party before moving west to Calgary.

We pulled out all the stops to ensure that the event was epic and memorable for all who attended. We set up a very large tent in our backyard, which allowed us to offer catering and a fully stocked bar. Mario, my brother-in-law, along with Stew Hedin, our technical supervisors in Barrie, tended bar and took care of our guests' needs. We wanted everyone to have a fantastic time.

Our backyard was large enough to host a circus-sized tent, a stage for live music, and catering for more than a hundred people, for an energetic and unforgettable twenty-hour event. It was an opportunity to bring together friends, colleagues, and associates in a fun and exciting atmosphere. Guests included many of Shaw's senior leadership team along with their families, as well as many working in community programming, local broadcasting, and even a few familiar news personalities.

Fellow musician and good friend Susan Ponting—an extraordinary musician and vocalist—performed with our band. Our guests partied and danced till dawn while our band played all night long! It was a band that Susan and I had formed during the short time I had lived and worked in Toronto. We loved to get together during the evening, and would occasionally play at a blues bar on Yonge Street.

Understanding that several of our colleagues were also accomplished musicians, we invited about six of them to perform at the party throughout the night. However, they weren't all drummers, and the one drummer we did have was so fatigued that he lay down and took a nap near the kitchen window, right behind his drum kit.

It was a party everyone still talks about today, one with a level of energy akin to AC/DC. It shook all night long!

When my new friends—band members, colleagues—and I weren't working hard or partying, we'd engage in spontaneous activities for fun.

On my fiftieth birthday, I had the Chinese symbol for the protector tattooed on my right arm. I had it done on Yonge Street, when I was out for dinner with Jim McHugh, our system manager in Barrie, and Susan Ponting, who was also our very talented community programming director. It felt appropriate, not just because people had often recognized my protective side throughout my life and told me so, but because it was something I strove to always be. I never wanted to forget that. Marking myself with this symbol was in honour of a trait I plan to take to the grave. The Protector, whom you can count on!

Italy

In 1998, JR rented a beautiful eight-room villa overlooking the ocean in Tuscany. During the three months they were there, he would invite senior management and friends of the family to join him and his wife, Carol, to spend a day or two with them. JR was respectful of Michael and treated him like a grandson. He would host dinners for the board members, and though the setting was relaxed and spectacular, in the beautiful Italian countryside, JR was still working. He could never get enough of work, and always wanted to be informed. So, even within the casual holiday vibe of that Mediterranean retreat, there were still Shaw-related topics talked about at the table.

It was a work ethic instilled in all the Shaws, as demonstrated by Julie when, during her visit to the Tuscan villa, she spent time installing solar panels to sustainably heat the pool!

Louise, Michael, and I stayed for two nights with JR and Carol in Tuscany, and for the remainder of the week we booked a room in a beautiful seaside hotel along the Italian Riviera coastal town of Viareggio. From there we explored the region in a rental car—a compact Hyundai—visiting Milan and Florence. It was a special time for Michael and me. He was just twelve, and it was a wonderful opportunity to create some fun father–son memories.

We'd go for long walks, exploring, laughing, and talking. One of the highlights of the trip for Michael was our visit to the naval museum in La Spezia, Northern Italy. This museum holds a significant place among Italian naval museums. It is a hub of naval history and technology, showcasing the evolution of Italian naval power and maritime technology over the centuries.

Michael was very interested, and asked many questions about the model ships and submarines that were on display. Their collection included models of ships from the Second World War. He was also intrigued by the diving suits and the claustrophobic underwater bells that divers had to use to explore the bottom of the sea to check for bombs and other threats that could sink a naval ship. Michael had a very active mind, and during our day, while touring the submarines on-site, he visualized the actual battles that these sailors endured to protect their small country with such a well-equipped navy.

Every day we got up early to drive somewhere new, taking in scenery, eating pizza, shopping, and navigating the helter-skelter traffic. All the while, I was practising my best lingua latina to converse with the local Italians.

It was a memorable and enjoyable time, although far too short. I hope to return to Italy one day to see the highlights of Rome and the Vatican.

The Move to Headquarters

After a year and three months in Toronto, Jim Shaw asked me to return to the West and take on the role of senior vice president of operations at Shaw's headquarters in Calgary.

It was during this time that 80 percent of Shaw's customers in Toronto signed up for the discretionary tier of services called the extended basic plan. This was a huge revenue contributor for the company and helped us to improve our operating margins to the same levels we had enjoyed in our Western Canadian cable operations. Things were going very, very well.

Moving to Calgary in a role that Jim himself had held before becoming CEO made me feel immensely proud. This move gave me greater exposure to the board and allowed me to present operating reports directly to the board at our quarterly meetings.

At the time, Shaw was growing at a rate of 10 to 15 percent annually, keeping analysts busy—one of whom, Paul Pew, would later join Shaw's board of directors. However, there was no time for complacency. There were always targets to meet, new goals to pursue, and higher numbers to achieve. While I was honoured to be recognized for my contributions, I stayed highly motivated and never allowed myself to get too comfortable.

Jim's comments, such as "If we don't make these numbers, Peter's going to get fired," were not meant to intimidate, but to emphasize the intensity of the competition. They served as a reminder that Shaw's success came from hard work in a tough environment. Every challenge was taken seriously, and once overcome, we moved swiftly to the next. There was no resting on our laurels.

When I moved to Calgary, I couldn't have predicted how much I would fall in love with the city. It became not only the headquarters of my career but also my home, the centre of my vast and influential network, and the place where I'd celebrate successes, form close friendships, and meet inspiring people.

However, all was not well on the home front. Within the first month of our move to Calgary, Louise befriended two ladies in a hair salon, who liked to partake in drugs. These ladies were pleased to have a new friend with the means to enjoy their company and lifestyle.

My objective at the time was to do the best possible job for Shaw and to demonstrate that their faith in me, having moved me from Toronto, was warranted. Throughout my career, I have strived to maintain balance. Employees and colleagues appreciate a leader who is even-keeled and predictable in their demeanour. No highs. No lows. No matter the circumstances, I always had time for our employees. My door was always open, and I was focused.

As my relationship with Louise devolved in our new setting, I faced challenges that tested my resilience and understanding. With so many positives occurring at Shaw during the day, it became increasingly difficult at night to navigate the impact of addiction on our lives together. I witnessed firsthand the toll that this took on my wife. It was painful to see someone I loved grappling with such challenging issues, often leading her down paths that hurt not just her, but our relationship.

The trust in our relationship began to erode, leading to feelings of hurt, confusion, and isolation for both of us.

Several years had passed since we moved to Calgary, and my doctor had cautioned me about my unhealthy, rising blood pressure readings.

In fact, he asked me, "When should I get the invitations prepared?"

"What invitations?"

"For your funeral."

I knew that my relationship with Louise was causing me stress. I worried about her recreational activities, and could see she had no respect for me. It had become impossible for us to communicate effectively. Louise and I had been seeing a marriage counsellor to try and resolve this. But the counsellor confided to me that in his professional opinion, Louise was not fit or willing to make changes to save our marriage.

I could soon see that he was right. Within weeks of being told by our counsellor that there was no hope in our marriage, I had had bone spur surgery on my ankle. The doctor had given me painkillers and instructed me to rest and elevate my ankle. I expected that, upon my returning from the doctor's office with a walking cast and a cane, Louise would help me with that first day after surgery. Instead, soon after I'd arrived home, she put on her short shorts and high heels and told me that she was going out with her girlfriends, and I better get used to it.

I had become suspicious of Louise's frequent disappearances with her girlfriends. Many nights, with no explanation, she would get up out of bed and leave the home.

My suspicions were confirmed weeks later. I flew to Barrie, Ontario, to give the eulogy for a Shaw manager who had been killed in a car accident. I had originally planned to stay overnight, but had work-related tasks I needed to attend to, so flew back to Calgary later that evening.

I arrived at the Calgary airport around 10:00 p.m., and after an hour's drive south, I arrived at my home before midnight. It had been a long day, and I was tired. When I opened my door, the only one to greet me, tail wagging, was Bobby, my Australian shepherd. Louise was not home. I tried to stay awake for her return, but to no avail. Surprisingly, I awoke early to what I thought was the sound of Jim McHugh's voice saying, "I am okay, and you will be too!" Louise was not at home.

I awoke again at 8:00 a.m. to the sound of Bobby barking and Louise driving into our driveway. Dressed in revealing silk shorts, she was surprised to see me at home, as she also thought I would be gone all night.

Louise was stumbling as she got out of the car. She was clearly intoxicated or high as she angrily told me, "Fuck off, it's none of your business," when I asked where she had been.

My friendships with Jim and Brad Shaw along with Bill MacDonald were paramount in my management of this situation. I confided in them, but through the course of time and public events, they had come to see it for themselves. I would not let this situation undermine my performance at Shaw, my role as a loving father to my son Michael, and my personal commitment to JR Shaw that he could count on me.

On August 1, 2001, I moved out of our home in Sundance and moved into an executive suite across the road from my office at Shaw Court. The horse was out of the barn. No more excuses would keep me from moving on with my life. My priority was to take my son for a trip to San Diego, to help him understand what had happened and how I was going to support him through this transition and onward. We spent a wonderful week together, visiting the sights in San Diego: the world-famous zoo, the naval ships in the harbour, and an NFL San Diego football game at field level.

Rivals in Business: Shaw vs. Telus

Competition benefits everyone. It sparks innovation and creativity, compelling companies to enhance their products, services, and customer relationships. It fosters a wider range of options and better pricing, improving the overall consumer experience.

During my years at Shaw, I witnessed firsthand how competition kept us on our toes. Telus was our biggest rival in the West. As the monopoly telephone provider for many decades, they had a long-standing presence in landline services, and as they rolled out their fibre-optic network, we fought fiercely to maintain our edge in cable and internet. By 1997, Shaw and Telus were engaged in what the *Calgary Herald* called trench warfare. Telus workers were severing Shaw's underground cables in Lake Bonavista to install their own. After witnessing the sabotage, Jim Shaw and I decided to take legal action against Telus, and we ultimately won.

By 2001, Shaw had secured 80 percent of the Western Canadian market, largely because we believed in our ability to grow, and invested heavily in technology. Our competition with Telus intensified through the early 2000s, with both companies accusing each other of false advertising and service issues. Yet, despite our rivalry, Shaw's local Canadian-based customer service set us apart. While Telus outsourced their call centres to the Philippines, Shaw's customer service teams were based in Canadian cities, making us more responsive to local community needs and strengthening our bond with customers. Competition drove us to be better, and even as we battled it out, we learned from this experience, keeping the industry dynamic and beneficial for everyone.

Pinetop Perkins—"Chicken Shack"

Pinetop Perkins, born in 1913 in Mississippi as Joe Willie Perkins, was a blues pianist. He died in 2011, two years and two months shy of becoming a centenarian. He had a long and influential career, known for his boogie-woogie piano style and his significant contributions to blues.

He played with notable musicians of the genre, like Muddy Waters and Howlin' Wolf. He received multiple Grammy Awards—one at the age of ninety-seven, making him the oldest Grammy winner ever—and was inducted into the Blues Hall of Fame.

To unwind after a long day at work, I would often go and watch live music with my good friend Terry Medd. The two of us were in a band together and would always open our gigs with a song called "Chicken Shack."

On one occasion, in the mid-1990s, at The Louie in Calgary, Pinetop Perkins—who had written "Chicken Shack" for his *After Hours* album—was performing with boundless vitality. At eighty-two years old, he still displayed incredible energy on stage.

That evening, Terry and I were able to chat with Pinetop Perkins for four hours and learn more about the man behind the song we'd been playing for years.

With a twinkle in his eye, Pinetop mentioned that he still loved to be in the company of women, even in his eighties. He told us he was born in Mississippi, and his music was influenced by the Delta blues players of the day. He gained fame and acclaim when he moved to Chicago to play in clubs with the likes of Buddy Guy, whom I had met at his Buddy Guy's Legends blues club when I was visiting that city. He autographed a T-shirt for me, and I knew I'd keep it forever.

Pinetop told us he had had some issues with the police. Lifting his pant leg, he proudly pointed at the tracking bracelet on his ankle. He said that he was on probation for a minor charge in Mississippi, which I thought was domestic, but he was such a gentle soul that I couldn't see him hurting a fly, let alone a helpless chicken in a shack.

Star Choice

It was May 1997, and Shaw wanted to expand its brand awareness and service coverage area in the East. With many customers in rural areas across the country, Star Choice satellite was the best option for us to accomplish this objective.

At the time we bought Star Choice, they were experiencing significant financial challenges, losing $800 million annually. Despite the financial losses, Shaw evaluated the situation and identified potential strategies for a turnaround, believing we could leverage our current strengths to enhance our strategic decisions, operations, and sales approaches.

Jim and I decided that Brad Shaw would be the perfect leader to take on the challenge of making Star Choice profitable.

And he was. In just one year, Brad and his team had transformed Star Choice into a robust and profitable endeavour. Under Brad's leadership, Star Choice quickly grew to serve 800,000 customers as they adjusted retailing deals, eliminated inefficient operating practices, and changed satellite and decoder procurement processes.

This was Brad's inaugural significant project with me, alongside Jim Cummins, who was then a regional manager, and it couldn't have turned out better.

As with every acquisition, there was a process of transition to ensure the smooth running of operations. One problematic issue requiring immediate attention was that Star Choice did not have sufficient resources to answer its telephones. This might not sound like a big deal, but when customers call your office, they must be answered immediately. They must be at the centre of every business decision. We must be readily accessible; excellent customer service must be a way of life. This is paramount for a business to succeed.

Every week, Brad and I would meet with the Star Choice manager, who repeatedly denied they were having trouble meeting the answer-time objectives we had established for our call centres. He was adamant it wasn't a problem, and believed they offered exemplary customer service.

So, in response to this denial, I said, "Okay, let's call them right now. Let's call Star Choice."

Tense were the thirty minutes it took for someone to answer the call.

I wasn't fond of bullshitters. It was obvious that Star Choice needed more customer service staff to answer the phones.

After a thorough analysis of calling patterns, we made the decision to relocate the call centre from Fredericton, New Brunswick, to our head-quarters in Calgary, where an entire floor was allocated to customer service staff to answer calls from Star Choice customers. In addition, we subsequently opened a new call centre in Montreal to handle the many francophones who were calling from Quebec.

Shaw expanded its Star Choice customer base into rural areas across the entire country. Quebec, which had experienced slower growth, started to improve with more targeted advertising, conveniently located retail outlets, and the offering of French specialty services from all regions of the province. Although we already offered cable services in our more urban communities, the availability of Star Choice in Shaw's service areas wasn't a problem. We were not competing with ourselves, as pricing was very similar. However, given the option, most customers preferred cable because of its convenience and the fact that you could receive high-speed internet as a part of the cable packaging. Star Choice did not offer high-speed internet over its satellite, as it was not economically feasible, given the limited number of transponders available on our satellites. We were simply offering customers options. It was an alternative that generated incremental revenue for Shaw, while expanding our reach and brand across the country.

In the long term, the acquisition of Star Choice, which was subsequently rebranded to Shaw Direct, proved to be a wise investment. This enabled Shaw to expand its service delivery throughout the entire country, which previously we could not reach with our cable network.

Our satellites had transponder coverage across all of North America. This enabled our customers to connect to our service from their recreational vehicles or cottages, no matter where in North America they were situated. This was a way to ensure that customers on the go weren't going anywhere.

The Tightners

I have been in multiple bands throughout my life. The first of them, which we formed in 1994 with encouragement from Terry Medd, was called The Lucky Dogs Blues Band. Terry is an accomplished guitarist and musician. To this day, he performs most nights in his hometown of Victoria.

Terry was a member of the famous Canadian band from Edmonton, Footloose. Their hit song "Leaving for Maui" still pays him royalties to this day. The bass player of that band was George Goodall, who also played in our Lucky Dog Blues Band.

In 1997, Kelly Cowan—whom I met while he was working as a salesperson at a guitar store in Calgary—and I formed a band called The Tightners. I admired Kelly's guitar-playing skills and we got along well, as we also worked together at Shaw. In addition to Kelly and me, this band was comprised of Henry Lees, our vocalist, who worked at Country Music Television in Calgary; Gary Reimchen, a flamboyant drummer known for his wild and crazy shoes and expressive drumming skills; John Parker, our formally trained keyboardist who had worked at Axe Music in Edmonton; and Steve Dueck, our grooving bass player from Saskatchewan, the home of so many successful musicians in Canada.

We loved to play together, and each night would gather in my studio in Calgary and practise songs we had written, along with cover songs to play when performing at gigs. Our music was mostly rock, blues, and country. After several years of playing together, we decided to record an album of our original songs. I had a well-equipped recording studio in my home and took on the enjoyable task of recording our first album.

One day, while I was flying home from a business trip to Toronto, I was seated beside Margot Micallef, Shaw's corporate counsel. She asked me what we were going to do with any money we made from the sale of our as-yet unnamed album. I told her that we would like to donate any money we received to a worthwhile cause. Margot told me about a woman she knew from Vancouver who had been diagnosed with lymphoma. Her name was Patricia Manson. She and her husband had five children, and her husband was a practising labour lawyer in Vancouver.

John Parker had just written a beautiful song—a tribute to a woman— that we thought could be the title song for our album. We discussed this, and our band agreed that we would donate our proceeds to the Lymphoma Research Foundation of Canada, which had been founded by Patricia Manson. Margot also informed me that her brother owned

Allegro Music in Oregon, and he would love to master and distribute our album. Once we agreed on that, we named our album *Magical Lady*. Wow, good things were happening!

The band spent several months in my studio, recording this album. I called John Parker at 4:00 a.m. one morning to discuss the song structure of "Magical Lady." The previous day, I had recorded John while he played the piano track for that song. Although in the middle of the night, I was now creating and recording my guitar part for the song. I wanted John to hear it, and so called him at that early hour. When you are involved in recording projects, there is no good or bad time to a day. The adrenaline flows.

John answered my call and was delighted that I was working on his song at that hour. I wanted him to hear what I had recorded, so played him the remixed song with my additional tracks. He loved it! I was delighted, and finally able to sleep.

No album is complete until the artwork is done. I had the pleasure of working with Deb Avis at Shaw. She was a creative force and our marketing vice president. I knew that Deb was also a very talented artist, as I had seen her work framed in her office. I asked Deb if she was interested in creating the cover art for our album. She took it on with passion. That modernistic oil painting still hangs in my recording studio in Calgary and graces the many albums that were created at Allegro Records in Oregon.

In June of 1999, I was introduced to the owner of Skyreach Place. He was a guest at the Shaw golf tournament. He had heard that we had a band and had released an album dedicated to lymphoma research, and asked me if I would be interested in being the headliner act for their New Year's Eve celebration in Kelowna. Our band's desire to make something good come about from our album was coming to fruition.

Everyone has a friend who knows a friend! We needed to find a replacement singer for that concert, because Henry Lees was moving to Toronto. The singer we chose was a well-known vocalist, Peter Laughlin, who had played in very popular bands throughout Calgary. I wondered to myself, "By accepting this gig, have I bitten off more than I can chew?" This was no different, in my mind, than some of the previous projects I had taken on during my life's journey. No different than business, we just needed the right mix of talent and commitment, and we would succeed. We could not let the Skyreach folks down!

Three months later, we drove to Kelowna and were interviewed by the local community television and radio stations. The focus of their interviews was "The president of Shaw and his band are coming to Kelowna to party with the locals and raising money for a good cause. Come one, come all!" And, come they did. It was a great success. Shaw Television promoted and used three cameras to videotape the event. An audience of several thousand enthusiastic revellers attended the concert. The venue was fantastic.

This entire experience reinforced for me that the principles that work in business can be applied to other areas of life.

Ted Rogers, himself a musician in his youth, known as the Song and Dance Man, was supportive of me and our band's pursuits, agreeing to sell our CDs at his countrywide chain of video stores for $14.99 each and offering to do all he could to promote them.

"We're a 'we' band, just like Shaw is a 'we' company. Everything we do in the band, we do as a team," I told the media.

When I started at Shaw, I learned that JR was very insistent on the minimal use of the *I* word in all correspondence. In fact, he would read correspondence that had been sent to him through the office mail and would circle every *I* that was used in that correspondence. In some cases, as a not-so-subtle reminder, he would return the letter to the originator, with its circled *Is*. *Let's chat, JR* would be handwritten on the letter.

Fortunately, my writing style most often had taken this into consideration, as we shared the same aversion. This *I* and *we* focus became imprinted in our daily conversations, so much so that new employees were confused when they heard a Shaw person referring to themselves in the third person. *We* was awkwardly being used in an *I* context. As JR often stated, "There is no *I* in *team*. We are a *we* company!"

Similarly, a good band depends on the relationship of its members—on their connection and their synergy. It relies upon each individual playing to their unique strengths, enjoying what they do, and giving it their best. They need to support, elevate, and celebrate one another.

The power of an effective team should never be underestimated—be it on stage or in the office.

Nibbly Fish

In 1997, my wife Louise, our son Michael, Louise's parents, and I went on vacation to Maui. Michael was eleven when I took him snorkelling for a day in a secluded bay.

While we snorkelled, calmly and unobtrusively seeking out native sea life such as yellow tangs, moray eels, and humuhumunukunukuapua'a—for real, that's what they're called—a woman who was too impatient to wait for such sightings was throwing handfuls of tiny breadcrumbs from a seemingly bottomless plastic bag into the water around her.

Within minutes, hundreds of fish began to swarm her from all angles, leaping over one another, splashing out of the water and nipping hungrily at her legs and bottom. Fearing she might be eaten alive, this panic-stricken woman began screaming.

There was no time to laugh. I swam over to her in the chest-high water and lifted her over my shoulder, carrying her out of the sea to the shore.

Between sobs, she said she was very grateful for my help, if admittedly she felt a little ridiculous. Her husband had been watching it all from the beach and offered no assistance. I wondered how their conversation might go on the ride back to their hotel.

Corus Entertainment

The dawning of a new millennium meant the dawning of new industry strategies.

In 1999, Shaw made the strategic decision to spin out its media properties into a separate entity called Corus Entertainment.

Corus was headed up by Heather Shaw as chairperson and Julie Shaw as vice chair. JR decided that Jim and Brad would be responsible for distribution and telecom, and Heather and Julie would head up media.

Over the years, Corus Entertainment expanded its presence in the Canadian media landscape by diversifying its offerings, ranging from television channels to specialty television and radio stations across various genres and popular digital streaming platforms.

The spin-out of media properties into Corus allowed Shaw and Corus to operate independently as specialized entities in their respective industries, contributing to the growth of the Canadian media and telecommunications sectors.

The changes in the way content is watched, and the impact this has had on broadcasters and their advertisers over the past twenty years, has been profound. I have observed our Canadian media companies trying to manage the consequences of these rapid changes on their respective businesses.

I once described this fast-occurring phenomenon to a retiring media company executive, Doug Murphy, as similar to that of a Zener diode. I learned about Zener diodes while in the air force. A Zener diode is designed to allow current to flow in the reverse direction when the voltage exceeds a certain level. The Zener diode has a phenomenon called *Zener avalanche breakdown*, which occurs when a certain voltage level is reached. This process results in a sudden and dramatic increase in current flow. In my mind, this sudden and dramatic change is what is being experienced in the broadcasting, media, and advertising businesses. It is catastrophic if not understood and managed accordingly.

Technological change, shifting viewer behaviours, and a plethora of niche streaming content has eroded the financial viability of the three largest media companies in Canada: Rogers, Bell, and Corus. In 1999, traditional broadcast television was the primary medium for content consumption. The advertisers who supported the linear programs being carried by these media companies were well served. They could capture the eyeballs of most of the viewers. More eyeballs meant more money. However, the rapid emergence of streaming platforms like Netflix, Amazon Prime, and later Disney+ has transformed viewing habits and the tried-and-true advertising models. Rather than being confined to linear television, viewers were drawn to programming on demand: watch whatever, whenever, and wherever they want. I call it the five Ws that wounded broadcasters.

The proliferation of mobile devices, and technological change, compounded the problem for traditional broadcasters. The more personalized viewing experience has resulted in a wider array of programming genres, including podcasts, live streams, and web series. It is no surprise that the broadcasting industry was so dramatically disrupted, and in such short order. Companies could either struggle to adapt or, in worst cases, cease to exist. The path ahead will be challenging and the content framework will continue to evolve. Stay tuned!

President, Shaw Cablesystems

Shaw Cablesystems Ltd. was a division of Shaw Communications Inc. which, as the name suggests, focused on providing cable television, internet, and telephone services to Canadian customers.

In 1999, I was promoted from senior vice president of operations to president of Shaw Cablesystems Ltd. The company continued to grow, another rung of the ladder ascended, and the next decade of opportunity beckoned.

Nine — President, The Early Noughties

It was the year 2000. Industry was thriving across Canada, especially in Ontario, with its vibrant arts and culture scene, passionate sports culture, and growing population. Finance, technology, manufacturing, tourism, and film and TV production were all contributing to a prosperous economy. And when computer systems avoided the feared Y2K bug, the sense that progress was unstoppable was in the air.

It was a great time for business meetings over dinner. One deal was literally written on a napkin. Jim Shaw and Ted Rogers were having dinner in Toronto, drinking a lot of wine. At the time, the companies' licensed service areas were becoming merged as Shaw acquired cable systems in the East, including Toronto, which had traditionally been Rogers' domain, and Rogers operated two large systems, Vancouver and Victoria, in the West, which was Shaw's predominant service area. The idea came up almost as casually, as a tipsy, "Wanna swap?"

As spontaneous as this impromptu proposal was, it made tremendous business sense. The idea was that Rogers would transfer its cable systems in Vancouver and Victoria to Shaw, while Shaw would transfer its Eastern systems—including New Brunswick, which Shaw had acquired a year earlier—to Rogers. They agreed on a subscriber-for-subscriber swap, with any excess subscribers compensated at $3,300 each. Rogers ended up paying Shaw the difference, as Shaw's systems in the East had more subscribers than Rogers had in the West.

I was thrilled when Jim called me after their dinner to tell me about the deal. I knew the Rogers' systems well, having worked in Vancouver and the Lower Mainland for Rogers and Western. My familiarity with the region and its labour culture would prove beneficial for Shaw as we transitioned.

The deal took a year to finalize, with all the legal and technical details to be hammered out. We never doubted it would happen. It was Ted and Jim's agreement, and it was my mandate, on behalf of Shaw, to make it happen.

My reputation throughout the industry was someone who was fair and knowledgeable. I knew that our operational leadership team was up to the task. We had done many deals previously. With our prior experience, we were well-positioned to ensure the transfer's success. And a success it was! It was during this period that I met John Tory, my counterpart at Rogers, who would become both a rival and a friend.

At our first meeting to coordinate the transfer of our respective cable systems, John Tory appeared holding a tube of K-Y Jelly: a lubricant intended to reduce friction.

Evidently, he'd heard I was a tough negotiator.

He looked me in the eye in front of our colleagues and said, "Peter, if you're going to screw me, please make sure you use this K-Y Jelly!"

I was quite taken aback that John would think this of me—unethical behaviour was, after all, against my very core beliefs!

John later admitted he had heard untrue rumours about me. These claims may have stemmed from the simple fact that we had successfully completed many cable system acquisitions fair and square. John had a great sense of humour and wasn't one to shy away from the shock factor or using negotiating tactics to try to catch me off guard. This made us a good match, given my own unconventional, fearless approach.

Our first meeting left a lasting impression, triggering a spirited competition that elevated the overall playing field. I always admired John Tory for his cerebral qualities and his ability to multitask effectively. These skills served him well throughout his career.

Sale of @Home

@Home was an industry consortium created to provide the cable industry with a North America–wide distribution backbone and user interfaces for broadband internet. In theory, @Home made perfect sense. In practice, however, it was a complete failure. @Home couldn't establish an operational organization or technical infrastructure to handle the rapid growth of broadband internet. In many ways, @Home was caught up in the internet bubble of the late 1990s. As an early investor and shareholder, Shaw did very well financially, but @Home was never an operating company we could rely on to grow our business.

Launched in the mid-1990s as a joint venture between several large American cable companies—including Tele-Communications Inc., Cox Communications, Comcast, and Adelphia Communications— and Rogers and Shaw in Canada, the goal of @Home had been to offer broadband internet access to consumers, capitalizing on the growing demand for faster and more reliable internet connections. Initially, the venture was a great success, expanding services across North America.

It was especially rewarding for Shaw, which was growing faster than any other company in the consortium. @Home's stock skyrocketed. Returns were so impressive and finances so robust that Shaw was able to distribute bonuses to all its employees, providing life-changing sums that allowed people to put downpayments on homes, pay off debts, purchase new cars, or go on dream vacations. We recognized that our success was the result of a team effort, and we rewarded that. It was a euphoric time for everyone.

The growth of internet customers, although good news for Shaw, was a problem for @Home. It could not scale its network fast enough to keep up with Shaw's growth. Michael D'Avella and I travelled to their headquarters in San Francisco to escalate our concerns. After many technical reviews, the expansion plans being suggested by @Home were clearly insufficient.

Shaw decided that it needed to build its own distribution and switching facilities. As such, Shaw's board approved a significant capital plan to build a superhub in Calgary. This digital switching, in concert with a much more robust backbone facility we had built, called Big Pipe, was of sufficient size and scale to meet our growth projections for the next five years.

We waited to announce our plans to @Home until after the facility was built and tested, ensuring that we could transfer our internet traffic without interruption. Upon transitioning to our facilities and our newly branded internet service, our customers were thrilled with the enhancements in service quality, speed, and capacity they were receiving from Shaw.

However, at that time, @Home filed for bankruptcy protection, as many of its members indicated they would leave due to the inadequate service levels that had been provided on the @Home backbone network. Michael D'Avella and I travelled to San Francisco to meet with the lawyers and trustee representing @Home during their bankruptcy proceedings. Prior to our meeting, I had asked our finance department to let me know how much in holdback we had accrued for the @Home payments we had held back. It was $11 million.

We convened in their offices high above the city. Initially, the meeting began amicably with the usual cordialities, but we soon got to the crux of the matter: our reasons for exiting the @Home consortium. We detailed to their representatives our experiences with the subpar network performance, the numerous meetings held to address these issues, and their failure to meet the minimum service-level agreements stipulated in our master agreement.

We highlighted the considerable cost incurred in constructing a redundant backbone network and a central switching hub to fulfill our customer-service expectations. Furthermore, we elaborated on the detrimental effects their poor service had on our growth trajectory.

In response, their lawyer, a confrontational and self-assured individual, argued that we had been taking undue advantage of the benefits afforded by the @Home consortium. He hinted at filing a lawsuit to recover $450 million in damages from Shaw, asserting that American judges tend to view Canadians unfavourably when it comes to taking advantage of American goodwill.

My immediate thought in reaction to his exaggerated claims was disbelief; I think I told him that it was inconceivable that a smart man like him could believe his own bullshit. It was evident that we had reached an impasse. In this meeting, I was the bad cop. We mutually agreed to disagree, and decided to leave the meeting.

Before our departure, I approached the trustee, who appeared reasonable, to request a follow-up discussion. Their lawyer insisted vehemently that the trustee should not communicate with me.

As we exited the lawyer's office and approached the elevator, I encountered the trustee once more. I inquired if I could speak with him the next day and asked him for his number. To my surprise, he responded with, "Eleven million dollars." I had been expecting him to give me his phone number. Michael and I exchanged smiles, recognizing that we had just, unbeknownst to the trustee, reached an agreement in principle; we just needed to confirm the financial details. The following day, I called the trustee from my office in Calgary, and within minutes, we successfully concluded an agreement for $11 million. Win–win always feels good.

At the turn of the millennium, as the internet landscape changed rapidly, many ISPs and telecommunications companies re-evaluated their investments and restructured operations. Parting ways with @Home had become a priority for Michael D'Avella and me. Joining @Home had been the right choice, and departing was equally the correct decision. In September 2000, Shaw divested a stake in @Home in pursuit of greater growth.

President

As the president of Shaw Cablesystems Ltd., I attended all of Shaw's board meetings. One very special board meeting was held in 2001. At that meeting, which was chaired by our founder JR Shaw, I was present to hear Jim Shaw's CEO report. As usual, I'd prepared my operational update. This included customer and product statistics and other high-level financial performance reports. Once I completed delivering my report, Jim thanked me and added, "Oh, I just remembered I have something I want to say. I want to introduce the board to our new president of Shaw Communications Inc., Peter Bissonnette."

I wasn't one to overreact or seek attention, yet I found myself flushing bright red with a wave of gratitude and shock. This unexpected recognition took me by surprise, and despite my disbelief, a beaming smile broke across my face, turning into a joyful laugh.

"Wow," I managed to say. "This is quite overwhelming. What a surprise!"

The board responded with a warm applause. I could feel their support and appreciated the moment more than they would ever realize.

I've always strived to be a thorough communicator, leaving nothing unsaid, explaining points clearly, and being realistic yet optimistic in my projections. Known for conservative forecasts but strong beliefs, I aimed to keep everyone aligned and, hopefully, delighted with results. The board seemed to appreciate my approach. Shaw's board has always been a powerhouse of knowledge and experience. The presence of influential figures like Don Mazankowski and J.C. Sparkman certainly added tremendous value to the strategic direction of the board.

It was impressive to work with such a diverse and accomplished group of individuals on the Shaw board. Each member brought a wealth of experience and expertise from the various sectors. Not only did this strengthen the board's strategic capabilities, but it also enhanced its ability to innovate and navigate the challenges in the telecommunications landscape.

With Brad Shaw as the executive chair and CEO, alongside Adrian Burns as a former commissioner of the Canadian Radio-television and Telecommunications Commission (CRTC), Shaw's board maintained a strong foundation of industry experience and regulatory knowledge.

Other board members included the Honourable Christina Clark, the former premier of British Columbia; Dr. Richard Green, former CEO of CableLabs; Gregg Keating, CEO of Altimax Venture Capital; Michael O'Brien, former CFO of Suncor Energy in Fort McMurray;

Paul Pew, our lead director and one of the sector's most trusted analysts before co-founding G3 Capital; Jeff Royer, a private investor with interests in the manufacturing, hospitality, and telecommunications industries; Mike Sievert, president and CEO of T-Mobile, the fastest growing wireless company in the United States; Carl Vogel, a private investor and industry advisor focused on media and telecommunications; Sheila Weatherill, former CEO of Capital Health and vice chair of the board of directors of Epcor Utilities in Alberta; Steven White, president of Comcast's West Division; and me, former president of Shaw Communications Inc. with over fifty years in the industry.

From when I joined Shaw in 1989, to becoming president of Shaw Cablesystems Ltd. in 1999, and now president of Shaw Communications Inc. in 2001, the company had grown astronomically.

By then, we were North America's fastest-growing internet provider, and our cable acquisitions had expanded Shaw's reach across the country. As is often the case when companies experience success, employment offers from various companies soon occurred, targeting many of our senior leaders.

Recognizing the importance of retention, Jim and JR devised a Supplemental Executive Retirement Plan—a SERP—to encourage key executives to stay with Shaw until retirement. Rather than massive annual salaries, executives received substantial retirement benefits based on long-term company performance. Shaw valued loyalty, offering its people a balance that JR felt was essential: Work was only one part of life, and he wanted employees to live well-rounded lives while contributing to the company.

While the company was flourishing, my life at home was becoming increasingly difficult to manage. Though Louise had been invited to the meeting, knowing it would be significant, she did not attend.

Later that evening, I heard a knock at our door. To my surprise, Jim and Brad Shaw had brought a special bottle of wine to commemorate the occasion. We had a few drinks, after which Jim asked Louise why she hadn't attended the AGM that morning.

Her response astonished even Jim, who knew Louise very well: "I didn't think it was important." It was evident—and not just to me—that our relationship was beyond strained. Jim mentioned to me the next day that he was surprised that this had happened, especially given how hard the Shaws had tried to include her in all the Shaw events. He called it a betrayal.

What Happens in Vegas

Las Vegas was a favourite for our team-building events, management meetings, stag parties, and operational reviews. Jim loved Vegas; the excitement, the lights, and the action suited his energy. By day, we'd be in meetings, our focus sharpened by the promise of Vegas's night-time activities. On one trip, Jim took us to the Nevada desert for a 4x4 adventure on the dunes, a bonding experience that blended exhilaration with laughter, grit, and a little leftover international cuisine from the night before.

At the blackjack tables, we'd often push through late nights. Phil Murray, with bleary eyes as sunrise approached, once asked, "Peter, we have a corporate decision to make. Should we be going to bed, or just stay up until the meeting ... which starts at nine?" Wisely, I chose a one-hour nap, and I even showered in my clothes to save time, though I arrived at the meeting in dry attire and—thanks to a few nudges under the table from Bill MacDonald and Randy Elliot—managed to stay awake.

We once enrolled in a machine gun training centre about thirty kilometres outside Vegas. This experience offered us a combination of excitement and learning. I was a little nervous at the beginning of the first training scenario.

I whispered to Paul, "These guys could steal our watches and then bury us, and who would know?"

With a fully equipped shooting range and multiple makes of machine guns, from Bren to M16s, we participated in simulated scenarios that both thrilled us and created a controlled but intense experience. Though I hit most of the bad guy targets, Jim's aim was less precise, catching a few good guy targets in the mix. The camaraderie we built on those trips was invaluable, with the pressure-cooker environment sharpening both focus and trust.

Under Jim's leadership, these gatherings weren't just a break from the grind; they were an opportunity to strengthen our connection to Shaw's values and our shared mission.

Tracy Belle

Back in 1969, as I was travelling by Greyhound from Ottawa to Vancouver with nothing but a dream of a better life and just fifty dollars in my wallet, Tracy was born in a small Alberta town called Spirit River.

Largely an agricultural municipality north of Grande Prairie in Peace County, Spirit River had a population of just 1,013. It was said to have a proud sense of community, a strong work ethic, and admirable family values. Like much of pastoral Alberta, it was also a place with Catholic and secular schools, oil and gas, and dinosaur bones.

Like me, Tracy was raised Catholic, along with her siblings. But unlike me, she and her two older sisters and younger brother were all very close with their parents, Mike and Beth, who gave them time, love, affection, and security as tremendous role models of family values. They remain close to this day, and Tracy and her siblings have always spoken fondly of their childhood.

Spirit River was a safe place where everybody knew each other, kids rode bikes and played noisily in the street, and fun was abundant.

Tracy's father had been a barber and later owned a flooring company. Like many of the boomer generation in the Western world in the 1960s and 1970s, it was an optimal time for him to make the most of his ambitious nature, expanding the business to multiple locations in the northwest corner of the province.

Simultaneously, Tracy's mother was also growing her enterprise—a chain of craft stores and florist shops in Fairview and Peace River.

Though busy with apparent aspirations, Tracy's parents were always present, embarking on adventures and tackling changes as a united entity.

And so, as her parents' careers truly took off, Tracy was uprooted from her cozy haven in Spirit River at age nine, moving to what she considered the big city of Grande Prairie, where greater opportunities awaited. There, she spent the rest of her childhood, and graduated in 1987 from St. Joseph Catholic High School.

Her subsequent studies at the University of Calgary were with the intention of becoming a social worker, a profession to which she felt called—to help people, particularly youngsters. But the reality of the endless hours of study was not what she'd imagined. She simply wanted to be out there, engaging with real people and making a positive difference in the lives of others.

Working at her mother's flower shop for several years fulfilled those desires in many ways. She got to know hundreds of people through her work, becoming familiar with customer service, and she offered a friendly, kind ear to patrons in their times of celebration or grief. It was a lifestyle that felt comfortable, content, and rewarding.

Having grown up witnessing her parents' grand example of making things happen for themselves, putting in the hours and effort to achieve a greater quality of life for their family, these became attributes Tracy admired and was deeply proud of.

In the summer of 2001, Tracy was working as a flight attendant for Canadian North—a company recommended to her by her brother, Todd, who also worked there as a flight attendant. It wasn't the same level of glamour she'd enjoyed for a very short time working for American Airlines; the destinations were typically remote and cold: Yellowknife, Inuvik, Tuktoyaktuk. The passengers were mostly those working in diamond mines or oil and gas, travelling on their biweekly rotations.

But the hours were more reasonable, the money was good, and she got to see some of the lesser-known parts of Canada.

At thirty-two, Tracy was just starting to navigate a new career choice after years of running a family-owned florist's business in Calgary and later working in flower shops in Canmore and Banff.

Though the thought of arranging beautiful bouquets in one of the world's most picturesque towns, amid the breathtaking backdrop of the Rocky Mountains, may sound idyllic, Tracy saw that period as the loneliest of her life.

She lived with her two little dogs, Lola and Hugo, and while Canmore could be bustling in the summertime, many of its residents were transient or tourists—a stark contrast to the vibrant city life she had come to love in Calgary.

While considering her options, her sister Brenda suggested she look for any openings at Shaw.

"They look like a great company to work for. Decent salaries, awesome benefits, lots of opportunity. They're a huge company, and they're only getting bigger! Plus, their offices are right downtown by the river; what a perfect location!"

So, while Tracy was venturing into the Arctic wilderness and wondering how the coming years of her life would unfold, that little mention of Shaw lingered constantly in her subconscious.

Meant to Be

July 20, 2001, was a bright and sunny Friday in Calgary, with endless blue skies and a warm twenty-five degrees Celsius.

Tracy had worked a long ten-hour day, flying the 2,200 kilometres to Inuvik, north of the Arctic Circle, and back again.

Her friend and co-worker, flight attendant Elizabeth Green—or Liz— wanted to celebrate her birthday. It was the last thing Tracy wanted to do at that moment; she would have much preferred to go home and cuddle with her two dogs. But Liz was from Edmonton, and there weren't many others around. Tracy wanted her to have a good birthday.

They headed to the pedestrianized, characterful, and always-ambient Stephen Avenue in the downtown core. Steve Hankirk, their co-worker and president of Canadian North, drove them to the Metropolitan bar around midnight.

Inside the Metropolitan, an increasingly popular spot for cocktails and gatherings since it opened in 2001 near the corner of 2nd Street, I was standing at the bar with Steve Dueck, the bass player from our band, The Tightners, cheering myself up after a complicated afternoon at the hospital getting an MRI on my shoulder. The claustrophobia while in that machine had been intense.

The attending nurse had asked me, "What do you think of this?"

I had responded immediately, "I think I need to get out of here," and I did.

I noticed Tracy as soon as she walked through the door. Though it was crowded where I stood by the bar, I'm a little taller than most, so I caught her eye. Something felt instantly unique about her. She disappeared for a few minutes, but the friend she was with made her way toward me as she tried to find a spot at the bar.

It was crowded and noisy in there. When Tracy returned, her friend Liz was holding a tiny space for her to come and squeeze in next to me.

Tracy said she had been to the Met many times before, but I didn't recall ever seeing her there, and likewise, she hadn't spotted me before.

That might not seem unusual, but I knew all the bartenders, all the servers, and most of the regulars. Every face was familiar. Only hers was new.

Tracy's friend Liz was doing most of the talking at first, but as time went on, I made it clear I was keen to chat with Tracy. Tracy seemed a little surprised. She was clearly modest and not one to seek attention.

As much of the world was experiencing a recession in 2001, Canada had avoided it. Economic growth was rapid in the prairies. And as was the hot topic among Calgarians in their booming city at that time, "What do you do?" seemed an exciting and appropriate first question. So, Tracy told me about her less-than-ordinary day flying to the boundary of the Arctic tundra.

Increasingly intrigued and always willing to share, I then told her all the details of my MRI before introducing Steve, and we all talked together about music and my guitar playing.

We hit it off right away; conversation and drinks flowed without pause or difficulty. Then Tracy asked, "What do you do?" and I responded by handing her my business card, depicting the Shaw logo. Her eyes widened, and I later found out it was because of her sister's recent words about Shaw being enormous and amazing.

"President?" she asked, as if she didn't really believe it.

It was fair enough that she didn't believe it at first, I suppose. Maybe she thought I wasn't dressed like a typical president of anything, because I wasn't wearing a suit and tie. Maybe she expected company leaders to be inaccessible, uppity, or too busy and important to chat casually. Maybe she was a bit confused by my lack of a superiority complex. Maybe I seemed real, fun, and easygoing.

I found out later that Tracy thought it might be a joke. In fact, she was momentarily suspicious. She wondered if I was a talented fraudster, if the joke was on her, and she questioned whether she should be talking to me at all.

As the night crept into the early hours of Saturday morning and the ongoing party at the Met was starting to make Tracy visibly tired, she said it was time for her to go home and cuddle her dogs.

I asked for her number, and as she departed, she simply said, "It's in the book."

The next day, I managed to find Tracy's brother Todd's number in the phone book and called, leaving a message for Tracy. Much to my delight, she called back the next day and spoke with my assistant, Derinda, leaving a message with her. When I finally called back, she answered.

She probably didn't expect me to follow through, to be honest, to be forward—not in an inappropriate way but in a way that expedited positive progress. But I was never one to procrastinate. I didn't dawdle with uncertainty. I was confident and proactive.

I had found a light in Tracy that felt warm and vibrant. She was so clearly a sweet, gentle soul, and I couldn't help but be magnetically drawn to her.

The Proposal

Clearly, Tracy knew it was coming because I had a hard time keeping a secret. It was impossible to contain my excitement, and when Tracy's friend Joyce Hansen visited our house shortly before we departed for San Diego, I showed her the ring I had hidden in the laundry room.

San Diego held special meaning for Tracy and me, as I had taken her there early on in our relationship. It was where we truly got to know each other, watching sunsets and talking into the small hours. It was where I invited Tracy to move in with me in the house I was buying in Calgary. And it was a beautiful, relaxed, sunny place with long sandy beaches, impressive waves, and chilled-out, happy people. It had all the good vibes.

Of particular interest to me, San Diego was home to a large, active naval fleet, and back in those days—and up until 2016—it was also where the San Diego Chargers football team played, at Qualcomm Stadium. My connections with Qualcomm, a supplier to Shaw, aided my proposal plans.

I thought Tracy might have known the big question was imminent. We had such a wonderful relationship; conversation was easy, humour was natural, chemistry was abundant, and everything just felt right. I could foresee our future together, looked forward to it all—and I was certain she did, too. I thought she'd say yes but until you hear that word, it's not certain. But where the element of mystery remained was where and how I would pop the question.

I don't think she expected it to be quite so grand and public.

The first clue came when we were sitting in the stands during the twelve-minute halftime break after the second quarter, and a videographer from NFL Films, with a huge camera on his shoulder, pointed the lens quite obviously in our direction.

Before she could decipher what this might mean, our images were up on the Jumbotron, our faces enlarged to fill the thirty-by-fifty-foot screen—her reaction projected to seventy thousand cheering, whistling, applauding football fans who could read the message, "Tracy Belle, will you make my day? Will you be my wife for the rest of my life?"

I got down on one knee to ask if she'd marry me. It was all a blur, with everything happening at lightning speed while seeming to move in slow motion, and suddenly, this beautiful ring was on her finger, and we were engaged.

And the crowd went wild!

Tracy was blushing and grinning as we kissed in front of thousands.

It didn't seem quite appropriate, romantic, or possible to focus on the rest of the football game after such a momentous event, so we shortly departed the stadium to head back to our hotel, stopping to pick up wine on the way. People recognized us, having just seen us on the liquor store TVs. Strangers congratulated us at every turn; it was all quite surreal, dreamlike, exciting, memorable, and spectacular.

As soon as we were back at the hotel, Tracy called her parents to tell them. Nobody was surprised, but everyone was delighted. There were joyful tears, celebrations, and a lot of laughter about the scale of attention the proposal received.

For me, there was no other way. I was feeling on top of the world with Tracy, and I wanted everyone to know it, to see how incredibly happy and in love we were, and to commemorate those immense feelings in a way that could inspire thousands of people we didn't even know. It was a demonstration of sheer joy, this one moment in a lifetime that would mean so much to us forevermore. I wanted it captured, frame by frame, for all to witness. And it was truly epic.

The Wedding

For all the luxury and glamour that a seven-figure income can ultimately afford, the most cherished and memorable moments of my marriage to

Tracy have been times when we've sat out under the stars, talking and laughing into the small hours.

The times spent around a dinner table with loved ones or simply playing a game of cards. Just being around those we care about, and each other, is what continues to be most precious to us. Appreciating health, valuing our shared interests, and supporting each other's creative passions.

These are life's riches that transcend anything money can buy.

Weddings are great fun. You get all dressed up, and friends and family attend your special day and smother you with love, attention, and often generous gifts. There are butterflies, adrenaline, excitement, and nerves. It's okay to have a stiff Scotch for breakfast.

It's a big event, a memorable occasion. There's professional photography, emotional speeches, delicious food, an elaborate cake, dancing, romance, euphoria, and inevitably some dainty ceramic kitchenware.

But as magnificent as it all sounds, these are not the reasons I got married three times.

Tracy and I got married on September 25, 2004. It was a wedding attended by three families: Tracy's family, my family, and the Shaw family. The Shaw family included JR and Carol, groomsmen and co-best men Jim and Brad, and Julie Shaw, along with many members of Shaw's leadership team who had grown to be close friends.

Regional vice presidents Colin Patterson, Terry Medd, and Shannon Donnici, as well as Phil Murray, our vice president of sales, and Deb Avis, vice president of marketing—they were all there. Bill MacDonald was sadly absent, having undergone a triple bypass two days prior.

But, of course, this was an occasion when nobody would be thinking about business. It was a day to celebrate love.

Tracy, who had always had a creative eye for interior design and floral arrangements, planned the décor for two large rooms at the hotel.

The Fairmont Banff Springs, opened by Canadian Pacific Railway in 1888, is a grand, luxurious hotel nestled amid the dramatic landscape of the Alberta Rocky Mountains in Banff National Park, a designated UNESCO World Heritage Site.

A luxurious, iconic, château-like building amid the wilderness of some of the world's most breathtaking scenery, it's a world-class resort in a truly magical place, inspiring the imagination and speaking to the soul.

Along with hundreds of mountains reaching up to 10,000 feet high, rivers and waterfalls, forests, cascading cliff faces, open green fields, turquoise lakes, crystal-clear ponds, glaciers, and wildlife like bears, moose, elk, and wolves, there are hiking trails, ski slopes, white-water rafting, paddleboarding, snowshoeing, quad riding, climbing, biking, hoodoos, caves, hot springs, canyons, hidden paths, elusive peaks, snow and ice or sun and warmth, colour and life, the smells of pine trees, fire pits, wildflowers, cozy pubs, quaint boutiques, unique and characterful houses and cabins, romance, history, charm, and the freshest air that makes you feel so very alive, fortunate, grateful, and happy.

Banff is beautiful. It's special. It's everything that's wonderful, endearing, welcoming, and adventurous about Canada. What a perfect setting for such a meaningful moment in our lives.

My mother was there, enjoying her time at the head table with JR and Carol. She finally appeared proud of me, as did all my close associates, though she looked a little surprised, too, as she took it all in.

My elder sister Cecilia and her husband, Ken, had made the journey from Ottawa, and my brother, Paul, had come all the way from Japan, where he had lived since 1975. And, most importantly, my son Michael was there, arriving in a limo as our special guest. Tracy's parents, siblings, and best friends from Grande Prairie were there. One hundred and fifty people in total joined together to celebrate our partnership that was undoubtedly meant to be. My final marriage, my only truly mutually loving marriage, my happy marriage.

Not one to feel uneasy in intimidating work settings or when faced with fearful situations, I was unusually nervous on the day of my wedding. There was adrenaline, excitement, and a desire for perfection because I knew the coming hours would sit in my memory for the rest of my life.

I took an Ativan—a mild tranquilizing pill used to treat anxiety and create a feeling of calm. It was just what I needed to get through my speech articulately, without haste, shaking, flushing, or error. *Wing it* was going to be the order of the day, as long as I could maintain my composure.

I also had a cigarette outside with my brother. I was not close to him—especially since he had moved to Japan some thirty years prior—but this was one of those brief scenes that tend to happen on important occasions, when the uncertainty around ensuring a flawless day inevitably invites small imperfections, offering a mirror and reminder of life.

Contrary to tradition, Tracy and I did see each other the night before the wedding. In fact, we shared quite a bit of champagne with friends, and awoke ever so slightly hungover.

On the morning of the wedding, Tracy told me she ran into Jim Shaw in the salon as he was having a pedicure. I knew he was making sure he looked his absolute best from head to toe for my big day.

At the reception, amid the elaborate but tasteful décor and ice sculptures, Brad, Jim, and Tracy's brother, Todd, all gave emotional and entertaining speeches.

Jim shared heartfelt words: "I've known two Peter Bissonnettes—the one before Tracy and the one after, when he opened up and found confidence. Tracy brought joy into his life and peace into his heart. All men are hopeless romantics, even though gals don't think so. Peter and I cry whenever we see Shaw commercials on air. We get emotional knowing we're bringing joy to millions of Canadians."

It was a magical, happy occasion in an idyllic setting, where we made treasured memories.

True Love

"Do you want me to cut your hair?" I asked, my tenth drink of the day in hand.

Tracy and I were watching the Stanley Cup playoffs from our hotel room in Hawaii. The Calgary Flames—whom we'd made a pact to support—were playing the Tampa Bay Lightning in the 2004 Stanley Cup Final.

I had been a barber in the seminary and again in the air force for spare change, so it wasn't a totally outrageous suggestion. Seating Tracy as if we were in a professional salon, I proceeded to cut her hair above her ears and around the nape of her neck—the stylish, confident, clean, and modern look that I loved about her. I did a very decent job, though slower than your average hairdresser—owing to all the romantic interruptions.

Of course, true love isn't always smooth sailing ...

In Pocatello, Idaho, on our first-ever road trip south from Calgary in our forty-five-foot motorhome, Tracy and I realized we were running low on gas.

We ought to have known better than to pull into the local Chevron. Giant motorhomes don't fuel up at an average pump; they use big truck stations, where all larger vehicles fill up.

The motorhome was so long that, to position the tank in the right place, the front end of it was partially on a hill, and we got completely stuck—wedged in good and proper.

Tracy looked awfully embarrassed as she rounded up our four wiener dogs and took off on a walk while I waited for the tow truck to come and haul us out of there.

It was a little tense and took some time. Eventually, once we were back on the road, it was a quiet drive. We would later look back on this incident and laugh about it—one of life's live-and-learn moments.

Tracy and I share a love of sports, music, and spectacular sunsets. We enjoy simple evenings where I play my guitar. While driving our motorhome to California, we listen to Howard Stern's controversial talk show together, enjoying his provocative but funny, authentic, and candid style—always thought-provoking and sparking interesting discussions.

Home Phone

At the end of 2004, Shaw had set the wheels in motion to enter the phone market—a move that would not only strengthen our position against Telus and allow us to enter a $10 billion telephone industry, but would also align us with another business rival, Bell, with whom the phone deal was struck.

Though competitors in the satellite realm, it made sense for all parties to team up on phone services, as it gave Bell a previously nonexistent revenue base in the West.

And, perhaps most exciting of all, this was a business evolution that would generate highly attractive offerings for Shaw's customers, as we rolled out a rather enticing and cute-sounding bundle option, where people could sign up for all three Shaw services—TV, internet, and home phone—on none other than Valentine's Day: a perfect occasion to spread the love and kiss your telephone company goodbye!

It might be remarkable to consider just how recently it was that the prospect of having a physical home phone that could ring loudly into your personal living space at any moment—interrupting your train of thought while completing a crossword puzzle, disturbing a pivotal moment of your favourite TV show, making you jump and scald yourself as you grab something from the oven, forcing you to hop precariously out of the shower mid-hair-wash, or pausing an intense family game of *Trivial Pursuit*—was not only considered a basic need, but also immensely appealing.

Once upon a time, people loved to answer the phone!

The move proved successful for Shaw, as we became a company offering all telecommunications services in a single, combined package. Canadians were finding us more lovable by the minute.

The launch of Home Phone was a particularly proud moment, as I recalled that decades prior, when I was working at BC Tel—of course, a telephone company—a young technical supervisor working alongside me named Ron McRae told me, "Peter, one day you're going to be the president of a telephone company."

And now, I was.

Ten — Heart-Stopping,
The Late Noughties

It was an average, busy Tuesday in the fall of 2006 when my day was interrupted by an unexpected phone call from a man in his late thirties who said, "I believe you are my father."

Though this event had not been listed on my packed agenda when I consulted my daily calendar that morning, it was not entirely the perplexing or gobsmacking surprise you might assume.

Patrick, 2006

In March 1969, I waited excitedly for Joanne, the rather lovely and intelligent bank teller I'd been dating for a few months, to appear at the international arrivals gate at Mirabel Airport in Montreal. She was returning from a two-week holiday in Barbados.

I liked Joanne a lot, but despite my hopes of a big smile and an enthusiastic leap into my arms, the feeling did not appear to be reciprocated any longer. As Joanne approached me with as much expression as her suitcase, I asked her if everything was alright.

"I'm sorry. Peter, I just don't want to go with you anymore," she said.

I felt a little gut-punch.

"Why?" I asked.

"You have holes in your socks," she said, "and I just think, maybe, I want better than that."

It was a line that stuck with me in the weeks and months that followed, as I debated how best to spend my horribly low salary at Northern Radio: on food or socks?

By August of that year, I had made the decision to seek out better for myself, and ventured via bus to Vancouver, where a month later, I got my job as a technician at BC Tel.

On December 19 of that year, one day after my own birthday, Joanne tracked me down and called me at work to say, "I had a baby yesterday."

And so it was that unbeknownst to me, on my twenty-third birthday, I became a father. Biologically. Genetically. Scientifically.

But in that moment, I didn't think of it as any of those cold, disconnected technical things. In utter shock, not knowing Joanne had even been pregnant as she dismissed me and my poor-quality, worn-down foot garments so heartbreakingly and unforgivingly at Mirabel Airport, my automatic response was, "Well, if the baby's mine, we should get married then."

But it quickly became clear that was not going to happen. Joanne had already made up her mind; her father had apparently warned her that I was unlikely to make much of myself and that she could do better.

"I don't want to marry you, Peter."

Our baby boy, who shared my birthday of December 18, was then given up for adoption to be raised by loving, united, stable parents who wanted him and could provide for him. It was a choice that seemed to make sense for Joanne at that time, and one that I did not know had been made.

The baby, named Patrick by his new parents, was adopted one month after he was born. One month after that phone call.

Almost forty years later, I met Patrick. As I got to know him, I learned about his happy, fortunate life and discovered our shared interests and talents. I couldn't help but wonder how much genetics might have played a part in those similarities as we played guitar together. Over time, through our phone calls and conversations, we began forming a bond, although our personalities are quite different. Patrick, who built a career in teaching, tends to be more methodical, taking time to weigh decisions carefully. By contrast, I've always been inclined to decide quickly, especially in a fast-paced industry where growth and new ideas drove each day. Patrick's life in Ottawa has instilled an appreciation for stability, whereas I left Ottawa seeking greater opportunities. Despite these differences, our shared passion for music provides a solid father–son bridge. We love each other.

Thinking Big and Living Large

The thing I really enjoyed about working with Jim was that he always thought big. I was in awe of how his brain worked. There were no limits. He reinforced my belief in the power of visualization: He'd have an idea, commit to it, see all the steps in his mind's eye, follow the process, and get things done. He made things happen.

In 2006, 2007, and 2008, I was the busiest I'd ever been. My calendars were so full they were overflowing: eighteen-hour days beginning at 5:00 a.m., back-to-back meetings, day trips to Toronto, flying all over. But it was that dynamic pace that kept me alive and vital. I loved every minute of it, always working toward the next goal, undertaking the next challenge, pursuing the next acquisition, and winning the next negotiation. Every success checked off the list was a dopamine hit, my energy was always high, my enthusiasm always at 110 percent, and I was switched on 24/7 with abundant adrenaline.

While the constant stress never felt bad or problematic, it could be overwhelming. And perhaps those of us leading the charge in these exciting projects and exponential growth were simply too busy to notice any negative side effects from working just that hard.

Jim self-medicated. It wasn't a secret. Everyone knew he liked to have a drink—or rather, *needed* to have a drink. He couldn't help but drink.

He knew he needed help in this regard, so he periodically spent time at the Betty Ford Center or Hazelden in Minneapolis to rest, recover, and hop back on the wagon. Yet, a week—or even a day—after he returned to his usual environment and work routine, he'd fall right off it.

On one occasion in 2008, Jim called me. He didn't say very much, but I heard it as a cry for help. I drove to his home in Calgary, where I saw Jim's mom, Carol, and his good friend Tim Hamilton. Tim had just dropped off groceries.

Jim had fallen and hit his head. He was just about standing when I arrived, but there was blood to clean up, and Jim needed care. I told Carol and Tim that they could leave, that I'd stay with Jim. He was my best friend, like a brother to me. There was never any question that I'd be there when he needed me.

Unfortunately, that was not an isolated incident. And some were far worse.

But we had a great team—Michael D'Avella, Steve Wilson, Peter Johnson, Bill MacDonald, Trevor English, Mark Porter, Zoran Stakic, Deb Avis, and Phil Murray—who all had immense respect for Jim and knew what a brilliant visionary he was. We strove to continue pursuing that vision, working together to make things happen.

While much of the world was entering the Great Recession, Shaw was growing. Our subscriber base soared to 2.29 million. We had almost a million satellite customers. Our digital subscriber numbers grew by 40 percent. Our internet services had the highest penetration in North America. Our annual reports were positive, despite the financial crisis the continent faced.

For all these against-the-odds successes, there was a lot of effort going on behind the scenes. And while rumours began to circulate on the outside, I was working to mediate, mitigate, and reassure—through actions more than words. We kept doing what we'd always done.

I never complained, worried, or got upset about any of it. I saw it all as part of the job. But perhaps I was unaware of how much I was absorbing, and of my inability to switch off. I could never switch off.

Spectrum

In 2008, Shaw acquired a wireless spectrum licence from the Canadian government. This authorized the use of wireless communication, specifically for mobile networks, indicating that exploring the realm of cellular was very much on our radar—insofar as we wanted to be prepared to break into and compete in that area, should we feel it a worthy investment.

Though acquired, Shaw ultimately did not utilize the spectrum licence for any significant wireless ventures, and sold it to Rogers in 2013.

Spectrum licences allow companies to provide wireless services like Voice over Long-term Evolution or VoLTE, high-speed data, and even 5G connections. While unused, it was something Shaw felt we needed to have if we were to launch a wireless business. Spectrum was a scarce commodity, and our competitors had had twenty years to accumulate spectrum, leaving very little for others to compete. The wireless land-scape was clearly divided between the haves and the have-nots—better to have.

It was a $200 million acquisition, and Jim was nowhere to be seen. As such, questions were raised throughout the process about who was going to run it. I reassured our board that, as with everything at Shaw, our brilliant team would run it.

It was becoming increasingly common for Jim not to show up to scheduled meetings where we expected him to attend. And we were getting quite good at filling in and taking over. We would conduct meetings in his absence.

It never occurred to me—or perhaps I simply didn't have time to notice—that amid all the positivity, productivity, and the good-stress environment in which I thrived, my physical body might be finding any of it difficult.

Good Times Bad Times

As Robert Plant of Led Zeppelin sang about his share of times both good and bad—through the internal sound system of the emergency operating theatre at Foothills Medical Centre in Calgary, Alberta— I ventured in and out of consciousness, having been defibrillated no fewer than thirteen times already.

Surgeons, nurses, and machines worked frantically on my sixty-one-year-old, flatlining body—as I somehow managed to stay both busy and rock 'n' roll, even while teetering on the edge of death.

Though my heart, which had pumped so automatically, predictably, and reliably since the day I was born, was now motionless, my past did not flash before my eyes. I did not see a tunnel of light or hear the voices of angels. Nor did I float serenely above my open chest and hover peacefully, witnessing every detail of the miraculous work being performed by dedicated and skilled doctors—many of whom were experienced enough to know that my survival was unlikely, given that the arterial obstruction causing my cardiac arrest was deemed a 100 percent blockage, something only 10 percent of those who suffer it live to tell about.

I experienced only darkness in those moments. I could no longer appreciate my favourite rock band's emotional lyrics—many of which were, ironically, relevant. I couldn't exclaim what a wonderful coincidence it was to have that very song as the soundtrack to this monumental moment between life and death, for I couldn't speak at all. Nor could I hear, see, feel, or think. Everything just went black—all-encompassing nothingness.

As a Catholic man, it would have been puzzling, if not horribly disappointing, if I had had the ability to be puzzled or disappointed in that moment. Those philosophical reflections would come later—when I was alive again.

It was October 1, 2008. Earlier that evening, I had been repeatedly striking the gargantuan arse of Daisy in my backyard out in Bearspaw. She was a beautiful, muscular beast, grazing nonchalantly on my much-loved, recently planted, and meticulously pruned landscaping.

Daisy was a moose. A regular visitor to my garden. A symbol of strength and resilience, endurance and survival. And, true to those traits bestowed upon her by the ancestors of that very land, Daisy wasn't moving.

"Come on, Daisy, dear, fuck off now! Go eat something else," I asked politely.

Insubordinate and focused on digestion, Daisy held her ground and proceeded to produce a rather large poo—seemingly her way of adding icing on the cake that had been my day.

I was a patient man, a tolerant man. I liked Daisy. She'd been the subject of some of my artistic photography. I admired her grace and grandeur—when she wasn't shitting on my lawn. But I was also tired. More so than usual. It had been an exceptionally long day, one filled with emotions, adrenaline, stress, frustration, and fury. I wasn't someone to project turmoil onto others, least of all animals. But that night, I'd had enough. Never had I simply wanted to go to bed more than in that moment. But, true to my lifelong work ethic, there'd be no retiring until I'd made every effort to get the job done.

I returned from my house with an air rifle. My intention was to scare her off, not to seriously hurt her. Sleep was beckoning. I shot at her enormous rear three times.

Daisy barely flinched. She appeared to give precisely zero fucks. Magnificent, majestic, and seemingly oblivious to her own impressive defiance, she carried on quite contentedly. Whatever she was gobbling up must have been far too delicious to abandon. She'd had a taste, and she wasn't going anywhere.

Staring at the moose, I conceded she had won and said with a sigh, "Fine. Carry on, then."

This might seem like a poetic metaphor, inaccurate or embellished to imply a profound simile: a parallel story of quiet determination, the calm but steadfast refusal to depart, the spiritual notion of a creature of God utterly uninterested in giving in, no matter how many hits it takes.

But it's all completely true. This all happened exactly as described. Led Zeppelin and all.

Ultimately, the moose prevailed. As did I. Which is most fortunate, really—not just for me, but for my loved ones and co-workers, and for those who indirectly and often unknowingly benefited from my efforts, influence, and charity.

That day, there was more than work-related stress on my mind. I had been to see my son, who was facing some challenges of young adult-hood, trying to navigate the difficulties of contrasting influences.

No doubt it's a familiar story for many during that age of exploration, that time of transitioning into a world of responsibility and maturity and expectation with uncertainty and confusion and, for many, a period of testing boundaries, chasing excitement, and finding out what sort of person you are by first eliminating, via trial and error, all the people you ultimately don't want to be.

And, through no one's fault but the convergence of overwhelming challenges and the misfortune of timing, I found myself in an already stressful period when my workload had mounted to an unmanageable scale. This was partly due to my own eagerness to please and desire to lead proactively. At the same time, my son was facing internal struggles and challenges of his own. I realized that I couldn't control the world. Unbeknownst to me, for the first time in my life my body couldn't count on me.

As every father knows, being there to help is not just part of the package you sign up for when committing to parenthood; it's a compulsion born of unconditional love.

It was a beautiful fall day. Tracy was sitting in the screened-in deck where we had a fireplace and a TV. She saw the moose wandering into the yard, chewing all the trees. And watched my attempts to move her on.

Once my attempts to get Daisy to leave had proved futile, I returned to the house, had a glass of wine, and went to bed.

I woke suddenly at two in the morning. I told Tracy I didn't feel well and was going to get up, watch some TV, and try to determine why my chest was feeling so tight, and see if I might be better once relaxed.

By 3:00 a.m., the pain was only intensifying, and I asked Tracy to call an ambulance. I guess I looked okay because Tracy seemed surprised. I was coherent and upright, so it was probably a perplexing request. But I knew something was not right and I insisted, so she called.

When the first responders, who were firefighters, arrived, they performed an ECG that showed nothing abnormal. They asked questions, which I answered, and nobody seemed especially panicked or acted in a real state of urgency.

It was as though I foresaw what was coming before it was even medically evident, because no sooner had conclusions started to be made that I was fine than I went into a seizure.

My claustrophobia was making things even more uncomfortable, and as the firemen brought out paddles to defibrillate me, I fought their closeness—attempting to battle the suffocating feeling of people surrounding me, holding me down.

Sudden cardiac arrest is a leading cause of death with no real warning signs or significant symptoms. It often happens far from any hospital or medical professional.

As my heart momentarily stopped, I was beyond fortunate that effective action could be taken instantaneously. There is usually only a window of mere minutes to restore the heart's rhythm before death is likely to occur.

My life was saved first in my own home, then again in the ambulance, and again at the hospital.

These defibrillator machines deliver shocks of electricity via electrodes that restart or restore the usual heartbeat. As my shirt was cut open to enable easier access to my chest, Tracy was taken out of the room so as not to witness my pain and convulsions. But she still heard everything from a nearby bathroom.

She later told me that in her state of shock, she felt detached from the moment, as if she were floating above the situation completely, hopelessly, unable to do anything.

As I was transferred from the floor onto a stretcher, Tracy was directed into a second ambulance to follow me to the hospital. I always liked to have my shoes on, and Tracy knew this, so she quickly picked up my sneakers—not really knowing why. Perhaps it was her way of telling the universe, or God, that she believed I would eventually walk out of this just fine.

I was intermittently aware of what was going on. "Watch out for the moose!" I shouted as we sped down country lanes toward the highway.

At the hospital, I couldn't say much to Tracy before I was quickly wheeled into surgery, but I did tell her at least three times to call JR.

Even in what could possibly have been my last moments, I was thinking about work—wondering what they'd do, how they'd manage, thinking of all the things on my agenda and worrying about how it would get done, and considering the burden, the delay this colossal inconvenience would put on so many others.

Around four in the morning, while I was having a stent put in, Tracy called my assistant, Derinda, asking her to let JR know what had happened.

By seven, the staff allowed Tracy in to see me. Her mom had been waiting with her for the last few hours.

I was in the ICU, awake when Tracy, visibly shaken, came quickly to my side. I instantly reassured her that I felt better, and I could see the wave of relief on her face.

This event was like hitting a giant reset button. For a while, I had to take a step back and put myself first. I had to let go of a few things. I had to relinquish control. I had to take it easy, take things slowly, and take care of my health. One step at a time on the road to recovery.

This didn't just mean reducing sodium intake, lowering cholesterol, getting more sleep, drinking more water and less alcohol, and exercising regularly. More than anything else, it meant learning how to lower stress levels.

Stress affects almost everyone. It's a silent killer that puts extra strain and pressure on a person, not just psychologically, but also physically. It's linked to six leading causes of death, not just heart disease. Prolonged exposure to overwhelming responsibilities is a trigger for chronic stress.

In 2008, there was a convergence of concerns in both my work and personal life. And although Shaw was doing very well, the broader context of a global financial crisis meant everyone, everywhere, was emitting anxiety like a viral pollutant.

In the days and weeks that followed, I felt enormous gratitude for my life and for what felt like a second chance at it. I also acknowledged that I had learned a very valuable lesson—one I had not considered before: that for all my ambition, good intentions, strong work ethic, passion, and drive, I had never conceded that such a busy, full, and demanding but thrilling lifestyle would inevitably come with great risk.

It was time to recognize the necessity for balance, for acceptance of delegation, and to surrender to the impossibility of complete control.

What could be more apt than returning home from the hospital just in time for our Thanksgiving celebration, which is held in October in Canada?

From that moment on, I have lived every day with gratitude for this second chance, counting each day as a blessing.

I thank God every day that I am still alive, and while I feel as though I am now on borrowed time, I don't take a minute for granted. I hope I can accomplish more, help and inspire others, and do a thousand things that will make people glad I kept going a while longer.

More than fifty thousand Canadians per year die from heart disease. In 2008, I was not one of them.

Those closest to me, who share my faith in God, believed it was never meant to be my time. Perhaps that's why I was not greeted by angels or a white light or became detached from my physical body—because my death wasn't due.

But coming so close to the end gave me a new appreciation for life, a greater awareness of my own mortality, a fresh perspective on priorities, deepened insight into what's most important, and strengthened gratitude for the seemingly smaller things in life. The beauty of nature and the soul connections I feel with my favourite people are, in fact, far from small things.

I consider every experience in life a lesson. The chance to learn and grow is abundant in every word we read, every conversation we have, everything we see, hear, feel—and in every near-death event that befalls us so suddenly.

Jim sent a note to the team informing them I had suffered *a minor cardiac event* and would take a slight step back for a couple of weeks to recover.

The wording he used was intended to avoid alarm and reduce the risk of any potential concern from analysts following our company.

I had visitors to my home to discuss work-related matters less than a week after I'd returned. Though I needed rest and would feel my chest tighten when I needed to contribute thoughts on decisions, I also longed to return to the excitement of work.

There was a balance I needed to learn.

Board of Directors

Shortly after my heart attack, I was appointed to Shaw's board of directors.

To be appointed to the board of directors was, of course, an honour, but perhaps an obvious move given that I already embodied the criteria sought for membership.

I already had enormous responsibility, not only understanding Shaw's vision and strategic goals, but pursuing and building upon them. I already played a role when it came to making big decisions, as my insight was valued by JR. I already had sustainability in mind, and was aware of risks and assessed them accordingly in every business move I made. And most of all, I was already an ambassador of Shaw—promoting, advocating, and networking on a phenomenal scale.

There was never any question about my commitment or my willingness to collaborate. My ethics were aligned with the company's values, and I was already recognized as a respected authority within the organization.

Being appointed to the board now gave me opportunity to meet regularly with the other members, as an equal with shared interests. Many of the members became close friends.

Ted Rogers

Ted Rogers had referred to me as *the one that got away* when I left Rogers Vancouver to take on greater challenges at Western, where we both served as board members. Ted had seen me in action during regulatory hearings in the industry back in the early 1980s, and indicated that he always knew I would go far.

Ted trusted me during my days at Western Cablevision, supporting the confidence that David and Steve McDonald held in me to manage the financial responsibilities and monumental business decisions of that company. That trust continued when I joined Shaw, as Ted knew I was a man of my word. He knew I was capable, that I'd follow through and get things done. Knowing this meant that communications between Rogers and Shaw were always respectful of each other's position and goals. We were open and honest about our intentions, negotiated fairly, and worked thoroughly to ensure the best possible outcome for everyone involved. JR and Jim Shaw respected Ted Rogers and looked at him as an example of a valiant leader who had invested all financially to build his company into the most successful of his generation. Ted was driven! JR and Jim took notice.

Born in Toronto in 1933, Ted built his telecommunications company from the ground up. Like JR, he had a strong and admirable work ethic and excellent people skills. He founded the company in 1960, at just twenty-seven years old. What began as a small city radio station, CHFI-FM would grow to be Canada's largest telecommunications company, offering cable TV, internet, home phone, and mobile to millions of customers nationwide.

Rogers' presence as a Canadian brand expanded into the world of sports when the company became the majority owner of the Toronto Blue Jays, later also acquiring the Toronto Raptors of the NBA.

Despite their rivalry in the business world, Ted Rogers and JR Shaw maintained a positive and supportive relationship, always acknowledging each other's accomplishments and appreciating the skills and qualities that made each of them formidable competitors. It was a friendship with a unique dynamic, one that combined fierce competition with genuine camaraderie. A consistent mutual respect set an example for the leadership teams of their respective companies.

Less than two months after my cardiac event, Ted passed away on December 2, 2008. I travelled with JR and Julie Shaw, both of whom were concerned it might be a bit too early for me to venture away from Calgary for any length of time. But it was important to me to be at

Ted's funeral; he had been a prominent figure in my life, and I held great admiration for him.

I sat in the church with the Shaw family. The number of attendees created an overwhelming sense of unity. It was uplifting to see so many come together to celebrate the life of such a brilliant man.

It was a solemn event filled with familiar faces, triggering memories of the past. Hundreds of colleagues, who had devoted so much time to Ted's dream, gathered—thankful for what it had given them and for how integral the company had been in their lives. There was an invisible thread of connection between them all, with Ted at the heart.

Ted used to tell me he'd die in the office. He never wanted to retire. Rogers was his purpose, his calling, his destiny. He was also very outspoken about wanting to buy Shaw for many years. JR and the Shaw family were not interested in selling back then, or any time previously when the topic had been raised. They had their own big ambitions to pursue. It wasn't out of the question, but it certainly wasn't time.

Shaw Direct

In April 2009, Star Choice underwent rebranding to become Shaw Direct. Though Shaw had acquired controlling ownership of Star Choice in 2000, it wasn't until nearly a decade later that they decided to rebrand the service under their own name, aligning it with their other telecommunications offerings.

The rebranding brought several changes, including the introduction of new packaging options for customers, offering improved customer service, customized channel lineups, and bundled service options.

It was a seamless transition that incurred no disruption of service. The change allowed Shaw to consolidate all its lines of business under one recognizable name and leverage its strong brand reputation in the telecommunications industry. It was representative of a strategic move to enhance Shaw's presence in the satellite television market and offer a more comprehensive range of services to Canadian customers.

Saskatchewan Launch

2009 was another busy year for growth and acquisitions as Shaw became the first cable company in Saskatchewan to launch digital phone service, in direct competition with the government-owned and established SaskTel.

We introduced our competitive telephone offering initially in Saskatoon before expanding into Moose Jaw, Prince Albert, and Swift Current.

Branding the phone service as digital as opposed to VoIP—Voice over Internet Protocol—was in recognition of the difference between Shaw's offering and that offered by Primus and Vonage at the time.

Shaw carried its telephone voice traffic on a separate network from that used to carry internet traffic. There was no conflict between the two types of traffic. Congestion on one did not affect the other. This approach ensured greater reliability, quality, and efficiency for our customers. The move into Saskatchewan came at a time when Shaw had just signed up 212,000 customers from the incumbent phone companies in British Columbia, Alberta, and Manitoba.

We were on a roll!

Mountain Cablevision

Throughout all the negotiations and acquisitions we were involved in during my time at Shaw, one thing remained true of the company: we always offered fair market value for the cable systems we were trying to acquire. Shaw would first determine the condition of the cable plant, the number of customers to each package, and the office facilities they owned. After this analysis, we would offer what was appropriate, what was deserved, and what made good sense for everyone involved. Our deals had to be win–win.

In October 2009, Shaw bought Mountain Cablevision of Hamilton, Ontario, from the Boris family.

The sale was an emotional one for Owen Boris and his family, who had owned Mountain Cablevision for fifty years. But in 2009, $300 million was a very appealing and fair offer. That figure came after JR, Trevor English, and I, while visiting him in Hamilton, assured Owen Boris that our offer was based on our determination of the true value of his business.

We also didn't make the offer without first discovering that someone had previously offered Boris a significantly lower amount.

That offer was very disappointing to Owen, so after rejecting it outright, he agreed to meet with JR and me, fearing he might not be able to sell his system for what he thought was fair value.

After much preparation, analysis, and oversight, we were able to come to an agreement with Owen Boris to purchase his cable system.

Rogers challenged the acquisition of Mountain Cablevision to the CRTC; however, we were able to convince them and the courts that we were eligible to be an acquirer, and the Commission approved our deal. Who knew that some ten years later, Shaw and Rogers would agree to the transfer of ownership of Shaw's system serving Hamilton to Rogers.

Canwest

In 2010, I was fortunate to be part of a wonderfully talented team from Shaw that included Ken Stein, Peter Johnson, Trevor English, and Steve Wilson, all of whom saw the potential benefits of my unconventional negotiating approach and encouraged it. In addition, Vince Mercier— one of Canada's most accomplished M&A lawyers—along with our team from TD Bank were assembled to take on the task of acquiring Canwest Global.

We were not intimidated by big financial ball-breakers, and I was never one to shy away from a challenge. At Shaw we always did our best to remain approachable and relaxed. Go in with a smile, and you're more than likely to leave with one!

On the way to meet Goldman Sachs at their headquarters in their brand-new, forty-four-storey building on West Street in the Battery Park City neighbourhood of Lower Manhattan to negotiate the acquisition of Canwest Global Communications Corporation—a popular broadcaster with numerous media assets—I was excited by the monumental challenge ahead. Before we left for New York City, JR had told me that he really wanted this to happen. Coming from the Chief—our term of endearment for JR—those words were enough to motivate our team.

The Financial District is known as a leading global centre for commerce. It's home to Wall Street, the Stock Exchange, the Federal Reserve Bank, and numerous other major financial institutions. There was no downplaying where we'd gone to play that day.

Although we knew Goldman Sachs owned over $700 million of the asset and was instrumental in getting the deal done, we weren't interested in complicated, ego-fuelled, drawn-out back-and-forths that would last infinitely longer than necessary. Perhaps my calm, casual, upbeat attitude was obvious, as the lead negotiator across the table from me sized me up as if I were a nobody. From there, he would not make eye contact with me as he was filing his nails.

I sat with Trevor English on my right and Peter Johnson on my left, with Steve Wilson, the CFO, also present. The trustee requested everyone at the table introduce themselves. As I announced that we were representing Shaw, I could almost hear the internal chuckles of the proverbial sharks sitting across from me, unsuccessfully concealing their doubting frowns and pursed lips.

I decided it was time to take control.

Leaning forward in my seat, I made direct eye contact with their pompous and cocky chief negotiator. The flashy dresser who was head of Goldman Sachs' Canadian division, Gerry Cardinale, seated directly across from me, continued to file his nails. With equal parts sincerity and warmth, I said, "You know, last night I had a dream about you and me." His eyes glanced up at me. "You won't believe it, but I did. I dreamed I was giving you a great big hug. A big hug because we did this deal." I now had his full attention as he fixed his eyes on mine.

Around the table, wide eyes, exhales, and grins manifested on the faces of the formal old fellows, who suddenly appeared visibly impressed by what I can only assume was my gargantuan balls.

The room went quiet.

"And that's why we are here," I added. "To see that dream fulfilled."

I paused to see what impact my words were having. Then continued.

"And if you want, why don't you and I go to another room, with no grandstanding, and we'll figure it out, in an hour or so—just the two of us."

Much to the surprise of everyone at the table, including Gerry Cardinale himself, Gerry took me up on this offer, and out into another room off the hall we ventured to walk, talk, and recognize our shared objectives as we got through our exchange of ideas. It was clear, after listening to the approach they were recommending, that we weren't going to resolve our issues at that time. I asked Trevor English to come into the meeting room with me to hear what they were proposing. When we came back into the main boardroom sometime later, the bondholder who we had an agreement with leaned into my ear and asked me what was happening. He was concerned that we had done a deal with the devil. I clarified this for him. "Not to worry, they just wanted to screw you over. We have no deal. We are proceeding to arbitration with Justice Henry Winkler."

My initial impressions of Gerry Cardinale changed as the bigger picture came into focus. With sage advice from Trevor English and Peter Johnson, we realized it would be necessary to buy out Goldman and the other bondholders, and rather than owning only 10 percent of Canwest, Shaw would have to buy the entire company. With the unanimous support of the board, this strategy was approved, and we were able to conclude the acquisition with each of the bondholders from Canwest.

We knew that if we agreed to have an ongoing partnership with any of the bondholders, it would be even more difficult to come to a buyout agreement with them in the future. They counted every nickel and never left one on the floor. Future extrication from those partnerships would inevitably become more costly, given Shaw's plans to add value through future investments.

So, proactive decisions were made all around, and our team was praised for getting the job done.

To be a chameleon when the situation called for it was thrilling to me. While others might find such scenarios daunting, I saw them as opportunities to deliver. Inspired by JR and Jim's bravery and out-of-the-box thinking, I strove to embrace those qualities in the work I undertook for them.

The Canwest acquisition was an important landmark and defining moment during my years at Shaw. It enabled the company to become vertically integrated, to own broadcasting services that allowed Shaw to compete with other key industry players and reap the financial benefits of advertising—which, at that time, was still flourishing on traditional linear television. Local news was always going to draw an audience, and that connection positioned us as a strong community partner, expanding Shaw's brand and boosting its already respectable reputation.

This acquisition was timely, as streaming platforms were in their infancy but already creating ripples; it allowed us to offer our own on-demand content that viewers found both convenient and attractive. It was the way of the future.

Vancouver Winter Olympics

Feeling like I had just won a gold medal myself, I couldn't think of a better way to celebrate a monumental business achievement than by cheering on my country in the Olympics on home soil.

The uplifting opening ceremony of the Winter Olympics in Vancouver took place on February 12, 2010, at BC Place stadium. The playlist of powerful, inspiring, and celebratory live songs performed by brilliant Canadians that evening could have served as the soundtrack to my mindset in that moment as much as to the start of an epic international sporting event. "Ordinary Miracle" by Sarah McLachlan, "I Believe" by Nikki Yanofsky, "Bang the Drum" performed by Nelly Furtado and Bryan Adams, and Leonard Cohen's "Hallelujah" sung by k.d. lang—it was enough to induce tears of happiness and awe as these phenomenal moments in my life coincided: a highlight of my career, and a highlight in Canada's history.

Shaw served as a sponsor and telecommunications provider for the Vancouver Winter Olympics, offering telecommunications and broadcasting services throughout the event. We were instrumental in supporting the infrastructure and technology required for smooth operations, including communications for event operations, media coverage, and broadcasting services—delivering the Games to viewers across the country and beyond.

Various venues were used for the hockey, figure skating, curling, and other indoor events, including BC Place, Pacific Coliseum, and Canada Hockey Place—renamed from GM Place just for the duration of the Games, and later known as Rogers Arena—as well as Richmond Olympic Oval and Whistler Blackcomb Olympic Park, the latter hosting most of the skiing competitions.

The Olympic torch relay spanned approximately 45,000 kilometres across Canada, and involved 12,000 torchbearers. The flame was lit in Olympia, Greece, and made its way across Canada before arriving at the opening ceremony.

As we watched the traditional Parade of Nations, where athletes from around the world entered the stadium, I celebrated with JR, who brought tears of happiness to my eyes as he told me how proud he was of me for the successful acquisition of Canwest.

Together with his wife, Carol, JR entertained Olympians on an entire floor we dedicated for them and their families at Shaw Tower. They included Wayne Gretzky and several other high-profile hockey players. The Edmonton connection was alive and well.

Never ones to turn down a party, Jim, Tracy, and I attended the events at Shaw Tower, too, celebrating daily into the early hours of the morning.

JR had arranged to buy a box from the Russian Hockey Federation for the gold medal game between the Canadian and American Olympic hockey teams. The Russians would only take cash for the seats. The game was played at Canada Hockey Place, home of the Vancouver Canucks.

Not surprisingly, Russia cheered for Canada. We watched that game alongside the head of the Russian Hockey Federation, a famous and rather large Russian former goaltender, Vladislav Tretiak, from the 1972 Canada–Russia series. It was an electric atmosphere. We even exchanged souvenirs from our respective countries, with the Russians receiving our Canadian hockey jerseys in exchange for a bottle of their finest vodka, as smooth as we had ever tasted.

When Sidney Crosby scored the Golden Goal, the guests in our box erupted with the most euphoric cheers. I captured this moment with my Canon camera, which I carried with me for that monumental game.

It was a hugely successful Games for Canada, who won a record-breaking fourteen gold medals, the most by any country in a single Winter Olympics.

While Shaw's purchase of Canwest would be forever remembered in the company's history—and indeed in the history of the country's media industry—the Vancouver Winter Olympics left a legacy on the host city, the province of British Columbia, and Canada as a whole.

It was a time of remarkable performances, memorable moments, and impressive wins.

Croatia Cruise

Following the successful acquisition of Canwest, JR offered a hearty thank-you for getting the deal done. These were the perks of a busy, often stressful job that made the long hours and tricky hurdles even more worth it.

In October 2010, Tracy and I boarded the superyacht *MonaLiza*—unbeknownst to us, owned by a Russian oligarch, and not a problem at the time—to cruise the Adriatic Sea in calm and luxury for seventeen days. We flew into Venice on the Shaw Challenger 601. Upon arrival, we were taken by water taxi to meet the Croatian captain of the *MonaLiza*, Ivan Sisevic, who took us to the famous Murano Glass Factory.

The chef on board the *MonaLiza* was from Serbia, and there was natural enmity between him and Ivan, who had lived all his life in Croatia, due to historical conflicts that they had to quell.

While on that cruise, I knew that my good friend and colleague Chris Johnston, Shaw's regulatory lawyer in Ottawa, was dying of cancer. He was on my mind. As Tracy and I witnessed the stunning scenes of the Adriatic—magnificent sunsets, awe-inspiring expanses of open water, impressive coastlines, and unique towns—we were reminded of the incredible natural beauty, vibrancy, and diversity of our planet. It was quite spiritual.

I attempted to capture those feelings through photographs along the journey, which I then compiled into a book and had couriered to Chris, who was confined to his bedroom at the time.

Like me, Chris believed in God and heaven, and, as I thought he would, saw these images as affirmation of God's benevolence. It was a gift of reassurance. He called me to tell me how much it meant to him, just days before he passed away.

Our itinerary called for a stop on the Greek island of Corfu, but a storm kicked up around midnight when we were about halfway from Montenegro. I suggested to Captain Ivan that we turn back and return to Montenegro, as we had just entered the open seas where three-metre swells were tossing our ship like a cork. Captain Ivan was pleased to turn around as I suggested an alternative plan. The crew would invite their families to visit them while they were aboard the *MonaLiza*, which would be moored in Montenegro. Tracy and I would leave Montenegro in three days rather than fly from Corfu. The crew were grateful, as many of them had not seen family for a long time.

They were happy to ride out the rough weather in the magnificent Porto Montenegro, which had, in fact, been built up by the funds of a famous Canadian businessman, Peter Munk, chairman of Barrick Gold Corporation, one of the world's largest gold mining companies. His yacht was in port while we were there—complete with more than one helicopter and its own mini-yacht on board.

Perhaps a very Canadian take on excess: We have lakes on islands in lakes. And so, our billionaires have yachts anchored upon bigger yachts.

When I was taking photographs on that cruise, I thought back to the photography classes I had taken many years prior, and was thankful for the gift of vision and the experiences Tracy and I had shared on our journey. It was a dream come true. Many of those pictures now hang on our walls and the walls of friends and family.

Eleven — The Fire and the Flood, 2010–2015

The reality of life is that we cannot—and perhaps should not—be winning all the time. No matter how good we are. No matter how prepared we may be. You can have safety nets and contingency plans that you never thought you'd need to use.

Challenges will inevitably arise. And sometimes they can feel a bit like wading through mud. It's exhausting, relentless, extremely difficult, heavy—and no matter how gracefully you attempt to navigate, how persistently you trudge onward, how confidently you continue to step, it's near impossible to tackle it all while still looking good.

The highs are best appreciated when you've seen and understood the lows. Perspectives are more valuable the broader and more varied they are. And it's a simple law of nature—that no matter how great the elevation or how far the distance you fly, eventually you'll need to come down. Nobody can fly forever.

A New CEO

In late 2010, news became public that Jim would step down as CEO, after reports came out about an investors meeting in which he had been a little too feisty and inappropriate.

Brad was leading Shaw Direct at the time, and was the obvious choice to replace Jim.

"Peter, you need to be CEO," Brad said to me.

Though flattered, I was never going to ask for that; it wouldn't have been right. It needed to be a family member, and Brad had proved time and again that he was more than capable of doing a fantastic job at the top.

"No, I can't. It's got to be you," I told Brad. "I'm behind you 100 percent. I believe in you completely."

Jim transitioned out, and Brad became CEO. It was a very tough time for the family because Jim needed some nudging, which JR provided. Emotions ran high, and difficult business decisions had to be made for the good of Shaw, regardless of family dynamics and the love between them all.

Everyone loved and was immensely proud of Jim for all he had accomplished and for how Shaw had grown under his leadership. But he had to step down. His personal challenges had become too great; he could no longer focus. It was heartbreaking for everyone to witness. Despite years of effort to help Jim remain in that role, it wasn't sustainable to run the company that way.

Brad told me he found it especially hard to see his dad in that position, as well as the impact it had on other senior leaders.

It was the right decision for the shareholders and for the team. And it happened just in time, because Telus was on our heels—a company we've battled competitively ever since.

Tax-Free Streaming

Netflix was in its infancy in 2010, but I could already see it had serious potential to become a significant competitor for Shaw's audience base.

We were seeing our network increasingly used for Netflix viewing, which was growing in popularity at an unprecedented rate, even in those early months of its broader availability. Shaw had invested billions of dollars into our expansive network, yet 20 percent of that capacity was now being occupied by Netflix—for free.

To get ahead of the inevitable problems arising from this imbalance, we submitted complaints to the CRTC about streamers having so much freedom, contributing very little and taking a lot.

The issue of tax-free streaming has since gained increasing attention in Canada, due to concerns that foreign online streaming services have not been subject to the same taxes and regulations as traditional Canadian broadcasters. This lack of taxation creates an obvious imbalance, putting Canadian broadcasters and content creators at a significant disadvantage.

Until recently, foreign digital streaming services like Netflix were not required to collect or remit GST—goods and services tax—or HST—harmonized sales tax. This allowed these services to offer lower-priced subscriptions compared to their Canadian counterparts, who remained subject to these taxes.

On January 1, 2022, the federal government implemented changes to tax laws, requiring foreign digital services to register for, collect, and remit the appropriate taxes based on their taxable sales to Canadian consumers. This meant services like Netflix became subject to the same tax obligations as domestic broadcasters.

These changes aimed to level the playing field and ensure foreign digital service providers contribute their fair share to the Canadian tax system.

For Shaw in 2010—twelve years before these laws took effect—it was an undeniable inequality that presented us with a level of competition that would only escalate.

It was around that time, as we sought to address the challenges of network management, that Shaw considered implementing usage-based billing, where we would charge customers according to how much they used the network. This would effectively penalize anyone binge-viewing shows on Netflix, as that would use considerable bandwidth.

After much deliberation, we concluded that categorizing our customers in this way was not in the company's best interest. And so, we continued to offer the ability to connect, communicate, and stream—equally to all, for whatever purpose they required, even if that was to watch Netflix instead of Global.

Although I acknowledged in 2010 the significance of proactively addressing an issue that would inevitably expand dramatically in the coming years, it has only recently become clear that more action is needed to compete with global media. The existing, outdated, and restrictive regulations are ineffective; they merely restrict progress. Canadian broadcasters are struggling, while the regulator is preoccupied with minutiae, essentially fiddling while Rome burns.

Tensions between Mark Zuckerberg and the Canadian government began in September 2021, as it was finally acknowledged that Meta—a massive online ecosystem—received unlimited free advertising from all news and original content providers across Canada and globally as they encourage people to follow their pages on platforms like Facebook and Instagram. Yet these social media platforms do not contribute financially to support the Canadian cultural sector, particularly news, which is a vital service consumers rely on for updates, especially on significant local events that impact them directly.

Meta pulls all its content from external sources who provide it for free. Without this content—whether from businesses, influential celebrities, information providers, or personal updates from individuals—Meta would have nothing to offer. It relies solely on input from others and gives nothing in return.

Although the functions and objectives of Facebook and Netflix differ, the recognition that such large and affluent companies should be liable for taxes or contribute financially to domestic content creators in the countries where they operate has been evident for some time. Had these matters been approached differently when initially raised over a decade ago, perhaps Canada and the world would not have to struggle so intensely to implement these changes. In hindsight, I believe this highlights the drawbacks of excessive regulation and the barriers to action that it encourages.

Always address a situation when it arises. Always get ahead of the game.

Shaw Court Fire

On the night of July 11, 2012, I was looking forward to taking Tracy to Italy the next morning, having been invited to a meeting with A&E Network.

But Shaw Court was on fire.

There had been an explosion loud and forceful enough to shake people and draw them to the windows of their high-rise apartments in Calgary's downtown core. Gazing out at the skyline toward the river, they could see smoke and flames billowing from 630, 3 Ave SW—the distinctive thirteen-storey office tower with the giant Shaw logo atop. It was around five in the afternoon, a busy time in the downtown core as people began leaving their offices to head home for the day. The Calgary Stampede was one day from opening.

Multiple floors were engulfed in flames. Sirens could be heard wailing from every corner of the city, growing louder as they neared Shaw Court, with flashing lights reflecting blindingly into nearby buildings.

The Calgary Fire Department arrived on the scene mere moments after the explosion, working diligently to battle the flames.

These were the scenes described urgently to me over the phone by Shaw's senior VP of operations at the time, Jay Mehr, as I was an hour away in Bearspaw. I called JR immediately—first to tell him I wouldn't be going to Italy anymore, then to explain, "because our headquarters are on fire."

I headed straight to the scene, where adrenaline would carry me and my colleagues through the next sleepless forty-eight hours.

On arrival, I saw that people had been evacuated, fire engines were everywhere, and ambulances were treating people for smoke inhalation, with some needing to be taken to the hospital. Flames were being progressively subdued, and water was abundant.

The fire had started with an electrical transformer explosion on the thirteenth floor, the top floor of the building. To ensure it was thoroughly extinguished, in addition to the sprinklers doing their job, water was now cascading from top to bottom—causing significantly more damage overall than the fire itself.

The most important thing, of course, was that everyone was safe. No one had been near the explosion, and no workers were left inside the building.

After confirming with the firefighters that the building was empty and there were no casualties, I felt immense relief—a moment to breathe amid the many questions we had, the confusion we felt, and the shock of watching our wonderful building being catastrophically destroyed.

For five hours, we were helpless as this magnificent office tower was turned into a giant water feature.

Eventually, authorities were allowed to enter to survey the damage and assess the situation. Jay and I approached the fire chief to ask for an update, only to be told, "Please leave. This is none of your business."

Of course, as vice president and president respectively of Shaw, it was very much our business. I reiterated as much and persisted, saying, "We are here to help you, to give you our utmost cooperation. But we have people I need to report to about this. We have customers—IBM, ATB, the Hospitals Association—all of whom are relying on us. Right now, we have a data centre downstairs that is still functioning, and clients relying on these services. We have very good reason to be informed and involved here."

None of what I said seemed to matter to the fire captain, who simply replied, "Well, I'm in charge."

Under the heated circumstances, it was difficult for me to keep my cool.

I said something along the lines of "I don't give a damn who you say is in charge! We know you have an important job to do here, and we really respect that. But there will be a point of contact with us. So, when you have your meetings in a few hours, we're going to be there."

And we were. Zoran Stakic, Julie Shaw, Jay Mehr, engineers, and others and I—Shaw was well represented at the fire response and evaluation table. SITREP—situation report—meetings took place at 6:00 a.m. every day for months, with senior fire personnel and our key management representatives.

Addressing the biggest problems quickly, we brought in generators to power the transitioning network, along with huge fuel tankers to keep them running. We were very much in emergency mode, doing everything possible to continue operations.

Amid the chaos, rumours circulated that 911 was down due to the fire causing service outages. This wasn't true, but it was an exciting story for the press to jump on.

And it wasn't the only ridiculous thing being implied by the media. Beginning with a CBC Radio interview I took at 5:00 a.m., I was faced with provocative questions suggesting major design faults in our building. Shocked, fatigued, upset, and with an awful lot to do, I remained composed while answering the most absurd and irrelevant queries with transparency.

The Westin hotel became our base for unfolding the contingency plan. Julie Shaw, Zoran, and members of the engineering staff needed to be in a hundred places at once. They briefed me daily so I could report to JR and the board.

We kept everyone informed, toured clients through the building as damage to their specific areas was surveyed, and found temporary downtown office spaces to rent so work could continue as normal while a more suitable long-term solution was sought.

Ultimately, that solution became the Shaw offices at Barlow in Calgary's northeast, which Julie Shaw and her design team reworked and redesigned to accommodate all the employees displaced from Shaw Court.

Fortunately, I enjoy the challenge of stressful, high-stakes situations where decisions need to be made quickly, problems solved effectively, and things accomplished. There were many sleepless nights for our engineering and design teams, and every effort made to ensure every angle was covered.

I hosted video press conferences in the building to inform the public about the extent of the damage and the ongoing remediation. Positive media relations were paramount. Global News was key to this strategy, and we maintained open and honest communication with them throughout, allowing them to relay facts over rumours.

As always, I was working with a brilliant team at Shaw who went above and beyond, conducting an extremely thorough post-disaster analysis and evaluation, which even included meetings with the European manufacturers of the cables used in the building's mechanics.

The damage to the building was so extensive that it sat empty for more than two years while undergoing renovations.

Italy would have been preferable.

Anik G1

In the spring of 2013, Telesat, on behalf of Shaw Direct, launched the Anik G1 satellite into orbit from the Baikonur Cosmodrome in Kazakhstan, signalling a new era of satellite TV.

A major addition to Shaw's satellite fleet, it was designed to push the boundaries of entertainment possibilities, offering the most HD channels in Canada, and giving Shaw Direct the most satellite capacity of any Canadian TV provider. This meant access to all the hottest, most talked-about TV series, plus the latest movies and hit shows, in stunning high definition.

It enabled Shaw to offer streaming-on-demand content at the push of a button. Shaw Direct put viewers in control of their TV experience, covering entertainment needs at home, at the cottage, and beyond, with future-ready hardware. Putting the universe at people's fingertips.

We had provided satellite-delivered services to Canadians from coast to coast since 1996, when Star Choice was incorporated.

We relished the opportunity to provide video services across Canada. Typically, our customers lived in rural areas, where the provision of cable services was not feasible. Extending wireline networks to these regions was costly, with very few subscribers per kilometre to amortize the investment. This created an attractive opportunity for Shaw Direct.

Calgary Flood

The song "Home" by Phillip Phillips, reassuring Calgarians they were not alone, formed the soundtrack to our video montage of the aftermath of the historic Calgary flood.

A catastrophic natural disaster, the flood devastated neighbourhoods along the riverbank and downtown core, caused over $6 billion in damages, displaced more than 100,000 people, and led to the tragic loss of lives. Yet it was an event that subsequently brought communities together, demonstrated resilience, opened hearts, broadened perspectives, and reminded everyone of what truly matters in life.

Fortunately, there was adequate warning to evacuate people successfully, as the flood resulted from a combination of rapid mountain snowmelt and persistent heavy rain over multiple days. This caused the Bow and Elbow rivers to swell to unprecedented levels, carrying debris as large as trees and even houses downstream. Massive, rushing brown waves obstructed and collapsed several bridges, while sweeping away entire segments of the road.

On Thursday, June 20, 2013, more than one hundred millimetres of rain fell on southern Alberta. Early that morning, commuters in the city centre rushed for buses and trains, holding tight to their umbrellas and realizing it was becoming increasingly difficult to avoid deep, dirty puddles as water accumulated in gutters, obscuring crossings as the rain fell harder, with giant droplets splashing relentlessly. The heavy rainfall was alarming and certainly noteworthy, yet downtown remained active with the typical weekday commuters heading to their offices.

Alberta is known for its strong work ethic, and record-breaking rainfall wasn't stopping anyone.

By the time people were settled at their desks, the City of Calgary issued a flood warning, and concern began to grow. Shortly after, residents in lower-lying areas or close to the river began receiving calls from family members and neighbours about evacuations in their communities.

Many initially considered it unnecessary drama, believing their biggest problem that day might be missed meetings. Yet, once outside with the river in sight, it was clear this was more than an inconvenience—it was indeed an emergency.

By early afternoon, the entire city was on alert. Evacuation orders had expanded, and offices closed. For those not residing in an evacuation zone, the lineups outside liquor stores were unprecedented.

One of the most significant natural disasters in Canada's history, the flood impacted major infrastructure and severely damaged the iconic Saddledome arena and Stampede grounds. Flooding lasted several days, submerging large areas of the city and causing power outages. Emergency shelters were set up to accommodate the displaced.

In the days that followed, Shaw stepped up, opening free Wi-Fi to all southern Alberta to keep people connected in a time of crisis. Brad Shaw's genuine love of community was evident in our company's outreach.

Employees were told not to return to work but instead formed volunteer teams across all affected areas—delivering bottled water, food, and essential items, and offering help with whatever was needed in flood-hit communities. They helped clean out basements, removed water-damaged furniture, cleared mud, and swept up remaining debris. Numerous businesses joined the response effort, expediting recovery and fostering a strong sense of unity.

Shaw raised funds for flood victims through various events, including concerts and the annual Shaw Charity Classic.

Since 2013, steps have been taken to prevent a disaster of this scale from happening again. It was a seemingly unlikely coincidence of what were once considered extreme weather events occurring in a perfect sequence—an event many never believed could or would manifest. Today, we are all too aware that these things can and do happen, and mitigation efforts need to involve a combination of preventive and proactive safeguards. Because, as we've witnessed, the spirit of people coming together in moments of need is powerful and inspiring—and worth protecting.

Shaw's ownership of Global was very important at that time. Brad and I convinced Global that they should discontinue regular programming and, in its place, broadcast shows each day from their Emergency Centre in Calgary. Viewership topped all regular programming, and Shaw was perceived positively in the community.

Big Valley Jamboree

Big Valley Jamboree—more popularly known as BVJ—is an annual country music event held in Camrose, Alberta. One of the largest country music festivals in Canada, it draws an audience from across the country.

Tracy is a fan of country music, particularly classic and traditional country. Every August, we would take our large Newell motor coach to the event, knowing it would be a fabulous few days.

The festival attracts 25,000 attendees daily and features well-known artists in the genre, like Tim McGraw, Brad Paisley, Luke Bryan, Alan Jackson, and Big & Rich.

It became a tradition for Tracy and me, along with Mike and Beth and our friends Joyce and Dale Clarke, to travel to Camrose in a motor coach convoy, spending time with good company, watching world-class musicians, photographing them, and participating in the antics of the fair.

Corus and Shaw's radio stations were longtime sponsors of the event, supporting it and contributing to its success. Part of our sponsorship involved promotion and coverage.

And, of course, having the company's president volunteer to take professional photographs of the performers and crowd was mandatory. Or, at least, I thought so. I loved everything about those three days. The rodeo, the backstage passes, and meeting talented artists up front and close. Then, at night after the concert was ended, sitting with Tracy, her family, and our Wiener dogs, reliving the highlights of the day over a glass of cabernet.

In recent years, the running joke is that I suffer from chronic and acute GAS—guitar acquisition syndrome. This relentless affliction has persisted for decades and has only intensified over the past twenty years. Fortunately, this is not merely something Tracy endures; she has come to cherish this aspect of me, as she has contributed to the collection of guitars that now fill our homes.

Guitar acquisition syndrome is a very real and serious condition. I have well over one hundred guitars. Typically, I never cull the herd. That is, I usually add to my collection rather than selling off any guitars.

I made an exception to this rule only once. As a sign of my happiness that we had found each other, I gifted Patrick, my son—a musician who loves guitars as much as I do—a vintage 1962 Stratocaster that had been given to me on my fiftieth birthday.

I was the one taking photographs at Big Valley Jamboree, but I'm known as something of a music man myself.

Hummy Mummy

In the spring of 2013, I delivered a eulogy at the funeral of Charles King, our vice president of regulatory affairs, in Ottawa. My theme was *Travel Safe*. I had been inspired by a family of hummingbirds, a mother and her two babies, nesting outside my home in California. Hummingbirds are seen as symbols of joy and peace: Their vibrant colours, delicate appearance, and rapid wing movements stir up a sense of positive energy.

They remind us of beauty, grace, resilience, and adaptability, evoking awe and wonder. Their ability to fly backward and hover in one place makes them appear to transcend the laws of nature, with some believing they, like dragonflies, can access a higher realm of consciousness.

For many reasons, the spiritual associations are abundant.

Like Chris Johnston, Charles King also died of lung cancer. After his diagnosis, I offered him the opportunity to fly from Ottawa to Calgary to meet with a healing Buddhist lama, Rinpoche. He agreed, as he was game for anything that might help him.

Through his interpreter, Sonam, Rinpoche joked that he could tell Charles had smoked a lot of marijuana. Charles had indeed, and he had a great sense of humour, so they laughed about it. Rinpoche said there was little he could do for him, as the cancer had progressed too far, but he would try to extend his life as much as possible.

Rinpoche had a long, silver spur, like an arrow, that he breathed on before our eyes until it became burning red-hot. He placed it on Charles's bare chest, leaving a burn, and then did the same for me in three places, forming a triangle across my chest. It hurt, but only momentarily.

Charles King was only forty-seven when he died. It is not possible to know if what Rinpoche did added a single day to his life, but it gave him hope—and an experience!

I created a book of serene hummingbird photos to illustrate the wonder of life. I captured the story of a mother hummingbird laying eggs, later feeding her newly hatched chicks, and eventually watching those chicks fly away. These photos serve as a reminder of both the marvels and fragility of nature, as well as its seemingly divine intelligence. We witness a delicate balance in this interplay of life.

The average lifespan of a hummingbird is just three to five years, so that mother and her babies are long gone by now, but those photos captured a moment in time in which their beauty, their love, their instincts, and their acceptance of their place in the world are forever still.

Directed Energy

On September 18, 2013, I was appointed an honorary captain of the Royal Canadian Navy. I was sworn in by the Minister of National Defence, Rob Nicholson, as friends, family, and guests gathered at Calgary's Military Museums for my official appointment ceremony.

Nine months prior, on December 18, 2012, I had been interviewed by Vice Admiral Maddison, and on that same day—which happened to be my sixty-sixth birthday—I was granted this prestigious position. It was the greatest birthday gift ever!

And while it was undoubtedly a gift for which I am forever exceptionally grateful, I do believe a certain amount of manifesting may have been at play.

People often think of manifesting and visualization as conscious acts. And it's true that you give greater power to your hopes and thoughts when you vocalize, share, and ponder them constantly. But I think there's another method for attracting abundance and bringing your greatest dreams into reality—it's all about directed energy.

It may seem obvious that I spent much of my life proving my mother wrong; evidently, this was a driving force that sat deep within my subconscious. It never faded, and, unbeknownst to me, these feelings at the back of my mind were directing the universe, angels, God—however one sees the omnipotent forces capable of guiding one's path—to extinguish the fire of doubt my mother lit all those years ago in a spectacular act of irony, by effectively dumping the entire oceans of the world upon it.

What better way to prove that my subconscious had indeed manifested this very occurrence—becoming an honorary captain in the navy—than to deliver such news on my birthday?

My mother, with whom I had long since reconciled, was proud that I had received such a wonderful honour. I told her that in my commissioning speech I mentioned that she had also been in the navy, serving as a nurse, and was proud that her son shared that service experience with her, although in different eras.

One of my first invitations as an honorary captain was to board the HMCS *Chicoutimi*, a submarine with a tragic history. At the time of my invitation in 2014, it had been in dry dock for some time. A fire aboard in 2004 had killed one person, and it was several years before it was ready to be commissioned to the Canadian Navy.

While I appreciated the invitation, it wasn't so much knowledge of that past incident as it was my own battles with confined spaces that led me to decline.

Instead of attempting to face my fear, as I had done so many times in the past, I was completely honest. I said, "I'm not going to bullshit you. I have claustrophobia. I'm not going."

Shaw Family Trust

In 2014, I was honoured to become a standby board member of the Shaw Family Trust. The Shaw Family Trust is a private family trust associated with the Shaw family, which, until the sale of Shaw to Rogers in 2023, was best known for their significant role in the telecommunications and media industry in Canada.

The trust held a controlling interest in Shaw Communications Inc. The trust was established by JR and the family to manage the family's wealth and control over Shaw Communications. It held voting shares in the company, allowing the family to maintain significant influence over corporate decisions and strategy. The family trust is utilized for succession planning, helping to manage and protect wealth across generations. The structure allows the Shaw family to ensure continuity in the management of their business interests. Recently, I became a board member of that trust.

In summary, the Shaw Family Trust serves as a key mechanism for managing the Shaw family's interests in their businesses, and plays an important role in the governance and strategy of the companies it controls. With the sale of Shaw Communications Inc. to Rogers, the family trust manages the proceeds of that sale in addition to its other investments for the best interest of the family.

Paul Robertson

Paul Robertson was the president of Shaw Media and a good friend of mine. He died of pancreatic cancer at the age of fifty-nine.

Just before Paul's passing, I received a call from his assistant, letting me know that Paul was close to death. I spoke with Brad, and we agreed to fly from Calgary to Toronto immediately to spend an afternoon with Paul.

It would be a long and difficult day, but an important, special, and treasured one.

When Brad and I entered Paul's home, his wife, Carole, took us to the bedroom where Paul lay in bed. I hadn't seen Paul for several months, so his fragility took me aback: a stark contrast to the strong, resilient man he had been throughout his career.

On seeing Brad and me, Paul's eyes lit up, and a big, recognizable smile crossed his face. He was thrilled to see us. Paul couldn't get up, so Brad and I lay beside him on his bed.

We had a wonderful visit, sharing memories, jokes, and tears.

When we were getting up to leave, Paul insisted on getting up too. The pain of trying was excruciating, and he stopped halfway, his eyes rolling back as silence fell over the room. For a long moment, I thought we might have lost him. Then, suddenly, he got his second wind. I looked at him and said, "Paul, you scared the shit out of me. I thought you had died." Paul had a great laugh over this and, with Carole's help, he came to bid Brad and me goodbye from his wheelchair.

About a week later, Paul passed away. I received a call from Carole asking if I would deliver his eulogy in Toronto.

I was struck by the honour and went about writing a eulogy that would reflect Paul's wonderful life and personality.

When I was in the cathedral, I sat in the very front row until it was time to speak. As I approached the altar and turned, I was delighted to see a tightly packed congregation, all there to celebrate Paul. So many familiar faces from his past filled the room. I perhaps should have felt nervous, especially since I was about to sing a cappella during my presentation. But I wasn't.

Paul had such a presence in my mind that all I wanted was to honour him and recount the special person he had been to each of those in attendance.

"Everything Paul did was an expression of the deep love he had for people.

"I know he would be annoyed at this attention because he never liked the spotlight. Paul, it is interesting that you spent so much of your working career in media, where lights and cameras are part of the gig, yet you always deferred to others to take the spotlight or the credit for work well done.

"We were confident that you were the best person to lead Media and welcome them to Shaw. Despite coming out of the uncertainty of bankruptcy protection, despite having reason to be cynical of larger companies, you inspired the team of Barb Williams, Troy Reeb, and Errol De Rae, who represented all of the employees at Shaw Media.

"Paul, this achievement is an essential part of Shaw's success and forms just a part of your legacy. Frankly, your legacy is building relationships and the power they bring to our lives. You saw the good in people, and you made things happen in an orderly, well-thought-out way. You were the consummate leader, mentor, and confidant."

Through my years at Shaw, I was extremely fortunate, blessed, lucky—to work with, get to know, and form close friendships with some truly remarkable people.

And inevitably, the more impressive the introductions—the more awesome the shared experiences—the more emotional the departures.

Retirement

By 2015, it was the biggest joke in the industry—that Peter Bissonnette was never going to retire. But I had set an internal clock for myself. My father retired at seventy, so to one-up him, I thought I'd work until sixty-nine. I retired at sixty-eight years and nine months of age.

Deciding where my retirement celebrations should take place wasn't easy, so we had three parties.

The first was in Calgary: my home at the time, the place where I spent the most notable years of my career, and the location of Shaw's headquarters. Then, a party in Ottawa, where I was head of regulatory, government affairs, and social giving at the time. Ottawa is the capital of the country and the city in which I was born. Finally, there was a party in Vancouver, which represented the genesis of my time in the cable industry.

Each event saw maximum attendance, and each felt like a lovefest where I could invite family members, former co-workers from my Shaw and pre-Shaw days who had all played a role in my career, as well as my colleagues of the time.

When I started working at Shaw, the company was making $100 million in revenue. By the time I left, we were making $5 billion. I was committed from the day they brought me on, and Shaw grew logarithmically. Opportunities came to me as part of that growth, and it meant that when I retired, I was in a comfortable financial situation thanks to the blessings of the SERP—supplemental executive retirement plan—and my investments in Shaw shares. I didn't hold shares anywhere else.

I felt tremendous gratitude that, in retirement, I could enjoy a damn good life.

As an altar boy, I always used to think, "One day, I'll be the priest up there." There's great pride in being able to lead, and I love leading. And so, to have had the chance to become a successful leader made me feel fulfilled, gratified, and blessed.

The years flew by. They were full, and they were fun. I felt nostalgic and a little sad that my time as president had come to an end. But I avoided the emptiness by maintaining relationships with those I worked with and by staying involved with the company's ongoing endeavours.

I continue to serve on boards today, so I consider it more of a transition than a full retirement—I'll never be completely removed from Shaw or from the industry, because it is well and truly ingrained in me.

Twelve — Good Grief, 2016–2020

On October 29, 2016, I participated in a fundraiser for the National Music Centre in Calgary. I had donated two recording sessions worth $40,000 each in my recording studio, which were both purchased at full price—one by the Mannix family, and one by Virginia Shaw, the niece of JR Shaw. Her husband was hoping to build his own recording studio in Barbados and was keen to view mine for inspiration.

At Studio Bell, home of the National Music Centre, I was honoured to play alongside some highly talented musicians. These included Canadian singer Sass Jordan, Nick Catanese of Black Label Society, and Brent Fitz from Toque, who also played with KISS and Slash from Guns N' Roses. Teddy "Zig Zag" Andreadis played with us as well; he had played with Guns N' Roses, Carole King, and Chuck Berry. This performance was part of a fundraising event spearheaded by Jim Carter of BANC, Benevolent Artists National Charity, to acquire and restore the Rolling Stones Mobile Studio, which would find its new home in the museum. Jim is an accomplished vocalist along with his daughter Erin, who both perform in that band.

When I moved from my house in Bearspaw in 2022, I donated my recording console to the National Music Centre for their recording studios. They were awestruck to receive such a high-tech audio mixer—an Avid S6 M40—and all the peripheral mixing equipment.

The console had been designed and installed specifically for me by Annex Pro of Vancouver in 2015, in readiness for my regular use once retired. It had been a lifelong dream of mine to have a professional-grade recording studio in my home.

Bryon Low of Annex Pro undertook the project, which included a Focusrite ISA 828 preamp, a Neumann U 87 mic, Genelec 1032 BPM and Focal Alpha 80 monitors, all integrated with Avid's S6 M40 control surface. The result was sound production like liquid gold!

Annex Pro has built custom studios for many big names in the industry, including Elvis Costello, Sarah McLachlan, Bryan Adams, and AC/DC—a list I was thrilled to join.

Freedom Mobile—Brad's Legacy

Because I remained on Shaw's board, I continued to participate in the business strategic discussions and company decision-making.

In 2016, under Brad Shaw's leadership, Shaw Communications made a significant strategic move by acquiring Wind Mobile, which it subsequently rebranded as Freedom Mobile. This acquisition marked Shaw's entry into the mobile telecommunications market, allowing the company to diversify its range of services beyond its core offerings of cable television and internet services.

The rebranding aimed to create a fresh identity that would position the company as a provider of affordable and flexible mobile services. It was positioned as a challenger brand, focusing on offering competitive pricing plans and innovative features to appeal to value-conscious consumers. Shaw introduced a range of monthly plans with options such as unlimited talk, text, and data. We emphasized providing customers with a Big Gig data experience, offering generous allowances at affordable prices.

Shaw invested in expanding Freedom Mobile's network coverage and improving its infrastructure to provide a reliable, robust network. We upgraded and enhanced our network technology to offer improved data speeds and expanded coverage areas.

By launching Freedom Mobile, Shaw aimed to challenge the dominance of existing operators in the country and provide consumers with more options in the market. This strategic move allowed Shaw to diversify its business portfolio and further establish itself as a leading player in the Canadian telecommunications industry.

While Freedom never became a mainstream competitor to Canada's longer-established mobile networks, it grew to be the fourth-largest wireless carrier in Canada, with more than 2.2 million subscribers as of 2023.

When Rogers acquired Shaw, Freedom was sold separately to Québecor for $2.85 billion.

Gravity Renewables

It had always been a dream of JR's to invest in renewable energy. Unquestionably, he saw this as the energy resource of the future. Having seen firsthand the ever-growing challenges faced by Calgary's once-booming oil and gas industry, JR understood the obstacles these corporations encounter in terms of environmental impact on an increasingly fragile planet, of a finite resource. Oil won't last forever.

When a rapidly changing need is identified in other industries, innovation and monumental growth typically follow. This has certainly been true of communications technology, especially when public opinion and consumer preferences are aligned. The resistance to transitioning to renewable, sustainable, green, clean, safe, nontoxic energy solutions will ultimately cost far more than the necessary, albeit costly and complex, initial changes.

All great progress and inevitable evolution require an ability to see the bigger picture, along with grand-scale courage and collective action. Today, investment in renewable energy is both a wise financial move and a source of new jobs and opportunities. Naturally, JR wanted to be involved in this change. He wanted to help growing renewable companies thrive and showcase their capabilities—and he asked me to help.

JR, together with the Shaw Family Trust, acquired 99 percent of the shares in Gravity Renewables. The goal was for this to be part of the Shaw legacy—a decision fuelled by hope, optimism, and the belief that, through this investment, our involvement might make a difference.

Despite JR's good intentions, along with those of Brad and myself, to make Gravity Renewables a success, we faced many obstacles. There was a lot to learn about the challenges of hydroelectricity. At the time of purchase, Gravity Renewables had eighteen plants across the United States, all situated along beautiful, scenic rivers in peaceful locations, doing their work without emitting pollutants. The plants operated in harmony with nature, helping to fuel the modern lifestyle.

In September 2017, Tracy and I drove from Montreal to Newport, Vermont, after celebrating our wedding anniversary in Montreal. We travelled there to meet with the senior management of Gravity Renewables to consider JR's interest in buying a hydroelectric dam on the Missisquoi River. This was to be my first involvement in an acquisition as a board member and Shaw Family representative for Gravity Renewables. The opportunity was particularly appealing because the sale of the dam included adjacent solar farms on the same land. Gravity Renewables hadn't yet expanded into solar energy—a highly lucrative market—and this looked like an ideal opportunity to begin that complementary venture.

After our visit, we purchased the company in Newport with optimism, but we soon discovered the complexity of regulations surrounding hydroelectric dams. Gravity Renewables, like many companies in the renewable energy sector, encountered significant challenges in achieving the scale necessary to ensure long-term sustainability. Renewable energy projects often require substantial upfront investment in infrastructure, technology, and development, which can be a barrier for companies on a smaller scale.

It is hard to run a renewable energy company from a distance. It involves managing multiple variables, including project development, maintenance, regulatory compliance, and customer acquisition. The complexity of these operations can strain resources and complicate decision-making, ultimately impacting sustainability. High risks associated with project financing, changing energy policies, and the unpredictability of energy generation based on environmental variables such as weather conditions, drought, and floods, can be enough to consider the business wisdom of these investments. Just after the purchase of the company in Newport, the pandemic hit the world, and this introduced just one more challenge in operating a company from a distance.

As Shaw sought to engage in sustainable energy initiatives, understanding and overcoming these challenges was crucial for success in this evolving and vital industry. Sustainable energy is not just a future goal; it requires a concerted effort to address the realities and hurdles in its path to widespread adoption.

Ultimately, it became clear that Gravity Renewables faced an insurmountable challenge, as the company couldn't achieve the necessary scale to make the venture sustainable. The high risk, combined with the effort required to grow the company with so many variables, triggered a reality check. Sustainable energy is essential for our future, but it's far more challenging than anticipated, and requires far more capital than the Shaw Family were prepared to invest.

Recognizing that the use of renewable energy is an essential need for the planet and our grandchildren, Shaw was able to sell its interests in these renewable assets to a company that had the requisite scale and local resources to continue with its growth. We are pleased that this need will be fulfilled for generations to come by a company with the ability and the will to make it a success.

Final Farewells

When faced with the passing of a loved one, we are reminded of life's fragile impermanence. As we focus on daily tasks, worry unnecessarily about the mundane, or relish moments of joy, we thankfully tend to forget about our mortality. We don't think about the inevitable fate we share, over which we have no control. We don't dwell on life's fleetingness, the eternity of death, or time's unstoppable momentum. Each time we hug a family member, we don't reflect on the finite number of hugs we'll share or the fact that every hug brings us one closer to the last.

Regardless of your beliefs, life is either an intentional gift or a one-in-four-hundred-trillion chance occurrence, but in both cases, it is miraculous, fortunate, and an opportunity.

Because of my faith, I am not afraid of death. I have gratitude for the wonderful life I've lived, and I accept the will of God. But I do love life. I very much love my life and all the people in it. And it is only human nature, through the freedom to love so deeply, that we anticipate great grief around our passing.

Throughout human history, people across the world have held innumerable beliefs about what happens when we die. An increasingly popular idea is that death is simply nothingness—much like the state before birth.

Whatever a person believes, death remains the inevitable, daunting finale we all share. We're anxious about the unknown; we fear pain; we don't want to be alone. We seek to avoid grief. And for all the love of God in the world, death is a reminder of our mortality on Earth, of our finite existence in this familiar form.

When loved ones pass, they leave a hole in our lives—but we can fill it with memories, love, and gratitude. For death finds us all in the end; we're all heading to the same destination, wherever and whenever that may be. Even more reason to cherish the journey.

Stan and Linda

We all know that death isn't always sudden or surprising. Sometimes it's foreseen, predicted, inevitably imminent, or slow yet apparent—and sometimes it's chosen.

I had always been very fond of Stan, one of Shaw's executive pilots. We'd spent many hours together in close quarters over many years. Often, while waiting for stopover refuels, we'd share cigarettes in Nuuk, snacks in Reykjavík, and unreserved conversations on long flights to and from significant meetings, urgent business, and unexpected events.

I had great respect for Stan; I trusted him, admired him, and enjoyed his company.

Stan had taken early retirement when he became very sick with a rapid and incurable degenerative illness that prevented him from even speaking. Hearing of his condition, I wanted to visit him before his imminent death. He was using a voice-controlled program on his computer to communicate.

At the same time, Stan's wife, Linda, was suffering from multiple sclerosis. She couldn't walk, and life was incredibly difficult for both. Neither wanted to continue, particularly considering the thought of outliving the other. They were deeply in love, the best of friends, inseparable soul mates.

In 2016, the Canadian Parliament passed legislation allowing eligible adults to request medical assistance in dying.

The Catholic Church opposes euthanasia or any kind of assisted suicide, believing that life is a gift from God, something to be embraced until its natural end. Though my religious roots are strong, I believe a benevolent God would bless such a decision, as it demonstrates love, empathy, and the ultimate exercise of free will.

Choosing medically assisted dying allowed Stan and Linda to plan their passing together. They could say their goodbyes while still able, leave this world at the same time, and prevent further suffering. They could approach this conclusion with contentment, reflecting positively on their lives and even joking with each other about backing out at the last minute.

I was one of many who had the chance to visit Stan and Linda to say a final farewell. In my studio, I performed and recorded a peaceful instrumental called "Sweet Dreams," a beautiful and moving piece made famous by Patsy Cline, and offered it from my heart to theirs. I later learned that the song I had created for them was what they chose to play as their injections were administered.

It was an incredible privilege—one I never anticipated, and forever humbling.

Jim

My best friend, Jim Shaw, led a fast and full life. An unforgettable character, he worked hard and played hard. While burning the candle at both ends is a trick few can master, he managed it for decades—until it finally became too much.

When expectations, demand, pressure, stakes, and impact are astronomically high, maintaining balance becomes increasingly difficult. Jim faced those challenges, but his strength eventually waned.

We have natural sympathy for visible, physical illnesses. For many, feelings of empathy and understanding come automatically when a person suffers from something clearly beyond their control. But with invisible illnesses like chronic pain, depression, autoimmune diseases, anxiety disorders, and addiction, sympathy isn't always so readily offered. In fact, it often isn't offered at all.

Invisible illnesses are easier to misunderstand. Society knows less about them, though awareness is growing. Stigmas and misconceptions often lead to blaming individuals for their own unstoppable mental health conditions. The brain, with its vast network of neural connections, is incredibly complex, and any one of its regions can be affected in ways that outsiders struggle to understand. Terms like *addiction* tend to imply singular, isolated problems, but addiction is rarely so simple. It takes hold gradually, and once it does, it affects decision-making, motivation, behaviour, and even personality.

Jim's journey with addiction was marked by challenges that changed him. He was supported by those who loved him: his wife, children, mother Carol, father JR, brother Brad, sister Heather, and me. We all gathered around his hospital bed during his final hours. His sister Julie was there in spirit, calling the hospital daily to support her much-loved brother.

Jim was only sixty when he died on January 3, 2018, in West Palm Beach, Florida. He had become ill after Christmas, fallen into a coma, and passed away peacefully with his loved ones by his side. He was remembered with immense love and admiration, recognized for his philanthropy, his contributions to the community, and his pioneering impact in business.

After hearing the news, Edward Rogers said, "Jim was a brilliant man and a fierce competitor. He was a confident entrepreneur who had a transformative and lasting impact on the Canadian cable landscape."

I held Jim's hand in his final hours. My closest friend for thirty years, we had spent countless hours together, pursuing big goals, strategizing, and sharing great times. As he lay in a coma, I whispered memories to him, recalling how we had bought the cable system in that very town years before. Though Jim couldn't respond, I believed he could hear me.

JR was there, too, sitting quietly by Jim's bed, heartbroken and exhausted. It was clear he was deeply sad, nostalgic, proud, and, undoubtedly, wishing for a different outcome. No parent ever wants to outlive their children.

In Jim's final moments, I held one of his hands while Brad held the other. Tracy stood at the foot of the bed, grieving someone she considered family. Jim took one last deep breath—a breath so deliberate it felt like he knew it was his last—and then he was gone. Peacefully.

I don't cry often, but as it hit me that my good friend was gone, I began to sob. Brad did, too. We were grieving the person we loved, grieving a past we could never get back. I treasured the memories I had with Jim, but there would be no new ones to add. That chapter had closed.

The grief over Jim's passing was felt by many, as shown at his Calgary funeral, when the Calgary Tower lit up in blue and hundreds of Shaw employees lined the motorcade route, standing silently in the bitter cold to pay their respects to a brilliant and trusted leader. Deeply moved, JR stepped out of the vehicle and shook their hands, one by one.

Shaw was more than a telecommunications company; it was a business at the heart of the community. Jim knew that, and it's why he gave so much back, supporting educational institutions that would impact future generations. Jim left behind a legacy of positivity that continues to benefit more people than he ever knew.

Luck

Sometimes, luck requires courage and the willingness to take risks. You need to be brave, to take chances, and to enjoy the thrill of it all. And when things don't go as planned, when things aren't going your way and you're not winning, don't stop. Don't feel defeated. Channel your energy into finding another path. Listen to the messages the universe offers. Whether they come from God, from guardians, or from your own projected consciousness, they're there, waiting to be heard, read, and acted upon. Opportunities are around every corner if you keep your eyes open.

Progress is regenerative, accomplishment is satisfying, and success feels good. It doesn't matter what that success looks like to others—only what it means to you.

I often think of Jim Shaw when I think about luck. What many may have perceived as luck from the outside was the result of hard work, a clear vision, and the fearlessness to make tough decisions. He created his own luck. Without the boldness to pursue his goals and strive for better, that luck wouldn't have materialized. Jim's mindset inspired me, teaching me, perhaps by osmosis, the same approach to life.

In sports, the term *luck* often comes up. "They were lucky to have won that game," some would say. As a pitcher, I would dream of the game the night before the game. I would see the field in my mind's eye, my teammates, opponents, the crowd, and myself throwing the perfect game. The following day, I'd be so focused that I could visualize each pitch and deliver it precisely. It wasn't luck guiding the outcome; it was preparation.

While I recognize that I've been very fortunate, I also believe certain angels intervene on our behalf, helping us make decisions that lead to positive outcomes. They're the subtle nudging angels.

JR Shaw

JR's passing was in stark contrast to the energetic life he had led, surrounded by people, always busy in business, and under the public eye. He left this world quietly, with only a few family members by his side: people who loved him dearly. He passed away in Hawaii, a place of fond memories, surrounded by abundant nature and the beauty of this planet we call home.

JR died on March 23, 2020, without knowing how long the stay-at-home orders and lockdowns triggered by the arrival of COVID-19 in North America would last. It would be a long time before we could gather in numbers to celebrate his life.

When JR passed, he left Canadians an invaluable gift at a time they needed it most: the ability to stay connected even while being forced apart. They could communicate, access information, binge-watch shows, and work from home—all largely thanks to Shaw's robust network: its scale, reliability, speed, and reach. Shaw's people—resilient, positive, and customer-focused—embodied these values, rising to meet this unprecedented challenge.

JR was a pioneer in telecommunications, witnessing the birth and growth of the internet and rising to the challenge of providing it, along with quality service, to millions. Though the pandemic was an unexpected, monumental challenge, Shaw rose to it magnificently.

Four days into Canada's mandatory stay-at-home order, where I was with Tracy in Calgary, I received a call from Brad, who was emotional as he shared that JR had passed away. I remembered the last time I saw JR, at his eighty-fifth birthday celebration in Newport, Rhode Island. On the flight back, he first mentioned it might be time for the family to consider alternatives for the future. The business was getting tougher; it needed enormous scale to keep up with the rapid shifts in consumer expectations. It was a different world from the one Shaw had grown and evolved with.

Little did JR know that Shaw would have one last monumental task to accomplish for its customers before ultimately merging with Rogers. Shaw went out on a high.

The night JR passed away, Tracy and I opened a bottle of Poetry wine from Cliff Lede Vineyards that he had gifted us years before. We toasted to his life, sharing memories of an incredible man: a humble mentor, a kind and gentle soul, a dedicated and caring father figure.

I miss him every day.

Rising to the Challenges

As battles wind down, despite all the wins along the way, there is inevitably a period of grieving for the losses.

During my final years with Shaw—as president and, later, on the board—the company faced numerous challenges and difficult days. The pandemic was an event nobody could have foreseen, and little had been done to prepare for a situation of that magnitude—a sudden, global shutdown with immediate economic impacts and, of course, the devastating loss of life and health.

In that first week of March 2020, when employees were instructed to work from home, nobody anticipated they'd continue to do so for at least two years, with some never returning to their office desks. Nobody expected a pandemic that would claim almost seven million lives, result in more than 770 million confirmed cases, and lead to the administration of over 13.5 billion vaccine doses.

If any company had previously chosen to switch its employees to remote work, for whatever reason, it would have required a change-management firm, at least eighteen months, and millions of dollars. In this case, COVID-19 forced that shift upon companies worldwide overnight—and they made it happen: some, like Shaw, with great success.

Those were years of loss and challenge. They were difficult years, and none of us give ourselves enough credit for not just surviving them but for coming out the other side, continuing to adapt, and making the best of things.

Life will inevitably test us, but within each struggle lies an opportunity for growth. It will test you. It will hurt you, and it will hurt those you love. It's okay to struggle. It's okay to break. It's okay to be down and out for a while.

Embrace the challenges you face, learn from them, and know that each of us has the strength to emerge even stronger than before. I call it resilience. It's what my story is all about. You must get back up. You will be stronger than ever imagined. You will have learned more than you thought possible. You will have been there, done it, and come out the other side with a story to tell and a perspective to share.

The order of chapters will differ for everyone. The highs and lows won't be even or predictable. But knowing, accepting, and embracing that—and going full steam ahead, regardless—is how you'll make the best of the journey. It's the journey that shapes us, and every experience enriches our outlook on life.

Thirteen — Pivotal, The Early 20s

Shaw celebrated the company's fiftieth anniversary a little late: after social distancing rules had eased and it was safe to be in a room full of people reminiscing, laughing, dancing, hugging.

The party was held at the Fairmont Château Lake Louise, arguably one of the most scenic spots on the planet with its pristine turquoise water, magnificent towering, snow-capped mountains, and year-round blindingly bright glacier.

The absence of Jim and JR was felt, but their presence within the memories of all those in attendance was evident.

It was April 9, 2022—a celebration JR had very much wanted to see happen, and Brad made sure it did. Brad was an exceptional host.

There was entertainment from Dave Matthews. Since their formation in 1991, up until the pre-pandemic days in 2019, the American rock band had sold more than twenty-five million concert tickets, and their debut major-label album was certified platinum six times over. Despite this, Dave Matthews remains extremely humble, as evidenced by his first words to the guests at Shaw's anniversary party: "I bet none of you know who I am." His humility very much aligned with the values Shaw embodies and seeks to promote in others.

Recognizing that, and as a genuine fan, I called out, "We know who you are!" A rocking time was had by all.

I think there was an immense sense of pride among Shaw's leadership in reflecting on how far the company had come. When Shaw sold to Rogers, they had nine thousand employees, but over its fifty-three years, the number was far higher. All those people whose lives were impacted by Shaw, hopefully positively for most, if not all of them. Those who made a career, a living, a lifestyle from their time with the company.

Every person celebrating at the fiftieth-anniversary event deserved a huge pat on the back for all they'd done personally. They all had stories. They all had accomplishments.

And there was pride, too, in being a great corporate citizen—showing leadership and reflecting the communities and people we served. We were extremely fortunate, but we also worked very hard.

As I review my time at Shaw, it's evident that the company's strength came from its people. From the values we shared. From our individual contributions, unique characters, ideas, commitment, participation, and roles within—our trust in and loyalty to—our teams.

But finding a workforce like this doesn't happen by magic. It's not luck. It's built. It takes time, thought, empathy—being real, being likable, creating a place where people want to stay, where people want to succeed.

Shaw: End of an Era

Throughout my career, there had been a theme of recent or imminent Rogers acquisitions. Rogers was the competitor Shaw loved to hate in an almost affectionate sibling rivalry. There was an undeniable closeness, a mutual understanding, respect on both sides, and a shared knowledge and history, as they grew up alongside one another.

I had retired as president of Shaw more than six years prior to completion of the Rogers merger, a sale worth $26 billion in its entirety. I had, of course, remained on the board and was a shareholder with an experienced voice to support those at the negotiating table.

It was an outcome JR had foreseen and hoped for. It was a takeover that, while signalling the end of such a proud and meaningful era, would make sense for the industry at large and for Canadian customers across the country as technology continues to evolve and the demands of the population increase.

On Friday, March 31, 2023, the federal government gave its final approvals on Rogers' acquisition of Shaw, enabling the transaction to proceed and be finalized the following Monday, April 3.

For Brad Shaw, his leadership team, and the board, there was clear relief after two years of talks and incremental progress as the deal finally closed. Likewise, Shaw employees, who had lived with daily uncertainty about the future, now felt a weight lifted. They could finally see their next steps clearly, whether continuing with Rogers in their current roles or moving on to a fresh start.

Executives and teams across both companies shared a unified enthusiasm for the future, eager to see the newly expanded Roger's brand turn the tide against their common competitor, Telus, with its increased scale and reach nationwide.

Maybe, for many Shaw workers, the transition was diluted in extremity, owing to the relatively recent changes in their day-to-day routines following the COVID-19 pandemic. Many office spaces remained empty, and the once familiar echoes of spontaneous team chatter within the building walls had become increasingly distant.

People had already made a forced and abrupt farewell to the old way of working—side by side, face to face—when lockdown rules led companies across the country and world to send employees home. Remote work quickly became the new normal, and after such a drastic shift, any further changes seemed far less significant by comparison.

In a pattern that seems to have repeated throughout my life, where notable turning points coincide in unexpected ways, my mother passed away on Wednesday, March 29, 2023, at the remarkable age of 102. This left me with just two days to grieve with my biological family before turning to celebrate with my longtime work family.

I'm no stranger to navigating monumental, contrasting events simultaneously, and I did my best to steer through both. Both occurrences had been long expected, and I was prepared for the emotional shift, which made processing the magnitude of it all a bit easier.

On the Thursday following my mother's death, I found myself spontaneously singing and recording the Rolling Stones song "Dead Flowers."

It was an unexpected choice, coming to me like a spark from nowhere. I'm not usually one to focus on lyrics, even though I perform my own vocals and learn all the words. It's the sounds, the feelings, and particularly the guitar riffs that inspire me.

However, when I later reflected on the meaning of the lyrics, I realized it was an interesting choice. The song speaks of a woman who considers herself superior to the man she treats with disdain. Though hurt by her, he promises to place flowers on her grave, symbolizing that he still loves her despite everything. When he outlives her, he will rise above her contempt, and forgive her in his own way.

Was this my subconscious message to my mother? A final goodbye through music? My mother wasn't a fan of the Rolling Stones—she found them far too wild. In fact, she thought "Dead Flowers" was a terrible song.

Then, in a strange twist, when I went to play back my recording, the file wouldn't open. I tried everything to access it, but despite all my technical experience, it was locked and inaccessible for no apparent reason. Was this a message from my mother? Did she corrupt the file because she disliked the song? Or was this her way of apologizing? Maybe she didn't want to be remembered as a mother who mistreated me. Maybe this was her way of sending a little love on her journey to the afterlife.

I then recorded a version of the Don Williams 1980s traditional country song "Lord, I Hope This Day Is Good"—the file of which opened just fine on the day the Shaw–Rogers' merger was finally complete.

As I listened back to that song, I reflected on my many good days at Shaw. Great days. The best days! Shaw was such a significant part of my life. It was where I forged lifelong friendships and bonds stronger than family. It was where I found a new father figure, new brothers, mentors, and became part of a community, all the while providing communication services to millions.

Effective communication was the key to making things happen: Working together, sharing ideas, and listening to others made Shaw a standout communications company. Individuals like Jim Shaw, Michael

D'Avella, Ken Stein, Bill McDonald, Brad Shaw, Ron Rogers, Peter Johnson, Trevor English, Deb Avis, and many more worked tirelessly to bring JR's vision to life. Their dedication and collaborative spirit were instrumental in shaping the journey and success of the organization.

My time at Shaw was the pinnacle of my life, and everything that came before it was preparing me for that moment.

Pivotal Places

The world may seem enormous, stretching on forever, but there are only so many places here on Earth. Only so many options for where you can visit, work, and live. Where you're born is a matter of luck. Whatever that place is, it's beyond your control, something you have no say in. Only as you get older and independent, as you recognize the array of possibilities before you, do you have any influence over where you might go. Even then, it's not always easy.

The places you live inevitably affect the person you become as you absorb the culture, climate, history, politics—the vibe of the community, the essence of the area. Places find their way into your soul, embed themselves in your memory, and offer you experiences to learn from.

Every one of us will spend our lives in a finite number of places. Some will be deeply meaningful to us, some will evoke feelings, ignite ideas, offer valuable lessons, and even change perspectives. Some places we will be deeply grateful for.

Asking me today where I consider home to be, you won't get an immediate, obvious answer. I was born in Ottawa, graduated preschool in Calgary, completed my earliest grades in Montreal, attended boarding school in England, finished secondary school in Vancouver, and ultimately left high school back in the city where it all began. An education summary that I find exhausting just to read.

But this movement back and forth across the world's second-largest country set the stage for my life to come. The adaptability I learned in those early days—the necessity to find my feet quickly, make connections right away, and feel comfortable in my surroundings—undoubtedly served me well throughout my career.

You'll often hear modern influencers echo a notion that's grown in popularity since the 1960s: that travelling is the best way to find oneself. This idea that identity enlightenment happens when the only constant is oneself. When the characters and settings keep changing, when difference abounds in the scenes you absorb—despite the greater freedom in such circumstances to be a chameleon if one chooses—inevitably, a sense of self-recognition grows and flourishes. You learn more about what you do and don't want, what you like and don't like, what you agree with, what you question, what you fear, and what pulls you with a powerful sense of belonging.

My love of exploring has taken me to multiple cities, towns, and countries around the globe. Beyond my years spent in various Canadian provinces and work trips to many states in the United States—particularly Texas and Florida—I have fond memories of travelling to France, Barbados, Mexico, Montenegro, Spain, Greece, Portugal, and Turkey, as well as frequent stopovers in Greenland on long-haul flights from Canada's West to Europe.

Just as one can grieve the absence of a person, it's also possible to grieve leaving a place—be it a home, a community, or a job. But in processing the loss, we look back and treasure the bits we loved most. And the places we loved most.

Kelowna and Rancho Mirage

Tracy and I bought our first property in Rancho Mirage in 2007.

After many visits to Jim's house in the same area, we had fallen for the reliably warm, dry weather and clear blue skies, the impressive landscape, the high-end facilities, and the convenience of having everything we could need in that small city with its spacious, suburban feel. Rancho Mirage is a safe, peaceful place that has been home to numerous celebrities over the years, including Frank Sinatra, Dean Martin, and Lucille Ball.

One of nine cities in the Coachella Valley, it's close to the popular tourist destination of Palm Springs and offers ample opportunity for an active lifestyle. It was certainly the perfect place to escape Canadian winters each year.

Not long after we bought our first home there, Tracy spotted a new build on a large lot that she dreamed of living on. I saw the owner gardening one day and inquired about buying it. At the time, the owner didn't need the money, so a whole year of negotiating followed before he finally agreed to sell. Whispering Wind truly became our dream home.

Shaw would often hold business meetings in Kelowna, a beautiful city in the Okanagan Valley in south-central British Columbia, known for its vineyards, lakes, and beaches.

From the first time I attended a business meeting at Jim's house there, right on the lakefront, I was in awe of the scenery and wanted to own a home there as well. The property we bought had over 150 stairs from the jetty on the lake up to the house, so for those arriving by boat, it was quite the climb. On one occasion, not long after his sixtieth birthday, Jim made the climb to the top to deliver a gift.

I loved walking around Kelowna. The breathtaking scenery and crisp mountain air were undoubtedly good for the soul—and the heart. It being a walkable city, I regularly strolled five kilometres to get the exercise needed for optimal cardiovascular health.

Despite the increasing threat of wildfires, Kelowna remains an attractive destination for Canadians to vacation and invest in. There is ongoing development, a diverse economy, a vibrant arts and culture scene, abundant opportunities for outdoor recreation, and a high quality of life supported by accessible and efficient amenities and services. The city is resilient and will undoubtedly continue to grow and thrive.

On Thursday, August 17, 2023, West Kelowna was on fire.

From my home across the lake, my family and I could see the billowing smoke blowing relentlessly toward us amid winds of forty kilometres an hour that carried ash and embers high into the night sky, threatening to ignite the trees around us.

At the time, 2023 had been the worst wildfire season on record for Canada, with over thirty-four million acres of land burned: an area equal in size to England.

Prolonged drought, persistent high temperatures, and an increase in dry lightning strikes, where rain evaporates before reaching the ground, are some of the climate-related causes behind this unprecedented scale and frequency of wildfires, a threat that will likely continue and worsen in the years to come.

Alongside climate change, there is also the increased human activity in areas once considered rural or isolated: campsites hidden deep within forests, more cars on the road, and more people hiking, biking, and adventuring through tinder-dry foliage.

The vast majority of people are careful; we are not a nation of unstoppable arsonists. Most people respect the nature they explore. But with increased presence comes higher risk of accidents, carelessness, and inattention.

In a country where forests are dense and primarily consist of closely packed coniferous trees, many of which are painfully parched, even a tiny spark on a breezy day can cause unimaginable damage.

As news of the West Kelowna fire spread, the prevailing opinion on social media was that it couldn't possibly jump the lake. Online, former firefighters and meteorologists weighed in with their expert knowledge, warning that it was indeed possible under windy conditions. They explained that, though rare, embers can fly up to thirteen kilometres, and this is even more likely to occur at speed when carried by the wind.

I watched in awe and horror as bright orange flames crested the ridge less than two kilometres from my home and family, with flickering reflections of towering flames visible in the lake before me. A crackle, a roar, and the density of the smoke rapidly intensified.

Before long, the firestorm was consuming structures. Unbeknownst to us, residents near Trader's Cove had been forced to jump into the lake to escape the inferno. Calls for help circulated on social media, and fortunately, they were picked up by boats and taken to safety.

Just before midnight, a neighbour banged on our front door, yelling that we needed to evacuate; the fire had indeed crossed the lake, erupting just a short distance away. My friend Scott Payer, a fire captain in the Kelowna Fire Department, arrived to place sprinklers around the house.

Adrenaline was pumping as Tracy and I, our dogs, and our visiting guests—my son Michael with his partner Chantel and daughter Evelynn, and my son Patrick and his girlfriend, Mel—quickly packed up and left, driving south in hopes of finding a safe hotel, uncertain when we would return or if there would be anything to return to.

At the Four Points hotel in Kelowna, I was told they had no rooms available. We were unsure of where to go at 1:00 a.m., but a man appeared in the lobby and directed us to the Manteo—about sixteen kilometres south, on the edge of the lake. He assured us they'd have a room.

Sure enough, upon arrival, we found that two rooms had been set aside. The hotel staff, however, had no idea who the man was who had told us to go there and couldn't explain how they'd prepared the rooms in advance. I considered it divine intervention. Someone was looking out for us.

Although it was ultimately over a week before Tracy and I were allowed to return to our Kelowna home, it remained unscathed. Sadly, this was not the case for all residents in the city.

Nearly 200 properties were destroyed in the area amid a fire that expanded to more than 13,000 hectares. Firefighters did a phenomenal job saving countless homes, as units were called in from across Western Canada and beyond to help. West Kelowna's fire chief described the situation as fighting a hundred years' worth of fires all at once.

It was a devastating time for the community—one that left a lasting scar on the landscape and brought a painful loss for all those who cherish the region. The abundant natural beauty was now charred and smouldering—a symphony of wildlife silenced. Once-towering, majestic trees, which had stood for longer than most lifetimes, were reduced to skeletal remains on a desolate canvas. Yet, it was a blessing and a miracle that no human lives were lost.

While wildfires raged in British Columbia, the first tropical storm since 1939 was heading directly for California, specifically toward the area between Palm Springs and Palm Desert, where my much-loved winter home sits in Rancho Mirage.

Hurricane Hilary, a Category 4 Pacific hurricane at its peak, churned over the ocean before weakening substantially upon landfall. Downgraded to a Category 1, it headed north up the coast of Mexico toward California.

The storm's remnants caused widespread flooding and dangerous mudslides across the Southwestern United States. Rainfall totals from the hardest-hit areas in California exceeded 330 mm over the course of this historic event.

The aftermath revealed hundreds of millions of dollars' worth of damage, uprooted trees, significant flooding at Eisenhower Medical Center, impassable roads, major business disruptions, and a dip in tourism for some time.

Worrying about simultaneous climate-related events affecting two of my treasured homes feels like more than a heartbreaking coincidence. Sadly, it reflects the times we live in. And it's a troubling indication of what more may lie ahead.

Phil Lind

On Sunday, August 20, 2023, Phil Lind, former Rogers director, right-hand man to Ted Rogers, and a friend of mine for many decades, passed away on his eightieth birthday.

Phil worked for Rogers for forty years—a career that spanned half his life and allowed him to pursue other passions. An avid sports fan, he orchestrated the launch of Sportsnet. As an environmentalist, he became a director of the Atlantic Salmon Federation, dedicated to the conservation and protection of wild salmon. His interest in politics and social issues as a progressive conservative led him to found CPAC—the Cable Public Affairs Channel—the national TV network delivering

House of Commons and other public affairs programming. He held a master's degree in political sociology and was awarded an honorary doctorate from the University of British Columbia. Phil loved the arts, culture, nature, and practical jokes.

Like me, Phil faced a near-death experience at the height of his career, suffering a stroke in 1998. He had to relearn how to walk, talk, read, and write.

I admired Phil from the moment we met in the 1980s. Like Ted and I, we were respectful competitors, operating in the same world with a mutual understanding. Holding similar roles in our respective companies, Phil and I shared a professional camaraderie and a mutual appreciation for each other's challenges and achievements.

Phil died on a day when I was still displaced from my home due to the wildfires. That day, Tracy and I decided to drive to Calgary rather than wait in smoky Kelowna to learn our home's fate. It was a long drive, and we didn't arrive until the early hours of the morning. Just as I was getting into bed at 2:44 a.m., I received an email informing me of Phil's passing.

I had seen Phil just three weeks prior at a Rogers board meeting in Vancouver. He was wearing a Toronto Blue Jays hat, and I gave him a big hug. Although I knew he hadn't been well, the news came as a terribly sad shock.

Broadcast Dialogue magazine asked me to share a few words for an article announcing his passing. I commented that Phil's character was marked by a sense of fairness and relentless preparation, even leading up to the Rogers–Shaw merger. I noted Phil's class and resilience in everything he did, never complaining, never letting anything—not even his stroke—slow him down. His character shone through when he attended Charles Keating's funeral in minus-thirty-degree weather not long after regaining the ability to walk. Phil was a great ambassador for Rogers and a wonderful person who will be dearly missed.

On Thursday, August 31, 2023, I attended Phil's funeral. Jim's son Parker and his wife, Megan, were there, representing the Shaws. Phil was like an uncle to Parker, having known him all his life, which reflects the deep connections between our companies and the industry.

After the funeral, Parker and I reminisced about the positive qualities of his father, Jim, and his grandfather, JR, as we shared time together in Toronto, nostalgically recalling days gone by.

Reuniting with old friends and revisiting fond memories shouldn't happen only at funerals. I hope that many of the people I consider family from my years at Shaw will soon gather again under cheerful circumstances.

There were many familiar faces present at the funeral of Phil Lind. On meeting John Tory at Phil's funeral, I warned him that the story of him jokingly offering me a tube of K-Y Jelly might end up in the autobiography I was working on—though I didn't tell him it would appear twice. Despite the friction and disagreements we'd had over our careers, John was thrilled that I was writing about it all. I suggested he owed it to his family to capture his own life's paths and experiences. Maybe we all do.

Writing offers the chance to explain ourselves, share viewpoints and beliefs, express motivations, and clarify values. It allows us to show that we are human, imperfect, with regrets, faults, and shortcomings. Writing it all down lets us share our story with future generations, so that our words echo and resonate long after life forces the story's finale.

Rinpoche

In Tibetan Buddhism, *Rinpoche* is a title of respect for an accomplished and revered teacher, translating to *precious jewel* in English. A Buddhist Rinpoche is considered a reincarnate lama or realized master, believed to have attained a high level of spiritual accomplishment. Rinpoches are often recognized as embodying qualities and wisdom from previous lives. They serve as guides, offering teachings, empowerment, and wisdom on the Buddhist path, often specializing in areas like medicine, astrology, or specific Buddhist traditions.

Though I still consider myself Catholic, I've felt an undeniable affinity for Buddhism as my beliefs have evolved. My brother, Paul, who has lived in Japan for fifty years, has moved further from Catholicism than I have and now identifies more closely with Buddhism. Rinpoche was the spiritual figure I took Charles King to see when he had lung cancer.

Brad Shaw, along with donating millions to local charities and food banks, has philanthropic interests in Tibet, contributing to an orphanage. Through Brad, and later Jim, I came to know Rinpoche, who attended Brad's wedding in 2023 and blessed his wedding ring. I have had many spiritual meetings with Rinpoche, learning about karma, healing, and the concept of reincarnation. I am open to all these ideas.

Rinpoche is adamant that he and I knew each other in a past life, though he won't say how or where. I don't dismiss the possibility, as I believe in God, an afterlife, and phenomena far beyond our earthly comprehension.

There's a slightly less appealing theory that could explain Rinpoche and me knowing each other before my birth: eternal return, presented in 1885 by the philosopher Friedrich Nietzsche. Some interpret it to mean living the same life on repeat, ad infinitum. The idea is that one should live a life they're willing to repeat … and repeat. This concept could account for premonitions, déjà vu, feelings of destiny, and instant soul connections. However, it's a grim concept for anyone with a life of pain or tragedy, as it offers no escape—only repetition.

Rinpoche is one of the unique characters who has influenced my belief system, broadened my views, and taught me a great deal. Whether our relationship transcends this lifetime, or if any of my relationships will extend beyond this timeline, remains a mystery.

Karma

Though often associated with Buddhism, karma also has roots in Hinduism, Jainism, and other Eastern religions. While interpretations vary, the general principle—also found in Catholicism, other faiths, and general ethics—remains the same. It's about cause and effect, reaping what you sow, and, to an extent, the law of attraction.

Some believe karma applies only to the current life; others believe it carries into an afterlife or even beyond. Some interpret karma as personal and instantaneous, while others see it as collective, with humanity's combined actions shaping broader outcomes over time.

Regardless of belief, the message is clear: be kind, act responsibly, consider the consequences, and do what's instinctively right.

We're only aware of this life—the one certainty we can all agree on. Here and now, there are choices to be made, opportunities to seize, moments to treasure, and much to appreciate. We share a duty of care to one another and to the world—a place we inhabit individually for a brief time, but collectively, forever.

Fourteen — Providence, The Future

Though I may not be a regular churchgoer these days, and my feelings about the institution have changed, I still pray every night. I still believe in God, I have gratitude for God, and I am certain that my faith was always integral to my success.

Angels

Sometimes it's a message you only recognize in hindsight; sometimes it's an unexplained but commanding feeling that pulls you in a certain direction; sometimes it's a premonition in the form of an illogical and unexpected dream; sometimes it's the intervention of something beyond your control that changes your life path in ways you didn't foresee or understand but that later reveal their purpose. Sometimes it's a hunch, an instinct, a spontaneous thought, a surge of creativity, a seemingly impulsive decision, or a feeling of kindness, comfort, or protective warmth.

Animals, in their thousands, will flee from oncoming natural disasters hours before they happen. They're in tune with the Earth and likely have a far greater respect and comprehension of its worth, meaning, and power than we do.

But for all the awful things that happen to people everywhere, every day, there is evidently a protective force, a guiding energy that can be accessed even in your darkest hour or final moments.

As I look back on my life, I can pinpoint the moments I felt what I believe was divine guidance. The first of those moments was in the summer of 1969, when I made the risky decision to leave Ottawa and go west.

My sister Suzanne believes it may be Granny Agnes looking out for me, but I'm not so sure. While I felt love from Granny Agnes more profoundly than I did from my mother, I cannot say who or what has directed these spontaneous, big decisions that came with an undeniable internal inspiration.

The drive to move forward in search of something better was a theme in both my career and personal life. Many people would choose, instead, to remain settled in a comfortable job, surrounded by co-workers they know, in a routine and environment that feels familiar and safe, as secure as a worn, warm blanket.

They might progress, albeit slowly, along a path that incrementally moves them forward, and it might feel safe, wise, and sensible, especially given their anxieties. But to truly excel, grow, and reach for your ultimate potential, I have learned that it's necessary to embrace a little fear. You need to be a bit scared, a bit uncertain. You need to make bold decisions and give things a try.

Time is not equal for everyone—not just in the sense that some live longer than others in a predictable, linear way, but in that some people live broader, fuller, multidimensional lives rich with colour, flavour, and depth. These lives are abundant with change, and change does something quite spectacular to the brain. In moments of transition, when our worlds begin to look and feel different, our minds become increasingly absorbent.

You notice more.

You appreciate the small things.

You experience awe and wonder, intense emotions that stimulate your soul and send waves of energy through your body. It's in these moments that time expands for you, pulling in more of the world around it.

Though it may seem to fly by as you navigate new surroundings and encounter new faces, later, when these memories are firmly embedded in the core of your mind, they feel richer, more alive. As a result, you can recall details more easily. These experiences, soaked up during times of change, form intense, vivid memories that, in hindsight, make your life feel longer.

All we have in any hour of the day are our memories. We cannot pause the present. Everything we ever see or do slips instantly into the past, and as time moves forward, the past drifts further away. The only things we truly hold on to and can revisit in our minds are memories.

Memories defy chronological order; you can call on them in any sequence you choose. You can dive into them, skim over them, share them, or suppress them. While the world marches forward, your memories remain still—always available to make you laugh, smile, cry, wince, or cringe. They are always there to teach, if you're open to learning from them. They are filled with clues, messages, and sometimes even predictions, if you choose to listen.

People may scoff at time travel, but you can revisit the past in your mind any time you like.

But when routine rules your world—when you're doing the same things in the same place with the same people, day after day, week after week—these millions of memories start to merge. They blur together, lost in the monotony of daily life within the same four walls. People who live this way may reduce their risks, but inevitably, they reduce their lives too.

Those who grow through change after change may face risks of failure, but with self-belief, hope, and positivity, they have a greater chance of succeeding. Ultimately, they will not only live longer but will live wider, deeper, higher—they'll live bigger. They'll live more.

I think those who have passed on are aware of this.

If death is final, and nothingness follows, maybe they aren't aware after the machine flatlines. And if that truly is the end, then even more reason to live the one life you have to the absolute fullest. This. Is. It.

And if there is something beyond death, as I and billions of others around the globe passionately believe, then the souls who have already ascended, gazing upon Earth with a panoramic view, would reflect and remind us of the magnificence of this world, the goodness of people, the opportunities waiting to be seized, and the amazing things we can do.

They'd guide us. They'd tell us to open our eyes and get on our feet.

They'd put thoughts and ideas in your head that seem to come from nowhere, and you'd quit your job and get on a bus, or end your marriage that's not making you happy, or apply for that job you thought was unattainable, or set yourself a goal to try something new, to be original, to innovate, to explore the world outside of the box and recognize that there's never no choice, never only one or two options. Even when the world seems to be offering up nothing other than option A or option B, remind yourself that there's always an infinite alphabet, and your heart and instincts will point the way.

It's not about running away when things go wrong; better yet is to move on when things are good. Seek better, aspire higher, trust yourself, and have faith that there's more out there waiting for you.

This was the case when I left the air force, in which I could have mastered a respectable trade and had a long, secure career; when I left BC Tel after thirteen years of internal ladder climbing, known across the company to be a rising star; when I left Amy because I wasn't in love with her and wanted a partner where adoration was mutual and butterflies abundant; when I changed paths after the sale of Western, not knowing what would be next, but being sure I wanted more than they could offer once they'd been acquired by Rogers; when I admitted to myself that Louise was not the one—that she didn't love me nor respect me, and I didn't have to accept the pain and anguish she caused me; when I bought properties in Kelowna and Rancho Mirage so that I could capture chapters of seasons in each place, so that the years wouldn't pass by in a single location.

And now, as a retired man, feeling accomplished and loved and happy, I can look back without regret on my varied and wonderful journey.

Though I know it took courage to venture beyond my comfort zone and my own hard work and efforts to make things happen, I believe without a doubt that I was helped along the way—by deific forces and the spirits of loved ones who have passed, looking out for me.

While I was the one at the wheel, I often felt a bit like I was enjoying a ride in one of those self-driving cars—as things I hoped for in my heart but never asked for out loud would happen.

The concept of angels has been present in my life for as long as I can remember: from my earliest education in Catholic schools to attending Mass daily every morning after my paper route. The perspectives and views of my parents and family, the broader belief systems of the communities I lived in, the impressive churches where certain sermons seemed to speak directly to my soul, and the harmonies of the choirs—their angelic voices echoing so eloquently and movingly, as if they were singing words that transcended time and space.

One morning, at Holy Trinity Parish in North Vancouver, I found myself staring at the statue of Mary, asking her if she could shed a tear to prove that she was ever present, there in that moment, and show me she was real. I waited quite patiently, but Mary did not cry. Nevertheless, I was satisfied that she appeared plenty sad enough—sort of melancholy and innocent—and that would do.

But surely, if statues the world over began excreting salty water from their stone eyes at the request of curious children, there would no longer be a necessity for faith. And is Mary truly in proximity to every artist's impression of her, waiting to be asked to prove herself?

We all do these things, at one time or another, allowing our scruples to instigate various tests. It's far from scientific, but it's just an extension of an automatic intrigue about a world beyond our human understanding. Nobody has all the answers; if they did, there would be no questions.

I believe that angels aren't always divine beings from heaven, living in another realm. I believe they can be human people you encounter here on Earth, within your lifetime.

I believe in providence, which differs from destiny in that providence is a process, whereas the latter is a destination. Part of providence may involve finding yourself meeting certain people at pivotal times, or being in a particular place as a significant event occurs. There are occasions when this is no accident, not merely chance. Some people are sent your way, perhaps guided by their own guardian angels. They have something to tell you, to teach you, to show you. They will change your life when you least expect it. This is divine intervention. These are human angels.

While destiny might feel like an idea that's overly grand and exclusive, providence suggests gentle nudges from wiser entities—a heavenly force looking out for our best interests. They aren't there to help us directly but to help us help ourselves. They see a broader view, one beyond our own limited vision.

Believing in God requires faith, because things happen that don't always make sense. But looking beyond ourselves and feeling that we are more than just perfectly formed biological matter—that there is something within us, whether consciousness or a soul, that can and will outlive our physical body—offers both inspiration as we live and comfort as we face death.

War or Peace

We are all just one aspect of an infinitely bigger picture. Our lives and experiences here on Earth are impacted, influenced, and determined by the broader connections of people, nature, and time.

The modern world is small. We have access to information about events happening in even the most remote locations, in countries thousands of kilometres away. We have livestream windows into the day-to-day lives of others, who voluntarily share their unique views and stories as they happen.

Events that occur in our lifetimes are documented extensively from all angles. They're analyzed and judged, repeated, and reflected upon. We hear the intentions of those in power—be they governments, corporations, or individual billionaires—and we form our opinions on them.

We can research the past, receive instantaneous access to the present from wherever we choose, and as such, our predictions for the future may now be better informed and potentially more accurate than ever before.

I am aware of the threats of our times—from global inequality, war, and famine to the looming inevitability of the dire consequences of catastrophic human-caused climate change.

For those in a position to help, however small their contribution, the choices are vast and ever-expanding: Which investments will be the most ethical, sustainable, and positively impactful to the greatest number?

In 1995, when the internet was in its infancy, I said to family and friends, "The next war will be an internet war." I could foresee how powerful this tool would be, and over time, this only became more evident as usage grew, with almost every person in North America having access to it—and soon enough, in the palm of their hands.

Every day at Shaw, teams worked to thwart thousands of attempted cybersecurity attacks on the network from across the globe—most originating from China, Russia, and some countries in Africa. Shaw employed dozens of people to work solely on cybersecurity, twenty-four hours a day. The motive behind most hacking attempts is money—like most crime generally. Perhaps more worryingly, it is also about control.

I recall once being informed of a very real and immediate threat of terrorism infiltrating telecommunications providers' networks, including Shaw's. This necessitated heightened vigilance when hiring new staff who might have ulterior motives for their employment.

Having served in the navy and having held top-secret clearance while working on radar systems with the Royal Canadian Air Force, I have taken a keen interest in these types of security threats for decades, and have observed their evolution.

Today, more than 9,000 satellites orbit the Earth, just over half of which are active and owned by more than eighty different countries. The United States owns the most satellites, followed by Russia and China, the latter operating primarily military satellites—more than eight times those operated by the United States. Most satellites are used for commercial purposes, are owned by corporations and communications businesses such as Shaw, and are launched privately.

A potentially concerning overlap emerged in the United States at the start of 2025, when controversial billionaire Elon Musk was designated a special government employee by President Donald Trump. Though Musk had never been democratically elected and did not have an official title in government, he was appointed to lead the new Department of Government Efficiency, or DOGE. DOGE was established by executive order, to modernize federal technology and software to maximize governmental efficiency and productivity. However, Musk was CEO of SpaceX, which developed the Starlink satellite internet constellation, raising ethical questions around conflict of interest and privacy.

At the start of 2025, Starlink had nearly 7,000 satellites in orbit, with each satellite costing around $1 million—significantly lower than the geosynchronous satellites used by Shaw.

Starlink benefits from a lower cost per satellite, but they require many satellites to offer their service. The lower orbit of Starlink satellites provides less coverage area than the Anik satellites used by Shaw, so this limitation is offset by having a larger number of satellites.

Many satellites require many launches, so this additional cost must be factored into comparisons, particularly when considering the shorter lifespan of Starlink satellites: typically five years. Anik satellites have a lifespan of fifteen years. But because Musk's SpaceX launches Starlink satellites, major stakeholders of both companies benefit by one set of costs being offset by another's profits.

Space junk is a negative attribute of the low-orbit Starlink satellites. When these satellites reach the end of their short life, they can continue to orbit, cluttering the orbital sphere and posing a greater danger to active satellites. In-orbit collisions with space junk are an ever-growing problem for LEO—low Earth orbit—satellites.

As of 2025, Starlink is unable to compete effectively with traditional terrestrial wireline networks in urban settings, as it offers internet speeds of 150 Mbps compared to the 800 Mbps to 1 Gbps offered by telecom providers. Bell, Rogers, and Telus have networks that will eventually support internet speeds of up to 10 Gbps.

I believe Starlink will primarily succeed in remote and rural settings where alternative wireline networks simply don't exist. With comprehensive global coverage, there is nowhere on Earth—from off-grid communities to the open ocean—that Starlink couldn't reach.

Starlink provided services in Ukraine since the beginning of the war with Russia. In the initial weeks after Russia's invasion, Ukraine's telecommunications networks were destroyed, and Starlink became the de facto national internet provider. However, three months into the war, Starlink determined that Ukraine was using its network to synchronize drones, which had become highly effective in disrupting Russian forces, and subsequently disabled its network for that purpose. Additionally, having invested over $100 million, Starlink decided it would not continue subsidizing the war effort.

Starlink still offers commercial internet in Ukraine, but as of 2025, it is funded by the United States government. Technology becomes politicized.

Within weeks of Donald Trump's 2025 inauguration as president of the United States, T-Mobile, the country's second-largest wireless carrier—with over 130 million subscribers—announced a new partnership with Starlink. Marketing themselves as the first space-based network in the United States, T-Mobile automatically provided their existing subscribers with this service—whether they asked for it or not. Days after the announcement, other wireless carriers in both the United States and Canada, including Rogers, shared that they too had the ability to connect with Starlink's Direct to Cell—or DTC—for sending and receiving text messages when out of range, and would be giving this to customers for free.

The issues this raises for anyone partnering with Starlink—and as such, with Musk—go beyond simple business considerations. The impact that public perception of Musk could have on brand integrity and customer trust are significant.

While connecting with Starlink satellites might present a great technical solution, is it socially acceptable? Knowing how carefully these decisions in the industry are made, I can only assume that data privacy, ethical considerations, corporate values, geopolitical ramifications, and the impact this arrangement will inevitably have on global markets must have been taken into account before agreements were made.

I predict there will eventually be a conflict in space—not with aliens, but over satellites. Without satellites, communications would become drastically limited, relying on terrestrial facilities running through transatlantic cables, particularly a single, lengthy 28,000-kilometre fibre-optic cable that links numerous countries between the United Kingdom and Japan. These cables, being on Earth, are more accessible and have already been known to have been tampered with, as attempts have been made to access data this way.

Ultimately, telecommunications technology is at the centre of how we move forward as a species. Information manipulation is the greatest means of control.

Data is the new currency. Once, whoever had the most money held the most power; today, the same can be said of data. Knowing this and having already achieved the most financial wealth in the world, I suspect Musk has moved on to the acquisition of global data. Data is knowledge, and "knowledge is power"—a phrase probably first said by Sir Francis Bacon, the English philosopher who served as lord chancellor of England and attorney general of England and Wales and was notably influential in the era of the Scientific Revolution, in 1597. So, it could be argued that this is not really a recent revelation—money just came along and distracted us all.

A war over satellites in space might sound futuristic and unlikely, but with the growing amount of space junk floating erratically above our atmosphere, it's increasingly probable that, even unintentionally, any satellite could be struck by debris and fail at any time.

Data breaches, security threats, spying, and wire-cutting may sound dramatic, but I predicted the risks of Huawei equipment long before that controversy unfolded. While some telecommunications providers were integrating Huawei technologies into their networks, Shaw made the conscious decision not to, considering the risk of spyware too great.

Our concerns were similar to those expressed by national security agencies. Many countries, particularly the U.S. and Canada, had expressed that Huawei's close ties to the Chinese government could enable espionage.

The existing legislation in China, such as the National Intelligence Law of 2017, required companies to cooperate with state intelligence work, raising concerns that these companies would provide data access and surveillance as a part of their compliance with this legislation. Poor cybersecurity practices and their equipment's vulnerability to attacks enhanced the risks of their use. Further, their lack of disclosure and transparency when asked about their corporate governance presented too much to risk using Huawei in our telecommunication systems.

As it turned out, doing business with Huawei was a bad move for some telecommunications companies, which have since had to undertake the painstaking and costly process of replacing that equipment—a task that takes time and causes disruption.

It wasn't until May 2022 that the Canadian federal government officially banned Huawei products from being used in the country due to national security concerns. This decision has led telecom giants to seek taxpayer compensation, as it was an unanticipated and retroactive policy. The conversations and controversies are ongoing, and it's most fortunate that Shaw—now owned by Rogers, who were equally prudent in their choice to avoid the Chinese multinational technology corporation—has sidestepped this significant problem.

The world has changed dramatically since 2018—a realization that is still sinking in for many.

At the height of the flower child era of the 1970s, the idea of peace on Earth almost seemed achievable in my then-hopeful, naive mind. But the reality is that it's a complex, long-term endeavour that is unlikely ever to occur. Achieving it necessitates addressing root causes. Often, these roots are impossible to identify accurately, not only because of historical complexity, but also due to human denial and cognitive dissonance.

We need to promote education, inclusivity, and tolerance to bridge divides. Our commonality is a desire for peace and survival. We need to work together toward that goal.

Advances in technology are indeed a double-edged sword. While they offer convenience and progress that feels exciting and forward moving, they also present unsettling risks and new challenges. The future of media is uncertain. How will artificial intelligence impact it? What will it mean for the economy and for existing businesses looking to grow?

Some of today's greatest global challenges involve containing the aspirations of conquering nations—whether they attempt to do so through brute force or electronic means. The internet and the control or elimination of satellite communications offer stealth capabilities beyond comprehension.

The destruction of the world through self-inflicted damage to the ecosystem has irreversible consequences that will challenge everyone and the world order. The goal must be in the best interests of all humanity, harnessing the capabilities of innovative technologies to mitigate these profoundly worrisome threats.

While none of us can single-handedly fix the world's problems and save the planet, in our own pursuits, we can be cognizant of our impact, aware of our responsibilities, and respectful of nature and others, with kindness and positivity. Little by little, we make a difference.

And through all of our choices and endeavours, we need to understand that communication is both the cause of and solution to all of our problems.

Final Track

As I reflect on my life thus far, I can hear the soundtrack—those significant, memorable songs that formed the background music to each chapter. These are the songs that influenced and inspired me along my journey.

It's been a journey I'm proud of, and I wish I could relive the highlights. There are a few things I might go back and change if I could ... but not too much. I wouldn't want to disturb the butterfly effect that led to where I am now.

As with all soundtracks, there's always a final track that plays as the closing credits roll. When I pass—and we all will, eventually—when my soul, like the echoes of soundwaves drifting into the ether, goes riding on the wind, I hope the song that will conclude my celebration of life is Jimi Hendrix's "Little Wing"—the first song I learned on guitar and one that holds great nostalgia for my younger years. It's been a consistent and deeply emotive favourite since my love of music began.

Fly on.

Fifteen — Count on Me

Amid the global challenges we see today, it's difficult to imagine a future in which everyone has an equal opportunity to thrive.

From the moment we are born, innocent and unknowing, the future is a mystery. Perhaps we'll reach and optimize all possibilities with ease. Or perhaps we'll face unimaginable obstacles. The truth for many of us is that we'll fall somewhere in between. But we all have gifts. We all have potential. Genetics and environment are not a formula that predicts destiny. It's possible to break away. Family isn't only biological.

For those of us fortunate enough to be born into a body and mind that enable the pursuit of dreams, and fortunate enough to be born into a country that supports those pursuits, it's important that you do—pursue your dreams, that is.

The world depends on each of us contributing our unique strengths, doing our best, being open to learning and growth, and showing kindness.

There's a good chance that the life we're living is the only one we'll get. Never tell yourself you cannot do something because you don't have enough time. For as long as you can make choices, to use your abilities, to feel hope—you still have enough time to make a difference.

At the core of all your actions and decisions is you. Though you may feel the forces of pressure, expectation, influence, and uncertainty, you have power over yourself. Take control. Envision the life you want and make it happen. Be brave.

Regret is more commonly felt in the absence of actions than in failed attempts. So go for it. The time is now.

If you get knocked down in your efforts, there will always be people willing to pull you up. People who see you struggling as you try. Even when you may feel your loneliest, there will always be someone, somewhere, rooting for you. So don't give up. And root for yourself.

Manifesting big dreams is possible when opportunities are seized, with self-belief and a commitment to hard work. Everyone has unique talents and valuable contributions to make. Everyone can make things happen.

The world needs a diverse workforce, from creators to critics. Competition makes us better. Opposition forces us to grow. If every one of us could radiate our most positive energy, collectively, we'd have the power to overcome great obstacles and implement the most innovative solutions. And whatever you hope for in life, faith in oneself is what is needed to succeed.

I never allowed myself to doubt. Failure was never an option. Because if I failed, it meant my parents had been right all along. And if my parents were right, then I was a blithering idiot who would never make anything of myself and never be worthy of love. This fear of rejection and refusal of doubt propelled me as I passionately strove to accomplish monumental things.

I didn't know, as a small child confined in a dark closet, that I'd become a leader one day. But I found my strengths, I found my purpose, I chased my dreams. I learned that it was possible to count on me. None of us is perfect. I have reconciled with my mother. I wouldn't be the person I am if it weren't for her.

I retired from my role as president of Shaw in August 2015 but remained a member of their board until April 3, 2023, when Shaw was merged under Rogers Communications. Shaw has now ceased to be. And that's difficult to accept.

I have served on many boards throughout my career. I have been a board member for CableLabs in the United States, Gravity Renewables, the Canadian National Institute for the Blind, the Society of Cable Telecommunications Engineers, and Western Cablesystems Ltd. None has made me as proud as serving on Shaw's board for sixteen years. I continue to serve as a director for the Shaw Family Trust. These things have kept me feeling relevant and connected.

Outside of my career, I've had a lifelong love of music, which truly became an integral part of my being when I learned to play guitar in the early 1970s. Today, I continue to seek learning opportunities in music and recording studio production. I will never stop learning!

My creative curiosity and desire to document and encapsulate moments, events, and chapters led me to photography in my early twenties. I became a published photographer, and my work has been featured on magazine covers.

From a young age, I showed an affinity for sports. I enjoyed the thrill of competition and the appreciation for teamwork, which was later mirrored throughout my career. Family members were never guaranteed to make good teammates, but good teammates would inevitably become like family. I played league hockey, basketball, baseball, and soccer, and competed in karate tournaments.

Perhaps my most poetic achievement, considering my mother's vocation as a nurse in the navy, has been that in 2013, I became an honorary captain of the Royal Canadian Navy.

I would love to be able to tell my six-year-old self all of this. He'd be so very excited for all that was to come.

Within these recollections of my life journey are embedded evocative truths about people and choices that challenge stereotypes and invite broader perspectives. The modern world is divided. But there's a layered context to reality that expands in all directions. We cannot make assumptions or place people in boxes.

I spent much of my life doing a job I loved, that fulfilled me, made me happy and proud. It was a job that broadened my human connections and allowed me to have some impact. I had a role that carried significant responsibility, which I never took for granted and always handled with care.

I enjoyed it. For all the ups and downs and setbacks and stress, it meant the world to me. I was glad to do my bit.

I can see the significance of serendipity in my life. And I trust in providence. While my perspectives have widened and my beliefs evolved, I have always had faith—faith in myself and in something greater than all of us.

Tributes

My sister Elizabeth sadly passed away at the age of seventy, following a battle with pancreatic cancer. Siblings are never guaranteed to be life-long friends. But, for those who do find a bond that stands the test of time, it can be impossible to imagine living without one another.

At the time of writing, my sister Suzanne is living her final days. For the past twenty years, I have been her primary source of income. I purchased a condominium for her to live in and have covered all living expenses each month.

As life unfolded unexpectedly, I found myself in a position where I would be providing substantial financial support for Suzanne, as she became very sick and required extended nursing care and a special care home twenty-four hours a day. A reminder of how unpredictable life can be. I have assured her that she can depend on me.

She has struggled with illness for much of her later life, and now has incurable stage 4 cancer. From childhood to now, we've had a friendship that's real and raw and eternally unbreakable—a connection that sits outside of careers, relationships, ambitions, projects, or present-day common ground. Her loving, supportive, and always-entertaining participation in my life story is coming to an end. We reminisce on the phone daily and speak openly about our inevitable parting. We say we'll miss one another. But we know we'll meet again in heaven.

Christine Oskirko

"For he will command his angels concerning you to guard you in all your ways. On their hands they will bear you up, so that you will not dash your foot against a stone." (Psalm 91:11–12)

This Way, My Child

In 1960, we lived in North Vancouver, and my brother Peter, who was about thirteen, had a paper route. He would have to rise at four in the morning to have the papers at the door before people awoke. Occasionally, my sister and I would sneak out of the house to do the route with him. It was dark and often misty—exciting but also frightening.

Peter said that, in the dark night, he would find comfort and safety whenever he saw an amber light shining from a window.

I created a painting that is a metaphor for Peter's life. The only amber light that gives us true safety is God. The almost translucent angel, seeing that Peter is about to stumble in the darkness, has her eyes on the stone at his feet, shining a heavenly light to guide him safely on his journey.

St. Joseph, the patron of our family, walks closely behind Peter, his hand on Peter's shoulder, guiding him forward in the way he should go.

The blue-green dots in the sky indicate the supernatural presence that surrounds him.

Peter was treated more harshly than any of his siblings. It was a real source of pain for us as children to witness this and to internalize the injustice. Yet, in a mysterious way, this mistreatment was a fire that forged an inner strength in him, without any sense of victimhood. Peter used all his emotional and psychological wounds constructively, striving to achieve success in his creative and business life.

God gave Peter a very gregarious, loving nature, many creative talents, and an intellectual curiosity that fostered his love of learning and studying. His hard work paid off and helped him get ahead. Some very good people, particularly one father figure, were placed before him to mentor him—people who clearly saw these gifts within him. Peter remained loyal to that mentor throughout his professional life.

I offer this painting, with all its limitations, as a labour of love to my brother, of whom I am very proud. I pray that the angels and saints continue to walk with him all the days of his life, until they bring him safely home to the heavenly shores.

— by my sister Christine

Suzapete

In 1958, our family moved from England to Southeast Marine Drive in Burnaby, B.C. Our parents rented a big, old house on a good-sized property not far from the Fraser River. Along the river's edges, Chinese and Japanese immigrants farmed rice paddies, as they still do today.

On one side of the property, there was an abundance of pear, peach, apple, and plum trees; on the other side, where we often played and swam in our knee-height plastic swimming pool, we had a view of a holly farm and a cedar mill. On rainy days—and there were many of those—the sweet smell of damp cedar would waft over to our house. It is one of my fondest memories of that time and place.

The property also included a greenhouse, and a rustic shed that served as a home for an eccentric older man with a goitre, named J.B., who seemed to come with the place. We were all a bit leery of J.B., but he never did us any harm. After he moved out, Suzanne and Peter tried to turn his shack into a clubhouse, which did not go over well with our mother.

All summer long, the youngest children had to play outside all day. Our mother would lock the door to prevent us from coming in with wet feet or muddy shoes. I remember us sitting on the wooden boards overlooking the garden, pretending we were in a chuckwagon and were cowboys. Imaginative play was constant.

Suzanne and Peter were always up to something and were both very active and athletic. One day, they found a dead sparrow, and Suzanne, being the animal lover, wanted to have a burial. So, Peter dug the grave and asked, "What shall we call it?" Suzanne piped up, "Suzapete!" So, Suzapete it was.

I wanted to paint a picture because it is one of my sweetest memories of the two of them playing. It wasn't as mournful a moment as the picture depicts.

They gave honour to Suzapete, and then, as all children do, they moved on to other forms of fun and looked for more mischief to get into!

Suzanne

I have terminal cancer, and my only thought is that I don't want to leave my brother.

I can remember my bond with my brother Peter from a very young age. Aunt Rosemary—my favourite aunt—always said that Peter and I were like two peas in a pod. We were always together.

I remember when we were sent to boarding school in England. The girls went to Sacred Heart Convent, and the boys to St. Michael's College, not far from each other in Hertfordshire. I would get so excited to see Peter on our walks with the nuns; I would yell out, "Peter!" to get his attention, and the nuns would get angry. I missed Peter so much!

When we left the convent and came to Canada, Peter and I grew even closer as we aged. I love his sense of humour; we really make each other laugh. We were always there for each other growing up. I have always felt a great loyalty to Peter, as he didn't have a good life with our mother.

I used to love visiting him every weekend when he lived in Vancouver. We'd always have a great time and lots of laughter with family and friends. I could always be myself at Peter's house.

Peter is an achiever; he worked so very hard to get where he did in the corporate world. The people who worked with him loved him because he was real; he treated them the way he wanted to be treated. I was so proud of his accomplishments. I think he wanted our mother to see that he was a valuable human being despite her unkindness toward him.

Uncle Peter truly adored us. He tried to make up for our mother's coldness. He could see how relaxed we were around each other, and we made him laugh.

Peter has been an extremely kind and generous brother to me in so many ways. If I'm feeling sad or want to bare my soul, I call him.

Peter has been such a loyal brother and a loyal friend to those he loves and cares for. There's no one I know who's more honourable and kinder than Peter.

I still see such youthfulness and beautiful, childlike qualities when talking with Peter that remind me so much of our childhood.

— by my sister Suzanne, written in January 2023

Brad Shaw

He always made me a better person. I always learned something from him, every single time. A little bit here. A little bit there. And he had a great sense of humour, and we had a lot of fun and did a little partying. He enjoyed life just as much as he worked hard. And that's important. You should celebrate success and the people around you and the love you have, just as much as the deal and the business driving it.

Peter came with tremendous knowledge of the business and was very supportive of what we were doing in the industry. He was so gracious and would give his time and his effort and his expertise to me or Jim. And I think JR thought he really fit into the culture and the values Shaw represented. I think he thought, "Wow, he's a special person. A special leader." And that's why he's earned everything he did and worked up the chain and proven himself time and again.

He built strength around him because he believed in, motivated, and inspired those around him.

He really became the key guy in our family. The four of us would talk about strategy and what he'd do, and his insight. JR trusted Peter completely—and he never let us down.

Timing was everything because it was around then, in 1989, that JR said to the family, "We're either going to sell, or we're going to grow."

We all said we wanted to grow. And we hit the turbos, man. Seventy or eighty acquisitions in five or six years. We were growing astronomically in that time! Peter was a big part of that.

I quit college. I didn't go to school. I felt like, *Who am I as a person? Who am I as a manager in business?* Peter was the guy who showed me the way. He showed me how you deal with people. He was such a straight shooter; he would always address a problem and always be fair to people—no matter who it was.

I think it motivates Peter to see others succeed. But boy, he's smart. Like holy shit, how he dealt with the unions or dealing with certain people or certain situations ... We had a lot of things come up dealing with programming and our customers, and he was always just so on it. He wouldn't wait a second; he'd always deal with it. It really made me make sure I don't leave things—that I get on top of it. Address it. He really exemplified that and was such a great example to me.

I knew he'd worked with the McDonald brothers in the Lower Mainland, and I thought when I saw his name, "Who's this guy? Why is he here? Why'd Jim hire him?"

But it wasn't long before I thought I'd won the lottery when I started to work with Peter. I'd go, *Wow, this guy's my boss. He's taking me under his wing, he is giving me his time, giving me the conversation, and always has his door open, and is always available.* Which is extraordinary, because he was a busy guy and learning Shaw at that time himself, but he was so gracious and so down-to-earth, and not only with me but with everyone. And I just really appreciated that because, you know, I could spin a little bit, not quite knowing what to do, and he always wanted to make sure I was successful and that I and everyone around always had support.

The name, the brand, everything! He cared about every little thing, and all it took is one customer to see that or someone to behave badly and it all impacts the company's reputation.

No one could represent us better than Peter could.

I know that tenure was incredible. I don't know if it was $300 million to $4 billion or something like that—the launch of internet, digital phone, the success of everything. Well, someone had to execute that. Someone had to drive that day to day. And it was Peter who did that. Jim was there too, for sure—and JR up here, and us down below. But I give Peter huge credit for a lot of the company's success at that time, because it does take someone to steer, someone to shift gears, slow down, speed up, make the call, and he would make the call. He'd be so thorough and complete and always make sure of everything. No loose ends. And the great thing is—he knows when to call bullshit.

I would trust him day in, day out. And I almost consider him like a dad in some ways—just for how much he's mentored me. The success I've had, what I've learned, where I've been—none of it would have happened without him. He never doubts you. He always thinks you're capable. I often thought, *Holy shit, I can't do any of this, and I'll never be like that.* But you learn and surprise yourself with what you learn, how you operate, how you deal with things.

I often think, when I'm trying to figure something out, *How would Peter do this?* or, *How would Peter do that?* And I never do it quite as well, I'm sure.

He's always been there, always saying, "Listen, if you ever need anything ..." And he's always gracious in opening that door and doing that. I wouldn't be the person I am, the leader I am—without him.

Peter's manual was his life experience and everything he learned from, everything he had to go through. He just seemed to understand every-thing. He had such a broad view and was able to put things in perspec-tive, to be relatable and personable when he could have stood on higher ground. But he had an unconventional way about him, and I think it was so powerful. I think it helped many, many people in their lives all around.

Howard Levitt

Shaw had shared cultures and values that Peter was instrumental in implementing. There were seven of them. Some companies have values, but they're usually not as specific as those seven. And not only are they specific, but they're in every contract of employment, every promotion, every transfer. You have to sign a contract committing to those values when you join the company. I used that in every single legal case I had.

Employees had to be trustworthy and reliable. They had to be accountable. These values were employee responsibilities. And then—lest they forget—they're at the formation of team huddles, team meetings, training sessions, maybe on emails, email signatures, letterheads, sides of meeting rooms, coffee mugs, ID badges. You could not pretend you didn't know what they were. And the team-player element was huge. The culture of *we* rather than *I*. People would think of themselves as part of the company as a whole.

If companies are listening to their people, then unions don't get in. Then people don't feel they need a union. People don't unionize for wages. More often than not, they unionize to be listened to and to feel important. If you looked at what Shaw paid—there's no benefit in being unionized. And because Peter was respected and liked, people thought Shaw would treat them well.

And he followed through with that. He proved they didn't need a union. People believed what Peter had to say, not only because he was personable and remembered people's names, but because he treated them like people, not just workers.

Though it's not unheard of, I do think it's a unique quality for a person at that level to be so personable.

I think perhaps his time in the seminary helped form his character and helped build those sorts of EQ skills. He has 100 percent in EQ. And that made all the difference when it came to negotiating.

I always found Peter impressive. I found him a counterfoil to Jim, with very different personalities. Peter would always defer to Jim, but he'd temper what might be considered excesses. And they were a brilliant combination, best exemplified by Jim increasing Shaw's market cap by six or seven times with Peter as his partner. He's handsome, a gentleman, articulate, smart, knowledgeable. And those were my very first impressions, which have lasted throughout the time I've known him. He's interesting, entrepreneurial, and had the same approach to a lot of things as I did. We really bonded over our shared opinions.

Michael D'Avella

During Shaw's golden era, we had a small but extremely effective team. Peter was a key part of that team with JR, Jim, Brad, Ken Stein, Randy Elliot, Billy Mac, and Ron Rogers. There were no egos, and we all understood our roles and responsibilities. This was the culture that JR created, and it was extraordinarily successful for many years.

Shaw was the North American leader in broadband internet. We realized very early on in the development of broadband that we had a competitive and technological advantage over Telus. We were singularly focused on deployment and growing market share. We invested strategically in upgrading our plant and cable modem technologies to provide broadband services quickly and reliably. Broadband internet was launched in the mid-1990s. By early 2000, our penetration was over 50 percent, and we had over 80 percent market share. It was and still is an enormous success and the single most important part of Shaw's business.

Peter and I had a reputation for being tough negotiators with programmers who felt entitled and privileged. Most cable operators would simply accept their carriage terms, rates, and conditions. We would push back and negotiate better deals for Shaw and, ultimately, for our customers. We were equally tough with equipment and service suppliers, because we understood the fundamentals of reducing input and capital costs in a competitive and capital-intensive industry.

Peter was—and still is—thoughtful, wicked smart, and a man of the people. Everybody in the company loved Peter. I relied on Peter for advice and guidance. Peter embodied Shaw's values and was, in many ways, our moral compass. A man of the people, loved by all. A team player, a great colleague, and my friend. He's smart, thoughtful, and remains fiercely loyal to the Shaw family and the company.

To be clear, none of us were very good at golf, because we all had day jobs, but I just loved playing with Peter, because we'd have cocktails, we'd be laughing, hitting shots in between, and just egging each other on and really being each other's best cheerleader. And it was just the most fun five hours you could spend with anybody. Every time we played, we did not stop laughing. We never got serious, but we were always competitive.

What company has that? What corporate culture allows that to happen, where it's a bit unusual, it's highly indulgent—but what a team! I was very, very fortunate to be asked along on those trips.

I think the golf course is a place where a lot of informal discussion took place—about what-ifs, hashing out ideas that had been lingering around boardrooms and meeting rooms for a long time. You had all the players who could make a decision—from the bankers to the lawyers—in one place. And it was very open. Everyone was available for those conversations. Everyone was in a good mood. And everyone knew why they were there: They were there to celebrate each other, but also to build the business.

Peter would counsel me on how to think about a problem as opposed to giving me the answer. His door was always open, and he always had five minutes, ten minutes, or more time to talk through—not *What should I do?* questions, but more *How should I approach things?* Peter was always about *How can I help you?* as opposed to *This is how I want you to do things.*

If they trust in what you're doing—*they* being the Shaw family and the senior leadership team—then the very least you can do is your best. When you hear JR say things like, "We're all employees; we just have different responsibilities," he's not saying it just as lip service. He's saying it because he honestly believes it. He honestly believes that there are some things you can do better than him and other things he can do better than you. And whether it's the person who is doing the installation in a customer's home, or somebody who is delivering a regulatory message to the government, or the person who's speaking to shareholders, there are different roles everybody plays. And your job is to play your role. To do the thing you've been trusted to do. Trust is what's motivating.

Peter was a hurricane passing through. I was at his office, ready for my interview, and he came in straight from a meeting. He was loud, he was excited, he was enthusiastic. He said, "Well, we just finished this strategy for the company for the next five years. I'd love you to look at it." And we just started talking. And then after that, we didn't talk about the company for the next forty-five minutes. All we talked about was music. We talked about his guitars. We talked about how he likes to play music, to produce music. We talked about people he liked in the music industry and people and music he appreciated. He asked me, "Are you a musician?" I said, "No. But I know lots of people in the music business."

Peter resembled a friend of mine who was in the music business. He was generous, he was laughing, he was telling jokes. He was treating me like I was already part of the team, coming to me mid-sentence and everything, assuming that I was following along. And I mean, it was not difficult to follow, but he was very familiar and comfortable in how he talked to me. And it was really something. I immediately thought, "Oh, this is a different company. This is a different place. These are different types of people. This is the president of Shaw who is talking to me about guitars and being on stage."

He was wearing a black T-shirt and had chains around his neck. This was not what I understood corporate culture to be, because I'd worked in banks, insurance companies, investment companies; I worked on Bay Street. And this was very, very different and very exciting. Peter was thrilled about what he had just finished. He was positive and motivated. And that was the thing that stuck with me. I really wanted to be part of a company like this!

We certainly had our fair share of crises, but nothing was insurmountable. I say that, because we dealt with them confidently. That was the thing, too—because of the way we all worked together, there wasn't any ownership of a solution. There was a shared accountability for a solution, so that whether it was a flood in 2013 or an email outage we had in another year, it was not *Whose fault is this?* It was *Okay, let's get this done.*

It's quite humbling to think about all the things we did, the success we had, and the freedom and trust that the family had in the management team to do the job that needed to be done. And that, I mean, I don't know how you re-create that. It was a great privilege.

It was challenging in every aspect: operationally, culturally, with people, with customers. The fact that the company had such operational success during that time is really a testament to the resilience of the people who were at the company.

Now that I've left Shaw, I really understand how unique what they had built was in Canada. And among large companies, it just can't be replicated.

Every company's quirky; every company's crazy in its own little ways. What's lovely about Shaw is its quirkiness is what makes it special. And the quirkiness is not different from what makes a family quirky—the sharp edges and the round corners that you love about people. And that is very, very true all the way down the line. Later on, as I would go and have meetings in different cities with different people, whether they were senior or more junior, you just got that sense all the way through. You really felt respect, but you also felt confidence that everybody had your back, and that you were supposed to have theirs. And you felt confident that everybody knew what they were doing, and that they thought you knew what you were doing, too.

Adrian Burns

The one thing about the Shaw company is when they came before the commission, they had provided every answer before you could start questioning. They were, as I have said, often in different circumstances, the gold standard of what a company should be when it comes to a tribunal. There were simply no questions left to ask by the CRTC, as Peter had answered them all before they even began!

Shaw was absolutely the gold standard, and they still are. And that's why the government was listening to them regarding the sale to Rogers.

I've had the most exciting time in my life in Shaw Communications because of the scale of the deals they did.

He doesn't get scared. Franklin D. Roosevelt, in his 1933 inaugural address, said, "The only thing to fear is fear itself." That's Peter. He's not afraid of anything.

I was the first woman on the board of Shaw at that point, and Peter's treatment of me was not patronizing—which was not true of everybody. I used to stop in front of the front door, having read the sports pages the night before, taking a deep breath before I opened the door to go in. Those were very intimidating days for a woman in a multibillion-dollar company. But he didn't mollycoddle me. He didn't help me, but he just treated me as an equal. And that's precious to me. Very precious. It's not a typical Calgary trait.

Peter doesn't see gender, he doesn't see colour or race, he doesn't see anything like that. He just sees confidence, humility, willingness, and kindness. That's what he sees.

He was always the last to speak on any occasion around the table when he was senior executive president, and that continued as a board member. He doesn't jump in with his opinions. He doesn't want to be heard for the sake of being heard. And I believe that was really the same approach he took when he appeared before the CRTC: When Peter spoke, you listened. He had something to say. It was relevant. And I cannot remember a single occasion when his advice or comments were not adhered to, followed, and most certainly given top priority. He was top-notch. He *is* top-notch.

I remember Peter appearing before me as a senior member of the executive of Shaw Communications when I was a newly minted commissioner. When applicants appear before the commission, there are two kinds of commissioners. I will call them, for lack of a better term, the *stuffed shirt, no smiling, demanding commissioners*. And then there's the commissioner who knows that the people advocating before them are spending enormous amounts of time and money just to make their companies better. Shaw fits in with me. I fit into the latter category. I think probably he liked me because I was respectful. I wasn't arrogant, and I really cared about what they were telling us because I knew it was going to strengthen Western corporations, which was what I was there to do.

I was raised by a self-made entrepreneur, so I understood how very difficult it is to run a business and help your personnel. And I knew that Shaw was first-rate in that department, and Peter was certainly at the head of that parade with the Shaws.

Peter is a man who spoke very little, but when he did, he had valuable information, was to the point, and never wasted time. He never, ever obfuscated on a question. He answered the question: He knew what we at the commission needed to know, and he provided it.

Also, although he was senior executive, then president, he had a lot of humility. There was no pretension to Peter whatsoever. And that came through in his very much Peter way of speaking, way of dressing. He wasn't putting on a position or a show for anyone. He was his own man. He was unapologetic for that. He was proud of that on both sides of the spectrum. He was just who he is, which is really compelling when you are a commissioner trying to figure out where people are coming from.

He really had what was required to appear in front of a tribunal.

He is a man devoted to music, with a love of music. And if anything takes us out of the trials of the day-to-day, we all know it's music. And Peter grasps that. Not only does he enjoy it, but he also participates in it and encourages others to take part in it. He is the music man.

Peter was speaking at the funeral service for Charles King, head of regulatory for Shaw, and he said a little piece on hummingbirds. It was just so gentle. That's why we love this guy. He's out in the desert; he's looking at hummingbirds—and they're touching his heart, and he's relating that to Charles King's wonderful personality. That's an example of the tender part of Peter.

My children say to me, and other friends say, "Why do you keep doing this? Why do you keep working? Why don't you just retire?" And I say, "I think probably I'm afraid of being irrelevant." So, the Peters and the Adrians and people like that—we're probably driven by that. We just want to be relevant in this world. That's the ego part. I think the overarching part of that for people like us is that we just want to do things that are good and make things better. It's a sense of commitment to a bigger picture.

I think they grew up through some very formative years and difficult times together. When Peter came over from Rogers to Shaw, Jim was very much working in the core of the company. I think they just bonded in a close friendship, which turned into a brotherly relationship. And I believe they were true brothers.

Peter was probably the first to recognize, maybe even before family members or others, how truly smart Jim was and how good he was for the business and the things that he did. His record is clear. During the time Jim was CEO, the company accomplished really great things—acquisitions, expansions, regulatory approvals. A lot of that happened under Jim. He was a really smart operator. And it would've been Peter who first recognized that and pushed him forward.

In a company like Shaw, which is a cyclical company, you have to take care of both your customers and your employees, but you're not going to serve your customers unless you've looked after your employees. Colleagues might as well say goodbye to the customers if they've got bad employees.

Peter never takes credit, and he seldom gives it, unless it's really, really something that needs to be done. And that will always be to staff—but he never takes credit for himself, ever.

There's an old expression that sadly applies to too many in the business world—*kissing up and pissing down*—but Shaw sought the antithesis of that.

Derinda Burton

Shortly after Peter met Tracy, I knew he had met the love of his life, and it was wonderful to see him so happy and be loved the way he deserved. She was wonderful, very caring, and instrumental in his recovery after he had a heart attack a few years after they were married.

From the first moment I met Peter, over twenty-two years ago, I thought he was different from any other leader I had been interviewed by. It was very relaxing, like just having a conversation with a friend.

He was very personable, and, I could tell, very passionate about Shaw. I knew after the first few minutes that this was someone I would enjoy working with, and I was thrilled when I was offered the position.

Working with Peter was never like working for someone in an employee–boss relationship; it was like he and I being a team, and he would always refer to us as working together, not me working for him. That alone showed how much he respected and appreciated me.

When Peter's circumstances changed not long after I started, he went through a long, difficult, stressful divorce. I was amazed at how calm, positive, and resilient he remained through the exhausting negotiations, still excelling in his very busy role as president of Shaw Communications.

Working with Peter was never boring. In the beginning, there was so much happening, and the company was growing extremely fast in so many directions, with Peter overseeing and executing so many exciting new products and developments.

He never ceased to amaze me with his bionic memory, whether it came to work correspondence or his life experiences. I loved hearing all of his stories, and it wasn't unusual for him to share these with our work colleagues, whether at a large roadshow with employees or in a casual encounter in the hallways.

Peter exhibits all the traits of a natural leader and a great mentor. He really is love in every sense of the word. He leads with his heart and has a big one. He is a great listener, a dynamic speaker whose presence commands a room, and has a special way of quietly sharing advice that inspires all to be their best. Hard to believe it's been over five years since Peter and I retired after an amazing fifteen years working together. I always felt appreciated and respected by Peter and Tracy. I think the biggest compliment Peter gave me was how much he trusted me with everything. I always joked that he had to keep me on as his personal assistant after retirement because I knew more about his life than he did. And he did, for over three years. Even though that came to an end, I still treasure our friendship very much and look forward to the times we get to spend together with Tracy and him, having a few cocktails and lots of laughs.

Peter is my angel who has blessed my life in so many wonderful ways, and I thank him from the bottom of my heart. He is the best!

Tracy Bissonnette

That was probably one of the very first things I noticed when I first met Peter: Even with him being president of Shaw and all that came with it, he was just normal. He was real. There were no airs to him. And he enjoyed the simple things in life. And I think we both liked just the simple things. You know, the nicer things are nice, but the simple things, the small gestures, can mean a lot. They matter more. There's a lot of quiet time. We can be quiet together, and it's always comfortable.

Every day is fun. I've been very blessed. And I think it was the right time in our lives for both of us when we met. I think it was meant to be. Serendipity brought us together.

Michael Bissonnette

I've always looked up to my dad. I've always felt proud that he's successful and very well-liked. He worked so hard to be able to do all these cool things—how could any kid not appreciate that and aspire to be that way? And so, it's an ongoing theme in my life—that I hope to embody as many of his characteristics as I can.

When I think of my childhood, I remember playing a lot of sports with my dad. He was always so encouraging and enthusiastic. He was patient, too. He'd take time to teach me, to help me get my pitch down. I was learning and improving, but it was always fun. We'd play roller hockey in the street too, football, baseball of course—and when I was around ten years old and started to play on teams, Dad used to umpire some of my games. I felt perhaps it was a conflict of interest, given that I was on one of the teams, but he was always fair. It was great for him to volunteer for that; I'll always remember it.

When it comes to football, Dad's always been a big BC Lions fan. In fact, he still is a die-hard BC Lions fan! We used to go to games together, and I remember he caught one of those little foam footballs that they shoot out of a cannon into the crowd. I cherished that thing forever!

One of my earliest memories—I guess I was about three years old—is sitting at the dinner table, and my dad handing me a Shaw teddy bear. One of those white bears, with the blue shirt and the Shaw logo on it. Shaw donated thousands of those bears to kids in crisis, and I think it was important to JR to be able to make that connection, to bring a little bit of joy to those homes. Of course, at three years old, I didn't know or understand any of that, but I really, truly loved that bear and remember it so well. So, I guess from an early age, I associated the Shaw brand with warmth and comfort and familiarity—I still do now! And those are things I also associate with my dad, of course.

I always remember my dad talking about the *fairness meter*, and making sure that your fairness meter is calibrated well and that you aim to hit the centre if you can. That applies to business and work but also, of course, to parenting—ensuring that you're level-headed in your approach to discipline, while also being very encouraging. Encouragement was always a big part of my childhood. Both of my parents were incredibly encouraging. So I try to be as encouraging as possible with Evelynn. As she gets older, I know I'll have a lot to draw on from what my dad taught me, which ultimately comes down to the persistence of love, even through those difficult times that kids inevitably bring. I know I was difficult as a kid, especially as a teenager. I had my bumps in the road, but he was always there to support me, no matter what. I'll definitely keep that in mind as I'm there for Evelynn, because I know it's not always going to be easy. She won't always be ten years old or necessarily happy to see me, but I'll always be there for her.

My dad has dug me out of many, many difficult situations in my life. I struggled as a teenager, and he was always extremely supportive of me. I put him through some grief in those days, but he remained steadfast, encouraging me through it all, setting me up for better days and future success.

Evelynn Bissonnette

He's very creative when he makes his songs and uses a bunch of different instruments. He has good vibes. When he walks into the room, it just feels good. He's really funny. He can always make people laugh. He's kind and has a very big heart. I remember last summer, when all the family were sitting on his boat and having a lot of fun. He's a good boat driver, and he's a good grandpa.

Patrick Lawlor

For as long as I could remember, I have known that I was adopted. My parents never kept it a secret. I remember my mother posing the question. She asked if I wanted to find my biological mother, when I was a very young boy. My answer was that I did not want to meet someone who would give me away. I felt that perhaps that was the right answer to her question—or rather, the answer she would most like to hear.

When I was eleven years old, my family was visiting my uncle in Vancouver. During the visit, he brought out a binder of the Lawlor family tree. I looked at it and could not find myself on the page where my parents and brother were listed. I was hurt. That may have been the first time I truly realized that being adopted meant I was not really considered a Lawlor. I felt left out. It took years for me to realize the impact that day had on me.

Years later, while studying psychology at the University of Ottawa, I was constantly exposed to theories on the nature/nurture debate, which reignited my curiosity around my own biological background, and inspired me to investigate. Though in the 1990s, it wasn't so easy, with the internet not being what it is today.

It was a process that took several years—first finding my adoption record, then following clues to my mother ... and then to my father, who was, at the time, an executive at Shaw. So, I called his office ...

Peter came to Ottawa shortly after we spoke on the phone for the first time. We went out for supper and talked about our mutual love of music and playing guitar. He told me about his time in the air force as a radar technician and his experience with tube technology. We were drawing many parallels between our hobbies and interests.

The following day, he sent me a lovely note saying it was a pleasure to meet me. I was delighted to have met such an accomplished man with so many interests and varied experiences. I was struck by how thoughtful and polite he was, but also that he was far from stuck up. He had a wit that was edgy.

In the years following my first meeting with Peter, we spoke quite often on the phone. I was going through a divorce, and he was very supportive of me. He would fly me to Palm Springs and Calgary to spend time chatting and drinking wine, having a jam or singing karaoke in his large studio room. It's always fun to visit him. We have lots of laughs. At larger social events, he's never missed an opportunity to introduce me to his friends and acquaintances as his son, often adding that I am a *fucking good guitar player*. It feels really nice for him to boost me up.

Peter is a man who is a lifelong learner. Whether it is his guitar playing, his recording studio, his photography—another hobby we both share—or his years of playing sports like hockey and karate, he tends to immerse himself into whatever he takes on, until he is operating at a high level. Clearly, he put the most time into being an excellent executive. The Shaw family appreciated his efforts. They treated him like family. I think he felt like he was part of the family. He was very proud to work for them.

When I was at his retirement party in Ottawa, I was astounded by how many people gave detailed speeches that highlighted Peter's professionalism, his kindness, and his humour. It was clear that he was very well respected in his career. It was a proud moment for me to witness such reverence for my father.

Katherine Emberly

Peter, I couldn't end this chapter without a special thank-you to you. I feel so fortunate to have spent time watching you lead at Shaw, and I always appreciated the time you shared with me. Watching you walk through a call centre and genuinely connect with every person is something that impacted me and the kind of leader I wanted to become. Around the boardroom table, you pushed us hard to be better, but always from a place of support.

Craig McCaw

These days, I don't remember what I had for breakfast or where I left my keys, but I remember everything about my younger years. And sure, I remember Peter Bissonnette!

He was an earnest, genuine guy with strong principles. I mean, he truly loved music and was always willing to put the work in to learn. Peter was a conscientious guy; I always liked him. He knew how to have fun too! It was evident he was in it for the immense enjoyment he got from music. And you know, I bet if he had chosen to pursue a musical career, he would have done very well. If he really wanted to be a rock star and that's where he put all his energy, he probably could have been! Though it's probably for the best he chose the path he did. I mean—look how well that worked out for him.

Chris Johnston

In a letter dated Sunday, September 10, 2006, Chris Johnston, once Shaw's regulatory lawyer, wrote a handwritten note, which read:

Dear Peter, although we have talked about your seminary experience in the past, I was struck more forcibly by how tough and lonely that experience must have been for you as you described it at Jim's reception.

I think it takes a special strength and character to emerge from that kind of background with one's values intact and the innate decency you continuously reflect unaltered. I could see others without your qualities becoming bitter and warped by the experience.

I was also touched, Peter, at your mentioning over dinner my beliefs about why we're all here and where we're headed. They have only become stronger over the years, notwithstanding that we are living through a time of horrendous acts committed in the name of various religious beliefs—a condition, of course, that is not limited to our age, unfortunately, but has repeated itself over and over through history.

Mankind reaps what it sows, and though God must weep at some of the infrequences, He has given us our greatest gift—free will—to choose our paths and learn the most we can from our journey here.

If there is a hell, it is of our own making here on Earth. I am absolutely convinced that on the other side, there is nothing but love so powerful and all-encompassing that we can't even imagine it, and total forgiveness— whatever the mistakes made here.

God doesn't judge. He only loves unconditionally. If only the world understood that, and tapped into it, what a change there would be! Mankind would become disciples of love rather than hate, of forgiveness rather than condemnation.

I'm sure God's plan is for us to learn this, but boy oh boy, what slow learners we are!

Chris passed away on November 16, 2010, from lung cancer. He was just seventy-five.

JR Shaw

We are blessed to have you as a big part of our company and family. It takes a special person to work between two brothers. You are the only one I know of who so admirably carries out this responsibility and remains a trusted friend. Thank you for going above and beyond in all you do.

— October 2004

Peter Johnson

I am so very grateful to have had you as my mentor all these years! You are a fantastic leader and have a gift for reading people and situations. Thank you for making my career as fulfilling as it has been. I wouldn't be where I am without your support. I look back at our crazy times and smile when I think of how we navigated through some choppier waters, always with you at the helm with a steady hand!

Paul Pew

I recall when you retired from the Shaw management team, JR spoke and expressed that if you could create a movie of a person's career and people would find it informative and entertaining, then it was a good career—and he thought that was the case for you.

Lucy Lynskey

Peter was a great leader at Shaw because he brings out the best in people—through encouragement, support, patience, and trust.

He never turns his back on a promise or a challenge. He's consistent, reliable, and he keeps his eyes on the goal. He maintains faith in people, even when they lose it in themselves.

Composition by Rick Mapes
(Sports and Music Illustration, rickmapesdesign.com)

Joan and Edmund, in their military uniforms

Christine (left) and Suzanne (right) with the flight attendant before boarding the plane to London

Peter (centre back row), Paul (third row, second from left),
Michael Tear (seated, far right); 1954

My first week in the RCAF, at boot
camp in Saint-Jean, Quebec

My classmates and I in Rivers, Manitoba

In my cut-off denim shorts at the Rideau Canal

TSPS base unit at 768 Seymour on BC Tel's 6th floor, in 1975. This system was the leading-edge technology. I worked with Bob Brose, Stu Hicks, and Marty Hinds, ultimately becoming their supervisor. The people who maintained the system include the three pictured here.

My first reel-to-reel recording studio in Vancouver

Taking a selfie

Bubble of Love, Yakima, Washington, summer 1987.
I took Michael on a camping trip to visit Auntie
Rosemary and Uncle Case.

Rogers' offices, Vancouver, 1985. Back row, L to R: Tom Makortoff, engineering staff; Frank Eberdt, VP and general manager; Peter Bissonnette, VP operations; Tom Hobley, VP engineering; Tony Van Wouw, VP engineering; Bob Peake, VP cable systems engineering. Front row: Ted Rogers, CEO: Rogers and George Feirheller, president: Cantel.

My access card at Shaw

What a thrill it was to bond with Michael.

With Tracy in San Diego

I took this photo of Tracy in 2005.

Our first dance, Banff Springs

*With my groomsmen: Brad
Shaw, Terry Medd, OD
Hanson, Todd Chahley, Darren
Lamoureux, and Jim Shaw*

"Kiss your phone company goodbye!" Me, JR and Jim, February 14, 2005: Valentine's Day

Making up for lost time: Michael, me, and Patrick

A photo I took of Daisy on another day

Cory Kraus, Shaw pilot, flying into Italy in 2010 on the way to the Croatia cruise

Taken by me at Big Valley Jamboree, 2013:
Big & Rich face-to-face

Taken by me at Big Valley Jamboree, 2013

Our home on the lake in Kelowna

Phil Lind and JR—photo taken by me at the National Cable Television Hall of Fame dinner in Chicago

My sister Suzanne

With Michael's family

Acknowledgements

I am thankful for my natural abilities and attributes—those that I have felt divinely inspired to unearth and nurture with authenticity and passion. I am also grateful that I met the right people at the right time—people who motivated and humbled me. They helped me pursue a career that became not only a joy, but my purpose. Having recognized this, I, in turn, hope to help others find their own purpose and embark on their own journeys of growth.

I would like to thank all those who participated in interviews and sent emails to contribute their thoughts and memories to this story:

Tracy Bissonnette
Michael Bissonnette
Brad Shaw
Michael D'Avella
Adrian Burns
Craig McCaw
Chethan Lakshman
Howard Levitt
Patrick Lawlor
Suzanne Bissonnette
Peter Johnson
Christine Oskirko

My publisher, Ingenium Books, cautioned me about trying to thank all the people in my life who have been a part of my story. As my list grew and grew, I would wake up in the middle of the night, having remembered another name that should be included in my list of acknowledgements. Pretty soon my list read like a Rolodex caught in time. I knew there would still be people whom I had forgotten. So, I have eliminated that list and now include special thanks to all those people who shared in my journey.

If you are reading my biography and recognize me, I also recognize you with great thanks and humility.

Lucy Lynskey—Lucy and I have worked together from afar on my biography for the past two years. What commitment it has taken for her to capture my narratives! I can't express enough gratitude to Lucy for her ingenuity and selflessness as she skillfully crafted this biography with me and infused vitality into my life story. I am eternally thankful; I could not have hoped to find a more genuine, varied, and seasoned blend of talent and determination. Her wisdom surpasses her age.

JR Shaw—There is so much to thank JR for. I am forever grateful for his strong leadership, his examples of how to live a life. I loved him, dearly. He was one of a kind, one in a million, and he built a company and a legacy that will forever be part of Canada's history. I am so fortunate that he was such a significant person in my life story, and that he had faith in me. He knew that he could count on me!

Jim Shaw—Jim was my best friend. He was like a brother to me. Some of the most unforgettable moments in my life were spent with him. He had a great passion for life. He was bold and brave and brilliant. And he was loved by so many. His influence is woven throughout my narrative and my leadership journey. He was a true business Rock Star!

Brad Shaw—Even now, Brad continues to be a beloved family member to me and always will be. Throughout his life, he faced challenges with strength and determination, consistently demonstrating kindness along the way. He recognizes the potential in others, providing encouragement and promoting positivity. He is an outstanding leader and a remarkable and loyal friend. I derive great joy from collaborating with Brad and experiencing his inspiring energy firsthand. He has a vibrant passion for excellence while approaching it with humility, lighting the way for everyone fortunate enough to work with him. He is a leader among leaders.

Michael D'Avella—I remember when Michael came to Shaw in 1991 from the Canadian Cable and Television Association. He arrived with outstanding qualifications, akin to a top draft pick in hockey terminology. He exceeded those lofty expectations in every endeavour he undertook for Shaw, and his insights were greatly valued. I had the opportunity to collaborate with Michael on many of Shaw's key initiatives and admired him for his consideration, teamwork, innovative thinking, and determination. The entire Shaw family treasured his wisdom, and rightfully so.

Dr. Susan Lea-Makenny—Dr. Susan has been my doctor for over two decades. She has been a remarkable and outstanding physician for me. In addition to her medical practice, she and her husband also care for horses at their ranch in the Priddis area southwest of Calgary. Since my cardiac event on October 1, 2008, Dr. Susan has provided me with care, and addressed the underlying causes of this incident through lifestyle modifications and follow-up testing. Dr. Susan is a highly skilled and exemplary physician who genuinely prioritizes her patients. She has played a significant role in restoring my health and enhancing the quality of life I enjoy.

Glynnis Prystae—Glynnis and I started working together on October 3, 1986. She was David and Steve McDonald's personal assistant at Western Cablevision. At that time, she also took on the role as assistant to the executive vice president and general manager of Western—that's me.

What a wonderful and loyal assistant she was all those years ago, and continues to be for Brad Shaw today. Her work ethic—in every day at the rise of dawn, discretion, and confidentiality—were appreciated by me. Glynnis was the barometer that indicated the atmosphere of the workplace at Western.

The staff valued and trusted Glynnis, often confiding in her about their concerns, which she would then relay to me for further action. I could have private discussions with her, confident that she would never violate those confidences. I will always cherish the privilege of working alongside her during this crucial time in my career.

Derinda Burton—Derinda supported me from 2000 until my retirement on August 31, 2015. She was my assistant during some challenging periods in my personal and professional life. The company was expanding rapidly, and I was thrilled when she joined our team, bringing with her a wealth of experience from her prior work at Nova before coming to Shaw. She was an incredible support and a truly wonderful colleague who was greatly respected by fellow staff. Derinda played a significant role in my success during our time together, warmly welcoming everyone connected with me though office visits or phone calls. I remain close with Derinda and her husband, D'Arcy; however, our gatherings are less frequent as we travel between Calgary, Kelowna, and California.

Lorie Burns—Lorie was my assistant for one and a half years when I moved to Toronto as a part of the CUC acquisition. She had been the executive assistant to Charlie Allen, who was the president of CUC. Lorie was very loyal to me and helped me integrate and understand the culture of CUC and their main leadership group.

From April until the CRTC approval in June 1995, my priority was to establish a leadership group that would head up the integration of CUC. At the same time, Shaw had come to an agreement to purchase Classicomm Cable, and therefore it was a part of my longer-term planning to establish a mix of personnel who could lead that new entity.

Extended days and countless hours of planning were the norm. Lorie assisted me during that transition, as she was regarded as a CUC employee and held the respect of those team members we needed to consider for ongoing operations at Shaw in Toronto. I continue to value and treasure her friendship.

Howard Levitt—From the first day I encountered Howard, he embodied one of my core principles: *Surround yourself with the best*. He is not only an outstanding labour lawyer, but also a genuine friend. His loyalty to Shaw was unwavering, and his support of Jim had no limits. Howard is truly one of a kind. Engaging conversations with him are a delight, as his curiosity broadens my perspectives of the world. Now, in his role as an extraordinary food critic, his palate explores global cuisines with finesse. There is no better friend I could wish for than Howard.

Bill MacDonald—Bill is one of my closest colleagues from my days at Shaw, where we collaborated closely for many years. We were practically inseparable as we worked on numerous acquisitions and integrated the staff associated with those new systems.

I first encountered Bill when I arrived in Edmonton in 1989 to interview for the position of vice president of operations for Vancouver and Vancouver Island. Although Jim Shaw was to conduct my interview, Bill led the initial part of the process. After what seemed like a gentle conversation, I met with Jim in his office; it felt like talking with an old friend, discussing our industry and the opportunities for growth. One month later, I began my career with Shaw.

Bill was incredibly supportive and optimistic. He was as close to embodying the essence of Shaw as anyone could be. We collaborated on many fronts, and when I relocated to Toronto to integrate the Cablecasting, CUC, and Classicomm cable systems, Bill spent every week in a Toronto hotel, living out of a suitcase. He conducted Shaw U courses for the new employees, and every Friday, we met to review their progress and discuss their fit within Shaw and in their respective roles.

He reminded me of Father John Bosco, who had a profound influence on everyone he met. Bill remains one of my all-time favourites and is a wonderful husband to Maureen, whom he cherishes. He was as close to the Shaw family as anyone I have known. Bill was an invaluable resource for me when we were strategizing human resources matters and their implications on the company and the family.

Harry Nutma—Harry was a great friend to JR Shaw and me. A jack of all technical trades, we relied on him for advice on everything technical. He managed to get JR's satellite working on his yacht and his Star Choice services running at his home in Hawaii, despite the drastically different azimuth from Canada. When JR bought a fishing lodge in Eagle Point, Harry was there to install backup power, communication systems, and monitoring for the lodge. He could work miracles.

Tracy and I loved hosting Harry and Miriam at our home in Palm Springs while they were working on a project for Jim Shaw. We spent many wine-filled evenings together, sharing stories and laughing over the ins and outs of operating cable systems and community programming equipment.

Jasbir Toor—Jasbir is a great and loyal friend. He works in our satellite division as a technical manager and is top in his job. He knows everything there is to know about satellite transmission, and can decipher satellite signals for every model of Shaw satellite receiver across Canada.

During my travels around Canada and California in my motor coach, I often needed to receive Shaw's satellite signals across North America. Many times, I'd struggle to get my receiver to lock onto Anik's satellites. No matter the hour, I could reach Jasbir. He would answer with his signature greeting, "Thank you for choosing Shaw. Jasbir speaking." He always seemed to be at work.

Jim Cummins—Jim and I worked together for many years. I first met him when his company was doing disconnect work for Western in Surrey. Later, when I moved to Shaw, I crossed paths with Jim again, as he provided the same support services for Shaw on Vancouver Island. Jim eventually joined Shaw, working closely with Brad Shaw at Star Choice.

Jim's loyalty to Shaw was remarkable. Once, during a management meeting at Jim Shaw's home in Kelowna, Jim found himself on the receiving end of some good-natured pressure to achieve specific operating margins. After dinner, Jim Shaw playfully put Jim into a headlock, jokingly trying to squeeze an extra million out of the satellite division. Jim's head looked like it was going to pop off. He took one for the team that night. I was sad when Jim eventually left the company, and I still count him as a lifelong friend.

Christine Oskirko—I am blessed to have a sister like Christine. She is a beautiful soul, a talented musician and artist, and a child of God. I am grateful for her contributions to this biography. When we refer to angels in my biography, she is one to be counted in that realm.

Todd Chahley and Darren Lamoureux—Partners for life. Since the day I met Tracy on July 21, 2001, Todd and Darren have had a profoundly positive impact on our lives. They have celebrated every home we've lived in, every milestone, and even the challenging times. They bring immense joy to our lives, sharing moments filled with laughter and sincerity. We are truly blessed and deeply grateful for their friendship and brotherhood.

Michael and Beth Chahley—Mike and Beth have been together since they were seventeen. They are my parents-in-law, and I love them dearly. They are incredibly loving and loyal parents, setting a high bar for their children. The example they set is evident in their children, especially my wife Tracy. They have brought immeasurable joy to my life.

Peter Johnson—Peter and I have collaborated for the past twenty-five years. When we first met, he was a young lawyer who had joined Shaw to take on the legal responsibilities associated with acquisitions, new product launches, regulatory submissions, and more. Peter has transitioned from those roles to become the most senior lawyer, corporate counsel, and head of government and regulatory affairs at Shaw.

In much of the growth and challenges at Shaw, Peter has been called upon for his insights, perspectives, and recommendations. He is a truly respected and sought-after member of the Shaw senior management team. His youthful enthusiasm, combined with his maturity during his tenure at Shaw, is noteworthy. The number of times we've faltered due to poor advice, legal overreach, or inadequately structured agreements is none.

I trust Peter and I've shared countless moments with him discussing corporate structure, careers, opportunities, personal fit, roles, and expectations, as well as subordinate and personal performance. We have engaged in hypothetical what-if scenarios, and these conversations have always remained confidential. They have been invaluable in my exploration of critical factors that inform my decision-making. He has genuinely met my need for wise counsel. To this day, although retired, I still look forward to my interactions with Peter.

Adrian Burns—Adrian and I are indeed contemporaries, having been born in the same year. Adrian has been a steadfast friend and advocate for the Shaws for many years. I remember how pleased JR was when Adrian agreed to become a member of the Shaw board; he was excited to share the news with us. Similarly, I recall Brad's positive remarks regarding Adrian's contributions to the board and her suitability to assume the role of chair for the human resources committee. She is a valued member and highly respected by every board member. Adrian is a successful businesswoman who offers valuable insights when strategic discussions are taking place at Shaw. I appreciate her willingness to engage in conversations and share her unique perspectives on pathways to success.

One of my proudest moments was when I was approved for the role of honorary captain in the navy; that achievement wasn't a coincidence— Adrian advocated for me, and then it came to fruition.

Adrian certainly belongs in the elite category of individuals we should consult before making decisions influenced by public perception. She is extraordinary and attuned to the world around her.

About Peter Bissonnette

Peter Bissonnette began his thirty-five years with Shaw Communications Inc. in 1989, as vice president operations. He became president in 2001: a position he held until his retirement in 2015. He remained on the board until Shaw's sale to Rogers in 2023.

As a child, Peter was an army brat moving from place to place. He attended a Catholic boarding school in England and for a time considered pursuing a life in the clergy. Instead, he joined the navy and later the Royal Canadian Air Force, where he discovered his aptitude for electronics and radar technology.

Always seeking new opportunities and growth, Peter left a low-paying job at Northern Radio in Ottawa with just fifty dollars in his wallet, and headed to Vancouver on a Greyhound bus. In Vancouver he found work with BC Tel, where he worked for twelve years, climbing the ranks, gaining a reputation for operational excellence, and attracting the attention of big telecom leaders like the McDonalds, Ted Rogers, and ultimately, JR Shaw.

Peter is an avid musician, with his own recording studio and an impressive collection of guitars. He is also a talented photographer, a subject he majored in at college and later pursued, photographing models and weddings.

Today, Peter spends his time between Calgary, Kelowna, and Rancho Mirage with his wife Tracy and their much-loved wieners, Winnie and Frankie.

About Lucy Lynskey

Originally from the Isle of Wight in the United Kingdom, Lucy Lynskey has a bachelor's degree in screenwriting from Solent University.

She has worked in Calgary, Alberta, as a commercial writer/director/producer for both Shaw Communications Inc. and Corus Entertainment, at Global Calgary.

She has been an English language teacher, a sales coordinator, and a project manager for high-profile events in Quebec City.

In England, she worked as a feature-film writer, freelance journalist, legal secretary, and a Sailor Jerry–promoting bartender.

Lucy lives in Maple Bay on Vancouver Island with her husband and two children.

You Might Also Enjoy ...

In the Thick of It:
Mastering the Art of Leading from the Middle

ingeniumbooks.com/thick

12 Elephants and a Dragon:
A Memoir of Survival
and the Kindness of Strangers

ingeniumbooks.com/12ED

Born and Razed:
Surviving the Cult was Only Half the Battle

ingeniumbooks.com/BORN

The Weaver's Way:
What an Ancient Art Can Teach Us About
Our Approach to Shaping Change

ingeniumbooks.com/WeaversWay

Recycled:
A Reluctant Search for True Self
Through Nurture, Nature, and Free Will

Screening for the One:
How to Gain an Edge in Your Hiring

ingeniumbooks.com/SFTO